Witches' Spell-A-Day Almanac

Holidays & Lore
Spells, Rituals & Meditations

Copyright 2012 Llewellyn Worldwide Ltd.
Interior Design: Michael Fallon
Cover Design: Lisa Novak

Background photo: © PhotoDisc
Interior Art: © 2011, Steven McAfee
pp. 13, 33, 53, 73, 93, 115, 135, 153, 173, 193, 213, 231
Spell icons throughout: © 2011 Sherrie Thai

You can order Llewellyn books and annuals from *New Worlds*,
Llewellyn's catalog. To request a free copy of the catalog, call toll-free
1-877-NEW WRLD or visit our website at www.llewellyn.com

ISBN: 978-0-7387-1521-6
Llewellyn is a registered trademark of Llewellyn Worldwide Ltd.
2143 Wooddale Drive
Woodbury, MN 55125

Contents

About the Authors

Chandra Alexandre is an initiated Tantrika and hereditary witch. On return from India in 1998, she founded SHARANYA (www.sharanya .org), a 501(c)(3) devi mandir (goddess temple) dedicated to social justice through embodied spirituality and devotion to Kali Maa. For over a decade she has worked to help those seeking the mysteries of the dark goddess and the technologies of Tantra find sanctuary and community through Daughters of Kali, Kali Vidya (www.kalividya.org), and public ceremony. Chandra holds a Ph.D. in Philosophy and Religion, a doctor of ministry degree, and an MBA in sustainable management.

Peg Aloi is a media studies scholar, writer, singer, and professional gardener. She was the Media Coordinator for The Witches' Voice from 1997 through 2008. Her blog, *The Witching Hour*, focuses on Paganism and media. With her writing partner Hannah Johnston, Peg co-organized two academic conferences at Harvard University on Paganism and the media. Their third book, *The Celluloid Bough: Cinema in the Wake of the Occult Revival*, is forthcoming from I. B. Tauris.

Barbara Ardinger, Ph.D. (www.barbaraardinger.com), is the author of *Secret Lives*, a novel about a circle of crones, mothers, and maidens, plus goddesses, a talking cat, and the Green Man. Her earlier books include *Pagan Every Day*, *Goddess Meditations*, *Finding New Goddesses* (a parody of goddess encyclopedias), and *Quicksilver Moon* (a realistic novel ... except for the vampire). Her day job is freelance editing for people who have good ideas but don't want to embarrass themselves in print. Barbara lives in Southern California with her two rescued Maine coon cats, Heisenberg and Schroedinger.

Blake Octavian Blair is an Eclectic IndoPagan Witch, psychic, tarot reader, freelance writer, Usui Reiki Master-Teacher, and a devotee of Lord Ganesha. He holds a degree in English and Religion from the University of Florida. In his spare time he enjoys beading jewelry, knitting, and is an avid reader. Blake lives in the Piedmont region of North Carolina with his beloved husband, an aquarium full of fish, and an indoor jungle of houseplants. Visit him at www.blakeoctavianblair.com or write to him at blake@blakeoctavianblair.com.

Boudica co-owns *The Wiccan/Pagan Times*, an online Pagan e-zine, with her husband and also runs the *Zodiac Bistro*, an e-zine focused on the solitary

practitioner. She is a working witch of over 30 years, has been a member of a few covens, and has taught at various events on the East Coast. She now prefers the solitary experience and supports various Pagan community events in her area. Boudica is a native New Yorker who has been displaced to the wilds of mid-Ohio, where she lives with her husband of many years and eight cats.

Dallas Jennifer Cobb lives a magical life, manifesting meaningful and flexible work, satisfying relationships, and abundant gardens. She enjoys a balance of time and money, which support her deepest desires: a loving family, time in nature, self-expression, and a healthy home. She lives in paradise, in a waterfront village in rural Ontario. Contact her at jennifer.cobb@live.com.

Scott Cunningham practiced magic actively for over twenty years. He was the author of more than fifty books covering both fiction and non-fiction subject matter; sixteen of his titles are published by Llewellyn Publications. Scott's books reflect a broad range of interests within the New Age sphere, where he was very highly regarded. He passed from this life on March 28, 1993, after a long illness.

Ember Grant, author of *Magical Candle Crafting* (Llewellyn, 2011), has been writing for the Llewellyn annuals for ten years. She is currently working on her second book for Llewellyn. Visit her online at EmberGrant.com.

Emyme returned to earth-based beliefs several years ago, having dabbled in witchcraft as a teenager. She is a practicing solitary eclectic who creates magick through gardening and art, in addition to the domestic crafts of cooking and baking. Her home, "Das Haus von schönen Frauen," is multi-generational and multi-cat and embodies Maiden/Mother/Crone. Contact Emyme at catsmeow24@verizon.net for news of her website and blog.

Anne Johnson was born and raised in Appalachia. Her great grandmother was a soothsayer who worked with a regular deck of playing cards. Anne attended the Johns Hopkins University and graduated Phi Beta Kappa in 1981. She is author of several books for young adults, including *Defining Moments: The Scopes Monkey Trial*. Anne has always followed the hedge witch path, having grown up in the mountains where home remedies and weather patterns were of ultimate importance. Her blog, *The Gods Are Bored*, was voted one of the ten best Pagan blogs of 2010 by the University of Phoenix Ph.D. program.

James Kambos learned about knot magic, as well as other folk magic practices, from his mother and grandmother when he was a child. He's been a student of magical traditions ever since. His favorite magical tools are the tarot and pendulum. He has a degree in history and geography from Ohio University. A regular contributor to Llewellyn's annuals, he lives in Appalachia Ohio.

Patti Larsen is an intuitive and a tarot reader as well as an author. She combines her years of spiritual exploration with her passion for growth and change, using these tools to help her clients move forward with their lives. A founding member of The Lovely Witches Club™, she embraces all belief systems in their positive forms and loves interacting and learning from other gifted souls. She lives on the east coast of Canada with her loving husband and four enormous cats.

Lupa is an author, totemic ritual tool artist, and shaman living in the Pacific Northwest. She is the author of several books on animal magic and related topics, to include *New Paths to Animal Totems: Three Alternative Approaches to Creating Your Own Totemism* from Llewellyn Publications, due in late 2012. She can be found at http://www.thegreenwolf.com and http://therioshamanism.com.

Mickie Mueller is an award-winning and critically acclaimed artist of fantasy, fairy, and myth. She is an ordained Pagan minister and has studied Natural Magic, Fairy Magic, and Celtic tradition. She is also a Reiki healing master/teacher in the Usui Shiki Royoho Tradition. She enjoys creating magical art full of fairies, goddesses, and beings of folklore. Mickie is the illustrator of *The Well Worn Path* and *The Hidden Path* decks, the writer/illustrator of *Voice of the Trees: A Celtic Divination Oracle*, and the illustrator of the upcoming *Mystical Cats Tarot*, coming in 2014.

Susan Pesznecker is a mother, writer, nurse, hearth Pagan, and Druid living in northwest Oregon. She has a master's degree in professional writing and teaches English and writing at Clackamas Community College and Portland State University. Sue teaches at the online Grey School (www.greyschool.com) and is the author of three books: *Gargoyles* (New Page, 2007), *Crafting Magick with Pen and Ink* (Llewellyn, 2009), and *The Magick User's Retreat: Making Time for Solitude, Intention, and Rejuvenation* (Llewellyn, 2012). Contact Sue through Facebook or at www.susanpesznecker.com.

Jenett Silver is a librarian, witch, and priestess, now living back in New England, the land of her childhood. She's fascinated by the interaction of music and ritual, the small daily actions that make our lives richer and more joyful, and the chance to share information with anyone who stops to listen. You can find her blog at http://gleewood.org/threshold.

Tess Whitehurst is the author of *Magical Housekeeping: Simple Charms and Practical Tips for Creating a Harmonious Home* and *The Good Energy Book: Creating Harmony and Balance for Yourself and Your Home*. She's also an intuitive counselor, feng shui consultant, and columnist for *Witches and Pagans* magazine. Her website (www.tesswhitehurst.com) and e-newsletter ("Good Energy") feature simple rituals, meditations, and musings for everyday magical living. Tess lives in Venice Beach, California, with two magical cats, one musical boyfriend, and a constant stream of visiting hummingbirds.

A Note on Magic and Spells

The spells in the *Witches' Spell-A-Day Almanac* evoke everyday magic designed to improve our lives and homes. You needn't be an expert on magic to follow these simple rites and spells; as you will see if you use these spells throughout the year, magic, once mastered, is easy to perform. The only advanced technique required of you is the art of visualization.

Visualization is an act of controlled imagination. If you can call up in your mind a picture of your best friend's face or a flag flapping in the breeze, you can visualize. In magic, visualizations are used to direct and control magical energies. Basically the spellcaster creates a visual image of the spell's desired goal, whether it be perfect health, a safe house, or a protected pet.

Visualization is the basis of all good spells, and as such it is a tool that should be properly used. Visualization must be real in the mind of the spellcaster so it allows him or her to raise, concentrate, and send forth energy to accomplish the spell.

Perhaps when visualizing you'll find that you're doing everything right, but you don't feel anything. This is common, for we haven't been trained to acknowledge—let alone utilize—our magical abilities. Keep practicing, however, for your spells can "take" even if you're not the most experienced natural magician.

You will notice also that many spells in this collection have a some-what "light" tone. They are seemingly fun and frivolous, filled with rhyme and colloquial speech. This is not to diminish the seriousness of the purpose, but rather to create a relaxed atmosphere for the practitio-ner. Lightness of spirit helps focus energy; rhyme and common language help the spellcaster remember the words and train the mind where it is needed. The intent of this magic is indeed very serious at times, and magic is never to be trifled with.

Even when your spells are effective, magic won't usually sparkle before your very eyes. The test of magic's success is time, not immedi-ate eye-popping results. But you can feel magic's energy for yourself by rubbing your palms together briskly for ten seconds, then holding them a few inches apart. Sense the energy passing through them, the warm tin-gle in your palms. This is the power raised and used in magic. It comes from within and is perfectly natural.

Among the features of the *Witches' Spell-A-Day Almanac* are an easy-to-use "book of days" format; new spells specifically tailored for each

day of the year (and its particular magical, astrological, and historical energies); and additional tips and lore for various days throughout the year—including color correspondences based on planetary influences, obscure and forgotten holidays and festivals, and an incense of the day to help you waft magical energies from the ether into your space. Moon tables are included at the end of each month and in the back of the book to help you find the perfect time for your rituals and spells.

Enjoy your days, and have a magical year!

Spell-A-Day Icons

New Moon

Full Moon

Abundance

Altar

Balance

Clearing, Cleaning

Garden

Grab Bag

Health

Home

Heart, Love

Meditation, Divination

Money, Prosperity

Protection

Relationship

Success

Travel, Communication

Air Element

Earth Element

Fire Element

Spirit Element

Water Element

Spells at a Glance by Date and Category*

	Health	Protection	Success	Heart, Love	Clearing, Cleaning	Home	Meditation, Divination
Jan.	13, 20	17, 29	15	18, 25	4, 8, 14, 28	12, 24	7
Feb.	5	9, 28	7	1, 6, 14, 19	4, 23	8, 18	11, 12
March	2, 17, 30	3, 22, 23, 26	15, 21	29	4, 6, 13	12	8, 10, 19, 20, 28
April		13, 16		5, 12	8, 29	9, 27	1, 4
May	6, 24	20, 29	8, 14, 23	1, 10, 11, 27	15, 30		
June	24	7, 10, 11, 29	26	1, 16	4, 28	9, 22	6, 20
July	5, 6, 24	10, 28	4		1, 13	3, 12	7
Aug.	5, 21, 31	24	4, 13, 26, 29	16, 23, 25, 30	2, 27		12, 18, 22
Sept.	18	16, 24	9		17, 23, 28	1, 22	6, 8, 11, 12, 20
Oct.	2, 14, 29	8, 15, 30	20, 28		23, 25, 31	3, 19, 21	7, 22, 24
Nov.	2, 24, 30	15, 27	7, 9		26	16	6, 20
Dec.	8	18, 19	30		1, 7, 9	10, 13, 29	3, 15, 27

*List is not comprehensive.

2013
Year of Spells

January

January is the first month of the year in the Gregorian calendar. On average, it is the coldest month in the Northern Hemisphere and the warmest month in the Southern Hemisphere. January is named after the Roman god Janus, the god of doorways. Janus is typically depicted with two faces, so he could see both what was behind him and what was in front of him. The side that faced the past was shown as mature and bearded, whereas the side that faced the future was youthful and full of hope. Janus's name came from the Latin word for door, *ianua*, and so January is the doorway into the new year. January is a quiet month after all the hustle and bustle of the holiday season. For those who follow the Wheel of the Year, it falls between Yule, when we celebrate the slow return of the light, and Imbolc, when we anticipate the first stirrings of spring. For many, it is a long, dark, cold month, but one that allows us to turn our focus inward and to prepare for the journey that is the year to come. Like Janus, may we turn our faces forward with hope and youthful enthusiasm.

Deborah Blake

January 1
Tuesday

 Color of the day: Red
Incense of the day: Cinnamon

New Year's Day – Kwanzaa ends

Setting Your Intention for the Year

What are your thankful for? Sit quietly until images or words float into your mind. Using a fountain pen (so your energy flows into what you're writing) and the finest paper you can find, write at the top: I GIVE THANKS.

Now write three really basic things you're grateful for. Examples: (1) My health is good. (2) Someone loves me. (Who?) (3) I'm employed and have adequate income. Write down three more things. Keep thinking. Write down three more things. Write neatly and legibly. No spelling errors!

Read your list aloud. Pause after each item and say, "Thank you, Goddess" or "Thank you, [name of other god or goddess]."

Fold your list into thirds and hold it against your chest. Visualize the words on your gratitude list flowing off the page and imprinting themselves on your heart in a beautiful calligraphic script. Carry gratitude on—and in—your heart for the rest of the year.

Barbara Ardinger, Ph.D.

January 2
Wednesday

Color of the day: Brown
Incense of the day: Lilac

Ancestry Day (Haiti)

Today is Ancestry Day in Haiti. Traditionally it is a day to honor one's human ancestors. However, our line of ancestry runs much farther! While we aren't descended from apes, we all share a common ancestor, the first primate. And we stem from a long line of mammals, reptiles, assorted aquatic beings, all the way back to the beginning of life.

This makes every living being our extended family. We really are connected to every other being on this planet, and this is a great day to celebrate that.

Instead of just putting out an altar for human ancestors, why not create one for a whole array of them? Obviously you can't include every single individual, and not even every species directly preceding humans, but you can create a general setting for them all.

Lupa

January 3
Thursday

Color of the day: Purple
Incense of the day: Balsam

A Food Drive Spell

Jupiter is the planetary ruler of Thursday and is known for qualities such as generosity and sharing. And since three is a number associated with goodwill, this would be an auspicious day to do spellwork for charity and giving.

With the holidays over, charity food banks begin to struggle. This spell will help ease their shortages. Work this spell with friends or coven members. Begin by asking friends to donate one item for the food drive, and request that they ask others to do the same. Then light two candles: one royal blue and one orange. Next, repeat this charm three times:

> Let our circle of sharing and
> caring expand. So mote it be.

Repeat this ritual for three nights, moving the candles farther apart each night. Hopefully this spell will turn into a regular charitable act.

James Kambos

January 4
Friday

Color of the day: White
Incense of the day: Thyme

Renewal Bath

A waning moon, a new year ... this is a good time for not only cleaning your physical space but clearing your emotions as well.

Use this bath spell for a fresh start and a positive outlook. First prepare an infusion of peppermint: you can simply brew a small batch of peppermint tea. Let the tea cool, or chill it if you'd like. Then prepare a bath (you can take a shower, if necessary, and wash with the infusion). Add the infusion to the bath water and, as you bathe, visualize the refreshing mint rejuvenating you. You can even add a few mint leaves to the water if you'd like. Say:

> Herbs and water on my skin
> Let your magic now begin.
> Fresh and clean, now renew –
> Help me have a cheerful view.

Ember Grant

January 5
Saturday

Color of the day: Gray
Incense of the day: Ivy

Twelfth Night

We come to the end of autumn and winter festivities begun on Halloween. Saturdays and waning moons are associated with endings and magical dormancy, respectively. Gather your friends and family for a quiet celebration to take down all Yule decorations. Wassail is the beverage of the day. Feast on fresh fruits and nuts—once a luxury, now readily available. Bake a cake with a bean hidden inside. Whoever finds it is the Lord of Misrule and owns the event, and will host the Twelfth Night party next year. As your guests depart, bless them with a small glass jar of the wassail (include the recipe) for all good and positive energy for the year to come.

Wassail Recipe

Simmer all ingredients for 2–3 hours. Enjoy hot or warm (not cold).

1 gallon apple cider

2 cups cranberry juice

½ cup honey

½ cup sugar

2 oranges

Whole cloves

1 apple, peeled and diced

Allspice

Ginger

Nutmeg

3 cinnamon sticks (or 3 tablespoons ground cinnamon)

½–1 cup brandy (optional)

Emyme

Notes:

January 6
Sunday

Color of the day: Gold
Incense of the day: Hyacinth

A Tarot Layout for the Journey

The dark depths of winter are a great time to work with divination, and early January is also a wonderful time to make plans for the new year. Joseph Campbell's "hero's journey" model frames all personal undertakings as a type of "quest" and divides each one into three phases: departure (during which one receives a call to destiny, meets a mentor, and crosses a threshold into adventure), initiation (during which one is tested and achieves the goal), and return (during which the questor returns home, filled with new knowledge and capabilities).

What are your plans and goals for 2013? Forecast one of your upcoming ventures with a tarot reading à la Campbell's quest. Draw one card to represent you—it's your adventure, after all. Below it, draw and lay three cards for departure, initiation, and return. Study and read the result: you're on your way!

Susan Pesznecker

January 7
Monday

Color of the day: Gray
Incense of the day: Rosemary

Triple Moon Tarot Spell

Select three different tarot decks from your collection. Pull out the Moon card from each deck and line up the cards before you. The card on the left is the Maiden, in the center is the Mother, and on the right is the Crone. From the first deck choose a card the represents something new you want to manifest in your life, and place it on the Maiden. From the second deck choose a card for something already in your life that you would like to grow, and place it on the Mother. From the third deck choose a card representing something you would like to remove from your life, and place it on the Crone. Meditate on these images for a while. When you are ready, state three times:

Maiden brings it new,

Mother gives it life,

And Crone sends it home.

Place the cards where you can see them, and focus on them daily until next Monday.

Mickie Mueller

January 8
Tuesday

Color of the day: Black
Incense of the day: Ginger

Time on Your Side Spell

It is common to look back on old deeds and feel the pang of regret or even the weight of guilt for what was done. This saps vital energy and continues a cycle that feeds the incident beyond its original effect. Often time and ego allow those moments of shame to become mountains, preventing forward growth.

Hold a winding watch in your right hand, as it is connected to your left brain or ego. This will focus the guilty feelings. Using your left hand, wind the watch backward as you remember the incident. If you can recall the approximate time of day the incident occurred, even better. But the process of rewinding while focusing on the moment is all that is required. When you feel the weight lifted, breathe three times across the surface of the watch to dispel the energy and wind the watch forward to the present time.

Patti Larsen

January 9
Wednesday

Color of the day: White
Incense of the day: Honeysuckle

New Day, New Choices

After the holidays it can be hard to get back into the swing of our daily lives. Here's a simple morning ritual to make that a little easier. Stand in front of your altar (or in some other meaningful place) and say:

> Today is a new day.
>
> I reach out and change the world.
>
> My words are wise and kind,
>
> My thoughts focused and clear,
>
> And my spirit seeks those of like mind.
>
> As I walk in my day,
>
> May I hold the blessings
>
> Of the Gods and the ancients
>
> And become a light in the world.

Afterward, take a moment for reflection, paying attention to anything that comes to mind. This is a good time to draw a card or rune for the day.

Jenett Silver

January 10

Thursday

Color of the day: Purple
Incense of the day: Myrrh

Ebisu Matsuri Business Blessing Altar

Today is dedicated to Ebisu Matsuri, one of Japan's Seven Lucky Gods and the god associated with business, luck, happiness, and prosperity. To bless your business or simply to enhance your cash flow, you might like to make a tradition-inspired altar by placing a small picture or statue of this smiling Buddhist deity on a small table or shelf—if possible, near the entrance to your workplace, office, or home. Add a red candle. Also add an offering or two, such as some shiny gold-colored coins (chocolate wrapped in foil will work), a bamboo or jade plant, and/or a small stack of rice cakes on a plate. Light the candle and say a simple invocation, such as:

Ebisu Matsuri, thank you for opening the way to ever-increasing prosperity and cash flow. Thank you for blessing my business (and/or life) with happiness and wealth. Thank you for paving my path with luxury and ease.

Tess Whitehurst

January 11

Friday

 Color of the day: Rose
Incense of the day: Violet

New Moon in Capricorn

Spell for Beginning a Project

In addition to being a new moon, today is also Carmentalia, a festival associated with Carmenta, the Roman goddess of childbirth. This is a perfect day to harness the energy of creation and new beginnings to help birth a creative endeavor or project into being.

Tonight take a piece of moonstone, go outdoors, and gaze up at the vast, clear, dark night sky. Visualize it as a blank canvas ready for you to create upon. Holding the moonstone in your left (receptive) hand, connect with the energy of the Divine and the cosmos, and ask for their guidance. Allow the inspiration to flow through you and the stone, filling both you and the moonstone with its vibrant energy. Meditate upon the first steps you need to take for your project. Then silently give thanks to the Divine for its guidance and begin taking action to give birth to your creative endeavor.

Keep the moonstone on your person as a talisman of the creative energy you have harnessed. If you ever feel stagnant or unsure of the next step to take, use the moonstone as a conduit to the energy channeled during this spell. So mote it be!

Blake Octavian Blair

NOTES:

January 12

Saturday

Color of the day: Black
Incense of the day: Rue

household harmony

O riginally a pagan holiday honoring Frigga, Norse goddess of the household, today was historically when women returned to the home following Yule visiting and celebrations. Though it was renamed St. Distaff's Day by the Christians, after a spinning tool used to make yarn, the original Pagan meaning was kept. Households require work—not just mundane cleaning, repairs, and maintenance but also the magical work of spiritual cleansing, protection, and blessing.

Today devote some time to mundane cleaning done with magical intent. Then bless your household, to create and maintain harmony within the house and among its inhabitants. Walk through each room, conjuring up feelings of joy and gratitude for all that your household means to you. Chant:

Bless this happy, healthy home.
Bless my people, wherever they roam.

Keep us safe, protected, and whole, and give us harmony in our wondrous home.

Use this blessing whenever you clean house, in the mundane and magical spheres.

Dallas Jennifer Cobb

NOTES:

January 13
Sunday

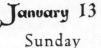

Color of the day: Yellow
Incense of the day: Almond

Festival of Brewing

Today is a traditional Druid festival of brewing. Brewing beverages from the local harvest is an ancient tradition, and festivals dedicated to Bacchus and Dionysus testify to the power of intoxicating beverages and their importance to the human experience. Preserving fruits and grains in this way also teaches us to make the most of our food supply: early American settlers drank cider and beer because they couldn't always count on having potable water. The famed Johnny Appleseed planted his trees so pioneers could make cider in their new settlements.

On this day, enjoy a beverage brewed from your area's harvest: beer from a microbrewery, wine from a local winery, mead from your coven's mead brewer, or cider (alcoholic or not) from a nearby orchard or farmstand. Buying local products stimulates the community's economy and encourages the self-reliance and reconnection to nature at the heart of the growing popularity in home brewing.

Peg Aloi

January 14
Monday

Color of the day: Lavender
Incense of the day: Narcissus

Cleaning Up Your Computer Spell

It's the beginning of the new calendar year, and there are several things you should do to keep your computer clean now that the holidays are over. Ask Techno-logika, goddess of all things tech, for another good year of no viruses, malware, or breakdowns for your electronic equipment. Then go through your Magical Technology List to make sure you are doing your part:

- Password for this year changed on all accounts
- Anti-virus program and definitions up to date
- Latest security patches up to date and installed
- Latest malware definitions up to date
- Keyboard and fans clean and free of debris
- Wireless network hidden and secured with a password

Then say the Spell of the Geeks:

I keep my machine(s) clean and up to date. Protect them, Techno-logika!

Boudica

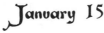

January 15

Tuesday

Color of the day: Gray
Incense of the day: Ylang-ylang

Mars Motivation Spell

Tuesday, carrying with it the aggressive energy of Roman warrior god Mars, is a perfect day to finish uncompleted tasks or tasks you've had trouble getting motivated to start. Gather a red candle and an appropriate holder and try out this spell to focus a bit of Mars' aggressive energy into executing your task. Hold the candle between your hands and visualize yourself starting, carrying out, and completing your task. Now light the candle and recite the following verses:

> Candle of red burning true,
>
> Mars guiding me all day through.
>
> Action, achievement, and forward motion too
>
> Fiery motivation please seep through.
>
> Guide and motivate me, intentions true
>
> The time for completion has come due.
>
> So mote it be!

Begin your task with a fresh sense of invigoration while you watch your candle burn itself out knowing you are drawing forth the energy needed for your task.

Blake Octavian Blair

NOTES:

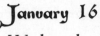

January 16
Wednesday

 Color of the day: Brown
Incense of the day: Marjoram

A Business Communication Spell

If you are going to give a presentation at a business meeting, have a meeting with your boss, or meet with a client, this spell will help you communicate effectively.

As you're getting ready for work that morning, use a lavender-scented soap and, if you have time, burn a lavender-scented candle. As you dress, say your opening comments out loud to yourself. Since yellow is a color that represents mental clarity, wear something yellow, such as a tie or scarf. In a small pouch or in a piece of fabric, tie up a small amount of dill. Dill is associated with the planet Mercury and mental sharpness. Carry your small bundle of dill in your purse or briefcase. One final tip: make direct eye contact.

James Kambos

January 17
Thursday

Color of the day: Turquoise
Incense of the day: Carnation

Sending Blessings into the World

To be sure, we live in challenging times. Most news broadcasts are filled with reports of fires, floods, hurricanes, and tornadoes, plus events involving people with weapons. What's a Pagan to do in such a world? *Live mindfully.*

I live in the city. Fire station #3 is two blocks from my home. At least once a day I hear a fire engine roaring up my street. I also hear police helicopters and sirens around the city. No matter where you live, you probably hear sirens, too. They're telling us that someone needs help. They're signals that someone needs a blessing.

Whenever you hear a siren, stop what you're doing. Speak this blessing to the firefighters, police officers, or ambulance drivers and their passengers:

> Blessings to you. Blessings to
> where you're going.

Send this energy out and see it touching the people who need it. Do this every day.

Barbara Ardinger, Ph.D.

January 18

Friday

Color of the day: Purple
Incense of the day: Vanilla

Fruit of Love

If you live in a temperate climate, this is the time of year when it's necessary to rely on the supermarket for fresh produce; we need it to nurture our bodies. Love is like this: we go through seasons of abundance, of need and fulfillment. Fruit has long been used to symbolize love. Find a piece of fresh fruit that you enjoy—an apple, perhaps, or a handful of berries.

Hold the fruit in your hand and visualize it being filled with nurturing energy, the love of Mother Earth. Take a bite, then another. Eat the fruit slowly, savoring it. Imagine the fruit filling you with love—the ability to give and receive it. Use this chant to help you visualize:

> Fruit of love, nurture me.
>
> Fill me with your energy.
>
> Fruit of earth, from vine or tree,
>
> I welcome love to come to me.

> Ember Grant

January 19

Saturday

Color of the day: Brown
Incense of the day: Sage

Water Work

Draw on the power of water today as you seek to hone your intuition, that perfect marriage of head and heart that gives rise to deep wisdom. You may wish to chant, sing, or utter prayers or mantras over a crystal-clear bowl of water and see what arises from your innermost sanctuaries. Remember to offer sprinklings around your home as a blessing. Anoint yourself, too, saying these words aloud to make clear your intention to cleanse all that obstructs your truest view of self and world:

> Mountain stream and water wild,
>
> Calmest brook and tide beguiled;
>
> Help me see through shadows deep,
>
> Mark my words this spell do keep.

> Chandra Alexandre

January 20

Sunday

Color of the day: Orange
Incense of the day: Marigold

Inauguration Day

Cure for the Winter Doldrums

Have the winter doldrums set in for you? Yule and New Year celebrations are well over. The house is no longer festively decorated. This time of year is said to be the most depressing. One definition of doldrums: a series of light winds or calm on the ocean. Starting today, take a positive slant and deem this a time of inward calm. Get plenty of rest. Eat light, nutritious, yet comforting foods. Work your body and muscles with yoga, tai chi, or simple stretches. Listen to soothing music or background noise. Ease your mind with meditation and inward reflection. Develop your spring and summer household or garden projects.

> Away from the winter darkness, toward the spring light,
>
> This calming time nourishes my weary spirit.
>
> Plans laid this day will bear abundant fruit.
>
> As I write, so mote it be.

Emyme

January 21

Monday

Color of the day: White
Incense of the day: Hyssop

Birthday of Martin Luther King, Jr.
(observed)

A New Pair of Shoes

Martin Luther King Jr. Day offers a chance to reflect on the challenge of discrimination and the power of social justice in our communities. During your day, pick out someone you see who is unlike you—in background, culture, religion, ethnicity, education, class, or any other category you can think of. Quietly put yourself in that person's shoes. What would be different from your life? What might be easy for you? Hard? Reflect briefly on what people might assume about you simply by looking at you.

Take what you've learned and act on one small thing you can change that will make life more equitable for others around you. You might suggest a change in a process at work, smile at someone on the street, or help out with a social justice cause. Simple acts can make a big change in the world—a potent kind of magic. Repeat as often as you can.

Jenett Silver

January 22
Tuesday

Color of the day: Red
Incense of the day: Basil

Inspiration Spell

Has your creative muse been napping? If everything seems solemn right now, the best way to get your creative juices flowing is to shake things up a bit.

Acquire a small, empty notebook and a pen, then place a mint teabag between the pages of the notebook, like a bookmark. Now take the notebook and go out and do something that is completely out of character for you. Visit a local place where you've never been, or try some ethnic food you've never tasted. Step outside your comfort zone. Jot down any random thoughts in the notebook.

When you return home, take out the notebook and brew that mint tea. Before you take your first sip, trace the shape of an eye in the air over the cup of tea. See what inspiration comes to you, and flesh out any notes that you made while you were out. Your muse is wide awake.

Mickie Mueller

January 23
Wednesday

Color of the day: Topaz
Incense of the day: Lavender

Elemental Connection: Earth

Immerse yourself in the earth element. Wear natural fibers in earthy colors of green, blue, and brown. Begin and end each day with a walk, at least part of which is spent with bare feet on the actual earth rather than on concrete or asphalt. Collect and work with stones and crystals; pay attention to which ones seem to call to you, remembering that stones are the oldest of Earth's denizens and bear the ancient memories. They'll share their stories if only you listen. Carry a piece of snowflake obsidian in your pocket for protection, and wear stones as necklaces, earrings, or other adornments. Use ceramic or wood to make a panticle for your altar, inscribed with a pentagram, an earth triangle sign, runes, or other relevant or meaningful symbols. Feast on unprocessed, organic foods. Revel in the solid-but-sensual nature of the earth element.

Susan Pesznecker

January 24
Thursday

Color of the day: Crimson
Incense of the day: Mulberry

Winter Comfort

In many areas winter has settled in, and we are possibly stuck indoors, with storms, short days, and bad weather. To pass the time, work with Hestia, goddess of the hearth, to make food that is warm, comforting, and healthy. Crockpot soups and stews are good on a cold, dark, and windy day. Chicken soup, beef stew, homemade spaghetti sauce, and vegetable soups are just some of the dishes that will make the house smell comfortable while they cook in the crockpot. Use Google to find a recipe that will appeal to you. Keep items in stock like root vegetables (potatoes, onions), herbs and spices, and frozen veggies to create your dish without having to run out to the store. And remember that bread machine you've got stashed under the kitchen counter? There is nothing like fresh, homemade bread with a good soup or stew.

Boudica

January 25
Friday

Color of the day: Pink
Incense of the day: Cypress

Pennies for Self-harmony

Venus is the planetary ruler of Friday. The Roman goddess Venus and her Greek counterpart, Aphrodite, both goddesses of love and the ocean, are also attributed to this day.

Here is a simple spell to bring a boost to your self-love and harmony utilizing today's energies. Gather three pennies, as copper also corresponds to Friday. Each penny will represent an area of your life or an aspect of yourself that could use more harmony, self-love, and acceptance. Hold the first penny, focusing on an aspect to which you intend to bring these energies, and proceed to blow your intent into the penny. When you have done this for all three pennies, either toss them into a fountain or place them in a bowl of water upon your altar for twenty-four hours in honor of the ocean goddesses who lend their energies to this day.

Blake Octavian Blair

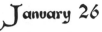

January 26
Saturday

Color of the day: Indigo
Incense of the day: Pine

Full Moon in Leo

Finding a Mate Spell

This is the perfect time to attract a mate. First make a list of qualities you value on a piece of paper. When done, fold it three times and place it on the bottom of the second drawer of your dresser. Then select an item representing your love needs, such as money or a gift of some kind. Now find an item to represent your ideal mate. Do you want him to be a professional? A nice tie will work. Or if it is a woman you are looking for, perhaps choose a pair of beautiful earrings. Mix equal amounts of catnip and ground cinnamon with three drops of jasmine oil in a small glass bowl and sprinkle rose petals over the mixture. Set the bowl in the drawer and encircle it with your mate's symbol of love, then yours. Repeat the following three times:

Love is mine as I divine.

When finished, close the drawer.

Patti Larsen

January 27
Sunday

Color of the day: Amber
Incense of the day: Heliotrope

The Law of the Power

The Power shall not be used to bring harm, to injure or control others. But if the need arises, the Power shall be used to protect your life or the lives of others.

The Power is used only as need dictates.

The Power can be used for your own gain, as long as by doing so you harm none.

It is unwise to accept money for use of the Power, for it quickly controls its taker. Be not as those of other religions.

Use not the Power for prideful gain, for such cheapens the mysteries of Wicca and magic.

Ever remember that the Power is the sacred gift of the Goddess and God, and should never be misused or abused.

And this is the Law of Power.

**From Scott Cunningham's
"Wicca: A Guide for the
Solitary Practitioner"**

January 28
Monday

Color of the day: Silver
Incense of the day: Lily

Detoxification Bath

Astrologically speaking, today is the perfect time to initiate a magical momentum related to the release of toxins—emotional, energetic, and/or physical. You might do so by lighting a white candle and drawing a warm bath. Add one cup of sea salt and place plenty of drinking water near the tub. Hold your hands over the bathwater and visualize it being filled with very bright white light. Inwardly or aloud, say:

Great Goddess, please infuse this water with vibrations of purification and love.

Now direct your hands toward the drinking water and repeat. Then soak for at least forty minutes, being sure to drink water often to replenish your fluids and help the cleansing process. As you soak, be aware of the toxins moving out of your body, mind, and spirit, and know that you are initiating a cleansing/releasing momentum that will continue throughout the remainder of the moon cycle.

Tess Whitehurst

January 29
Tuesday

Color of the day: White
Incense of the day: Cedar

Hecate at the Crossroads

The twenty-ninth of each month is dedicated to the Greek goddess Hecate, goddess of the crossroads, of magic and the occult, and the "dark face" of the earth mother archetype, often associated with death. Her Roman name was Trivia, literally "three roads" or crossroads. Trivia's modern meaning is based on folklore about Witches, an old saying that "nothing of importance happens at the crossroads." These words conveyed that the sight of women/Witches meeting at the crossroads (on their way to a sabbat, perhaps?) was trivial.

In the dark days of winter, Hecate is close to us. Honor her with a plate of bread and cheese on your hearth or altar; eat some yourself, feeling nourished against winter's cold. The next time you come to a crossroads, leave a small offering there for Hecate, and ask her to help you reach your destination safely.

Peg Aloi

January 30
Wednesday

Color of the day: Yellow
Incense of the day: Bay laurel

Magical Getaway

Invoke Wednesday deity Mercury, Roman god of travel, as you prepare for a winter getaway. When traveling, overprepare and then go with the flow. Make a list—not the usual "clothes, shoes, toiletries" list, but what you'll to need to take, and to do, to care for your sacred self while traveling. What will bring you safety, security, peace of mind, relaxation, acceptance, and joy? Don't forget your toothbrush and sunscreen, but pay careful attention to the essentials of magical self-care. Take multi-use items, such as magically charged jewelry, sacred cloth sarongs, herbal dream pillows, or a journal for magical observation, journaling, and note taking. Avoid athames and unidentified herbs or oils, as these may slow you down at customs.

While on vacation, make time for sacred routines, rituals, meditation, and spellwork. Do protective spells daily to ensure you always travel with good spirits, and remember to always give thanks.

Dallas Jennifer Cobb

January 31
Thursday

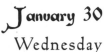

Color of the day: Green
Incense of the day: Clove

Feast of Hekate

Also known as Lucifera, Bringer of Light, Hekate is a keeper of ancient wisdom often locked in the dark recesses of your body's memory. Invite her in today using drum and dance to help free up what lies trapped and untapped within you. Release her healing powers, too, with a prayer as you move:

Hekate, Goddess of Cross-roads, show me the path to my woundings and weaknesses that I might heal and grow strong.

Ancient One, accept my offerings that I might hear your honest guidance, your naked truth.

Three-headed Hag, teach me to laugh at myself, bringing the gift of humility.

Chandra Alexandre

January Moon Table

Date	Sign	Element	Nature	Phase
1 Tue 12:35 pm	Virgo	Earth	Barren	3rd
2 Wed	Virgo	Earth	Barren	3rd
3 Thu 8:11 pm	Libra	Air	Semi-fruitful	3rd
4 Fri	Libra	Air	Semi-fruitful	4th 10:58 pm
5 Sat	Libra	Air	Semi-fruitful	4th
6 Sun 1:09 am	Scorpio	Water	Fruitful	4th
7 Mon	Scorpio	Water	Fruitful	4th
8 Tue 3:28 am	Sagittarius	Fire	Barren	4th
9 Wed	Sagittarius	Fire	Barren	4th
10 Thu 3:54 am	Capricorn	Earth	Semi-fruitful	4th
11 Fri	Capricorn	Earth	Semi-fruitful	New 2:44 pm
12 Sat 4:01 am	Aquarius	Air	Barren	1st
13 Sun	Aquarius	Air	Barren	1st
14 Mon 5:49 am	Pisces	Water	Fruitful	1st
15 Tue	Pisces	Water	Fruitful	1st
16 Wed 11:07 am	Aries	Fire	Barren	1st
17 Thu	Aries	Fire	Barren	1st
18 Fri 8:36 pm	Taurus	Earth	Semi-fruitful	2nd 6:45 pm
19 Sat	Taurus	Earth	Semi-fruitful	2nd
20 Sun	Taurus	Earth	Semi-fruitful	2nd
21 Mon 9:04 am	Gemini	Air	Barren	2nd
22 Tue	Gemini	Air	Barren	2nd
23 Wed 10:00 pm	Cancer	Water	Fruitful	2nd
24 Thu	Cancer	Water	Fruitful	2nd
25 Fri	Cancer	Water	Fruitful	2nd
26 Sat 9:20 am	Leo	Fire	Barren	Full 11:38 pm
27 Sun	Leo	Fire	Barren	3rd
28 Mon 6:27 pm	Virgo	Earth	Barren	3rd
29 Tue	Virgo	Earth	Barren	3rd
30 Wed	Virgo	Earth	Barren	3rd
31 Thu 1:36 am	Libra	Air	Semi-fruitful	3rd

Times are in Eastern Time.

February

February is a month of extremes. It begins with the sabbat of Imbolc, has a romantic celebration of Valentine's Day mid-month, and, just to keep us on our toes, ends with an extra day some years. February is a magic in-between time when anything can happen. Often the most brutal of winter storms occur now, and even though we get caught up in the romance of the middle of the month and the revelry of Mardi Gras, spring can seem far away. But the light increases every day, and we should remember that February is all about the light, possibilities, and the hope of new life to come. Deities associated with the month are the Celtic goddess Brigid and the Greek deities Eros and Aphrodite. Folks born in the month of February are assigned the violet and the primrose. The violet's magical qualities include faery magic and good luck and cheer, while the primrose has the enchanting qualities of protection and love. The amethyst is the birthstone for the month of February. A very popular stone with most magic users, the amethyst's magical properties include protection from manipulative magic and the power to enhance personal protection and your own spellcasting.

Ellen Dugan

February 1

Friday

Color of the day: White
Incense of the day: Alder

Love Yourself Spell

Like many people, you probably don't take time for yourself. We've reached the middle of another cold winter, and since this is a Venus day it's time to love yourself for a change, and this spell will help. Run a luxurious bath for yourself using a soothing body wash—vanilla, rose, or gardenia are good choices. Light pink or white votive candles. Ease into the tub and visualize every care leaving your body, being cleared away by the water. Later, as the water drains, "see" your worries and concerns going down the drain, too. Dry off, use your favorite moisturizing body lotion, and wrap yourself in a favorite bathrobe. Feel the Goddess surrounding you; she wants you to take care of yourself. Then brew a cup of herbal tea, such as almond or lemon/rose. Sip slowly. Love yourself for a change—you deserve it!

James Kambos

February 2

Saturday

Color of the day: Gray
Incense of the day: Sandalwood

Imbolc – Groundhog Day

Bringing Light and Creativity into the New Year

Imbolc, or Brigid, celebrates the rising of the light that was reborn with the winter solstice. Let's celebrate the sun and work for a manifestation of creativity. Think about creativity in your life. How do you want it to manifest? In specific projects? Generally?

Set up your altar with symbols, candles, and incense holders in the four directions. The incense holders should be gold, though abalone will work as well. Be sure to set your charcoal briquettes on a bed of sand. Set a figure of Brigit in the center.

As you cast your circle, light the candles and the briquettes. Invoke the goddess:

> Great Brigit, goddess of the sun, goddess of light and heat, smithcraft, and poetry—be present with us on this holy day. Fill us with the power of your light and let it manifest as creativity in our lives.

You can add to this invocation, if you'd like.

Sprinkle Vesta powder on the briquettes. As they spark and

sparkle, visualize each little spark growing stronger and flying up into your soul, touching your imagination, your hands, and your heart. Visualize the ways creativity will manifest in your life this year. Add more Vesta powder for more power. Carry the sparks of Brigit's power in your heart throughout the year.

Barbara Ardinger, Ph.D.

NOTES:

February 3

Sunday

Color of the day: Orange
Incense of the day: Frankincense

Religious Freedom

In 313 the Edict of Milan was passed, ending persecution of Christians in the Roman Empire. Today many small religions, including Neopagan paths, still seek religious freedom in many countries. Here's what you can do to help support this civil liberty.

Remember that religious freedom is for everyone, not just the people you agree with. It can be tough to support those with beliefs you dislike, but like the freedom of speech, religious liberty is strongest when everyone has it.

Write letters to your elected representatives urging them to support everyone's right to—or from—religion.

If you're out of the broom closet, be a positive example of your Pagan path. Don't shove your beliefs in everyone else's face, but offer information if asked, and politely correct misinformation.

Lupa

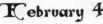

February 4

Monday

Color of the day: Gray
Incense of the day: Neroli

Setsubun

In Japan, Setsubun means "dividing the seasons," and this tradition involves throwing roasted soybeans while shouting "In with good luck, out with demons!" This is a kind of symbolic spring cleaning ritual. Today perform this ritual in order to clear negativity from your environment. Visualize the end of winter and the beginning of spring (even though it's a bit early in most areas). Imagine the soybean bringing good health and vitality while chasing away any unwanted energy. You can freely toss soybeans around your home and yard, if you'd like, or choose a more methodical approach. Place a bean in each room and, as you set it in place, use this chant:

Bring good fortune to this place.

Purge all harm without a trace.

Ember Grant

February 5

Tuesday

Color of the day: White
Incense of the day: Geranium

Solo Dining

This week, "Solo Diners Eat Out" is observed. Tuesdays are the domain of Mars, passionate and courageous. Begin a tradition of solo dining at a local establishment with the eye to becoming a regular. Before departing your home, and before and after the meal, offer appreciation to Mars for his protection. Should an evening meal prove too expensive, lunch (or even breakfast) is a fine substitute.

Great warrior god Mars,

Guide me in this project/ process.

Infuse me with a passion for dining.

Smile upon me with your courage and protection.

Emyme

February 6

Wednesday

Color of the day: Brown
Incense of the day: Marjoram

Aphrodesia (Festival of Aphrodite)

String together six beads today: one for love, one for passion, one for joy, one for sex, one for play, and one for beauty. Six, the number sacred to the Goddess of Love, is also the number of sides on a honeycomb, the sweetness of honey a reminder of life's pleasures. Throughout the day, finger the beads and enjoy meditations on these aspects of the goddess known in various parts of the world as Aphrodite, Venus, Ishtar, Astarte, Freya, Lakshmi, and Oshun. If you desire to fulfill a particular wish, bring the strength of repetition to your work, speaking a prayer or sacred intention on each bead for a total of six times six.

Chandra Alexandre

February 7

Thursday

Color of the day: Purple
Incense of the day: Apricot

Snow Bird Prosperity Spell

Build a full-figured snow goddess with her arms folded and cupped in front of her, creating a bowl made out of snow. Think "snowman with dangerous curves"—it's not about the skill, but the intention. On the inside of the bowl, with your finger carve the shape of a dollar sign (the kind that looks like an S with two vertical lines, not just one), then make a triangle around the dollar sign for manifestation. Fill the bowl with birdseed and repeat:

Birds of the air, food of the earth,

I offer you wealth for all that it's worth.

Eat till you're full, every dear feathered friend.

Generosity shall return much more than I send.

Keep the bowl full of birdseed until the snow goddess melts away. As the birds eat the seed and the snow goddess melts, may the obstacles between you and prosperity disappear.

Mickie Mueller

February 8

Friday

Color of the day: Rose
Incense of the day: Orchid

Blessing the Food

Food fills so many roles in our lives. It nourishes our bodies, nurtures us when we're ill, provides a unique type of sensual pleasure, and, for those of us magickal folks, comes with an arcane element as well. Yet we often zip through our days, gobbling food and too often relying on processed, pre-cooked, or fast foods. Even worse, most of us only rarely pause to show gratitude for the life-sustaining gifts food provides.

Today make a plan to pause mindfully each time you eat or drink. Think about the food or drink you're about to enjoy, and offer a simple blessing:

> I take this food
>
> With gratitude.
>
> May it nourish me.
>
> So shall it be!

Use this blessing throughout the day. Eat slowly, chew mindfully, and visualize the nourishment moving through you. Honor the gift.

Susan Pesznecker

February 9

Saturday

Color of the day: Black
Incense of the day: Patchouli

Create a home Guardian

Ruled by Saturn, Saturday is a good day for protection magic. There is an old saying that "home is where the heart is." That is certainly something worth protecting!

Our homes are a sacred sanctuary from the hustle and bustle of the world outside. You can create and train your own home guardian to serve as protector of your home. Find a statue of a protective creature such as a gargoyle, dragon, or Asian Fu Dog. Anoint the statue's third eye, and walk with the statue around your entire home and even around your property. Explain to the guardian as you do so that this is its domain to protect and what you wish for it to do. When you are finished, place the guardian near the main entryway to your home, either on the inside facing the entryway or outside directly next to the main entryway. Feed your guardian periodically with appropriate offerings.

Blake Octavian Blair

February 10

Sunday

Color of the day: Amber
Incense of the day: Eucalyptus

New Moon in Aquarius –
Chinese New Year (Snake)

Shake Things Up and Get Things Flowing

Like water and air, our lives feel healthy and invigorating when we're aligned with natural movement and flow. When our lives feel stagnant or stuck in any area, often all we need to get the energy moving is a fresh perspective.

Good news: there is perhaps no better time to infuse our perspectives with freshness than at the Aquarius new moon, which is associated with unconventional ideas, ingenious inventions, and creative solutions. To celebrate this moon, shake things up, and get in alignment with the most ideal, blessing-filled life flow possible, make a rattle out of a metal salt and pepper shaker and some dried white beans (or use a rattle you already have). Now move around each area and room of your house in a counterclockwise direction shaking the rattle loudly, taking precautions not to scare your animal friends. Then shake the rattle loudly around yourself and anyone else who'd like to participate. Next ring a chime or bell in a similar way, moving clockwise this time in each room and area before you ring it around yourself and any other participants. Conclude by holding your arms wide and chanting:

> I welcome in the dawning moon.
>
> I sing and dance to my own tune.
>
> My mind contains the whole world wide,
>
> And I sail along the blessings tide.

Tess Whitehurst

NOTES:

February 11

Monday

 Color of the day: White
Incense of the day: Clary sage

An Amethyst Dream Spell

The February birthstone, amethyst, is good to use as an aid to encourage prophetic dreams. You'll need either an amethyst cluster or a smooth, polished amethyst stone you can hold. Send your intent into the amethyst by holding it, or gently rub it with a white cotton cloth. At bedtime hold the amethyst and think or say:

*Send me the dream I should
have, and tell me what I should
know.*

Don't try to control the dream by thinking about a specific issue. Let the amethyst do its job; don't worry, it knows what to do. Then place the cluster on a bedside table, or, if using a stone, put it beneath your pillow. Relax and drift off to sleep. You should experience a clear dream. In the morning, record your dream and see if it comes true.

James Kambos

February 12

Tuesday

Color of the day: Red
Incense of the day: Bayberry

Mardi Gras (Fat Tuesday)

Beneath the Mask

Mardi Gras, or Fat Tuesday, is the traditional day of celebration before the austerity of Lent begins. In New Orleans, Mardi Gras is a huge event that goes on for days. Although the observance stems from Catholic tradition, Mardi Gras itself is a very decadent pagan festival, similar to the European tradition of Carnivale, where people wear masks and behave in uncharacteristic ways. The energy of these festivals lies between the realms of the mystical and the mundane, where we might meet another version of ourselves.

This ritual lets you explore your hidden potential. Get a basic mask from a craft store. Put it on and look at yourself in the mirror. Light a candle and turn off the lights. Continue to look at your reflection, particularly your eyes. You may find you see some odd things, but let these images offer you insights into your true self.

When you feel ready, remove the mask. Your face will look slightly different, because you have glimpsed your hidden self and all the potential that lies within you. Repeat this ritual whenever you are feeling unsure of your path or your place in life.

Peg Aloi

NOTES:

February 13

Wednesday

Color of the day: Yellow
Incense of the day: Lavender

Ash Wednesday

honoring Those Passed Spell

The Romans used this night to connect with the spirits of those who had gone on in order to clear away any old, negative feelings in those relationships and to reinforce their love and happy memories of their lost loved ones. Sit in a dark room facing a window (make sure the curtains are open) with one white candle in front of you on a table. Light it with a match as you say:

I welcome you to my light in peace.

Focus on the flame and allow your most powerful need to rise. Who is it you must make amends with? Have forgiveness for? Or simply renew love and laughter with? Focus on that person and repeat the following:

Open heart, open mind, open spirit.

I see clearly, I hear the truth, I feel you with me.

I thank you, I forgive you, I love you.

When complete, blow out the candle.

Patti Larsen

February 14

Thursday

Color of the day: Green
Incense of the day: Jasmine

Valentine's Day

Love Yourself

You must love yourself in order to create healthy relationships with others. For this spell you will need a mirror and a fragrance that is special to you: a perfume, incense, or essential oil. First pamper yourself today. Treat yourself to a nice meal, a walk in the woods, a massage—whatever brings you joy. To encourage an attitude of self-love, look at yourself in the mirror. Remember that we are all unique and beautiful. Speak out loud the things you love most about yourself—not just physical characteristics but also personal ones. Inhale the aroma you selected as you look at yourself in the mirror and name your beautiful qualities. The goal is to associate the attitude of self-love with the scent, so that when you wear it or smell it, you are reminded of your true beauty. Chant:

> I see myself, and I see love.
> I love myself and take care of
> My body, mind, and soul—
> To be happy and be whole.

Ember Grant

February 15

Friday

Color of the day: Pink
Incense of the day: Yarrow

Packing Your Porta-Witch Basket

Who knows where or when you'll want to do some magical work. Be prepared. Pack your Porta-Witch basket.

Buy a picnic basket with handles and a lid. What do you need for magical work? Make a checklist. It may not be what everyone else would use, but this is your unique toolkit. Some suggestions:

• A goddess or god you're dedicated to, such as an all-purpose deity like the Statue of Liberty (America's goddess), a mother-creatrix, or a powerful and generous father god. Find an unbreakable figure.

• An altar cloth that will stand up to repeated use and in a color that can be used for any ritual.

• Directional symbols (unbreakable and in the proper colors).

• Candle holders (unbreakable and in the proper colors).

• Incense holders.

- Sand and charcoal briquettes in plastic bags.
- Matches.
- Oils and other important supplies.
- Ritual jewelry.

Keep your Porta-Witch basket in the trunk of your car. You'll always be ready to work.

Barbara Ardinger, Ph.D.

NOTES:

February 16

Saturday

Color of the day: Indigo
Incense of the day: Magnolia

Connecting in the Ether

Today is the anniversary of the first online bulletin board systems, the ancestors of our e-mail lists and social networking sites. That makes it a great day to review how we spend time online. Does it make you happy or leave you upset? Do you have time to focus on longer projects, or are you always in crisis response mode? Consider taking a break from the 'Net (once a week, once a month) to rebalance.

Make it easy to focus on what matters most to you (family, friends, passions) by putting those bookmarks, files, and apps front and center. Remove any that are no longer part of your life, and hide those that distract you. Change your desktop image or profile photos to something that reminds you of a current goal or passion. Technology can be part of a rich and full life—as long as you're intentional.

Jenett Silver

February 17

Sunday

Color of the day: Yellow
Incense of the day: Juniper

Sunday Three-Day Prosperity Spell

Sunday is always a good day to begin prosperity spells. I like a three-day working because it gives the job extra energy. Start with a yellow or gold three-day candle, available at most esoteric shops. I like to add an oil that says "prosperity," so some sunflower oil mixed with some honeysuckle or cherry and a few drops of cinnamon is a nice mix and will make the house fragrant.

Next draw some dollar signs on a piece of paper and burn it with your intent to be profitable. Remember, prosperity does not necessarily mean a big check; it could mean a golden opportunity or a special increase somewhere that can be turned profitable. If you need help with funds, dollar signs will do. If you need help with an idea, draw an illuminated light bulb on a piece of paper. Do not limit yourself.

Boudica

February 18

Monday

Color of the day: Silver
Incense of the day: Rosemary

Presidents' Day (observed)

Invoking Hestia

Mid-winter, a time when pantries are emptying out, is a time to invoke Hestia, the Greek goddess of hearth and home, the "keeper of the reserves." Take stock of home and hearth. What's needed for comfort, protection, and nourishment? It's cold outside, and time to create warmth within. Cook hot oatmeal and invoke Hestia. As the oatmeal warms you, be with Hestia:

> Hestia, make this house a home, a sanctuary to all who enter.
>
> Bless this doorstep. All who cross, come in peace.
>
> Bless this home. Family and friends feel welcomed and nurtured.
>
> Bless this kitchen, the spiritual heart of this home.
>
> Bless this stove, warm center of sacred space, creator of nourishment for body and soul.
>
> And bless this pantry, with reserves to see us all through winter,

Warmth to provide comfort
and respite from the outside
world,

And your sweet spirit to warm
us within.

Blessed be, Hestia.

Dallas Jennifer Cobb

NOTES:

February 19

Tuesday

Color of the day: Maroon
Incense of the day: Cedar

Cheer Up!

Some days just stink. If it's been one of those days for you, here's a bit of a pick-me-up.

First think of one of the very best days you've ever had, no matter when. Immerse yourself in the memory and remember how it felt to be in that day. Next take that feeling and give it a name; it could be something like *Joy* or *Fun*. Don't name it something more specific, though, like *The Day I Learned to Ride a Bike*. You want to transfer the feeling to many other days.

Next take a stone of a color that reminds you of the good feeling, and hold it over your heart. Visualize the feeling welling up out of your heart and flowing into the stone.

Then, when you have a bad day, hold the stone next to your heart. Visualize some of the good feeling flowing back into your heart, and invite it to make your day feel better.

Lupa

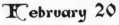

February 20

Wednesday

Color of the day: Topaz
Incense of the day: Bay laurel

Basic Wand Use

First let me say that I do not use my wand primarily to cast spells; I use it to focus my energy into positive channels. If I'm angry or anxious, I use the wand to bring me back to a place of calm. I face west (my preferred direction), point the wand toward the floor, and channel the negativity through the wand and into the ground. Personally I prefer channeling thoughts, not words, but the object is to exchange raw emotion for calm, rational thinking. When finished with the channeling, I endorse my wand for its assistance. I keep my wand on an altar.

Wands can be particularly soothing during transitional moments in life, such as births, weddings, funerals, new jobs, and new homes. Touching a newborn baby with a wand can endow that baby with your positive energy. Those old fairy tales have grains of truth in them after all!

Anne Johnson

February 21

Thursday

Color of the day: Crimson
Incense of the day: Nutmeg

Day of Nut

Sky goddess of rebirth, the Egyptian Nut provides inspiration today, inviting us to be born again truer to our souls. From the time you wake until the sun begins to set, practice mindfulness in all you speak and do. Invoke Nut:

> Carrier of a Thousand Souls,
>
> Hear my prayer this day;
>
> I give myself to your potent embrace,
>
> Birth me come what may.

With the setting sun, gather grasses and herbs that you can burn, making a sacrificial fire into which offerings of incense, flowers, and fruit may be made. Give Nut your gratitude and release that which keeps you entangled in the past. Extinguish the fire with wine and wear white to bed. Arise reborn.

Chandra Alexandre

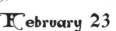

February 22

Friday

Color of the day: Coral
Incense of the day: Mint

The Cup of Concordia

This is a feast day of the Roman goddess Concordia. It is a good day to make peace within the family or household. We often take our families for granted and expect that our relationships will function on autopilot. But maintaining trust and compassion can require effort at times.

Perform this ritual when you want to preserve peace in your home and/or among family members. Take a cup or chalice and place it on your altar or a central location, such as the dining room or hall table. Every time you perform a kind act or say something positive to a family member, add a tablespoon of water to the cup. Every time you speak sharply to or lose patience with a family member, or otherwise cause friction, take a tablespoon of water out of the cup. After a week, see how empty or full the cup is. Try to keep the cup as close to full as possible.

Peg Aloi

February 23

Saturday

Color of the day: Brown
Incense of the day: Sage

Communications Breakdown

Right now Mercury starts its retrograde motion, so communications may be rerouted or blocked.

Work on clearing your throat chakra. Check to see if it is blocked. Do this by closing your eyes and taking a "look" inward at your throat chakra. It should be a nice royal blue color. If it is not a rich blue, but instead pale, visualize the color deepening and becoming rich and vibrant. Concentrate on that till it appears corrected in your mind's eye.

Our choice of words always says volumes about who we are and how we consider ourselves and each other. Improve your vocabulary by learning a new word each week. Use it in a sentence daily and try to include it appropriately in casual conversation. You will be surprised at how much you can learn, and how much it will speak about your sincerity.

Boudica

February 24

Sunday

Color of the day: Gold
Incense of the day: Marigold

Purim

Abundant Blessings

Call it luck or good fortune, karma or kismet, but call it! The energies today invite you to believe in the abundance of blessings all around and to call them in.

Start with a visualization of the things you want to manifest in your life. One by one, bring them into focus and send them a kiss of acknowledgment that they are indeed within your reach. Next call on earth, water, fire, and air to provide the right mix of substance so that the manifestations you seek—and the ones that are closest to actualization—may appear. Then, when you have finished, take a length of string and tie it three times around your wrist (left to invoke the energy of the moon, right for the sun) to carry the spell with you. Within three days you will have your first reward.

Chandra Alexandre

February 25

Monday

Color of the day: Ivory
Incense of the day: Hyssop

Full Moon in Virgo

A Group Lunar Ritual for Cooperation

Tonight is a full moon, with the moon moving from the fire sign of Leo into the earth sign of Virgo. When the moon is in Virgo, we tend to feel a sense of responsibility. We become aware of what needs to be done and may be anxious (even a bit antsy) to get started doing it. If we're not careful, we may become frustrated with those who don't share our same work ethic. Create a communal lunar ritual to inspire these strong feelings of desire and intention while also reminding each participant to be gentle with each other. The full moon is, of course, a wonderful time to raise energies, whether by dancing, drumming, chanting, or singing. As the energies spiral up, speak aloud of the work that is waiting to be done. Then, as the energy ebbs, focus on the need to create peaceful cooperation toward the end result. Have each participant tie a silver cord around one wrist; allow these cords to remain until the next full moon, serving as reminders of the shared intention.

Susan Pesznecker

February 26

Tuesday

 Color of the day: Black
Incense of the day: Basil

Share Because You Care

Over the holidays and during other busy times, some of our friendships can slip from our minds. Use the chant below to focus your attention on a relationship or friendship that might have been a little neglected recently.

> Thought, word, action, deed,
>
> Help me now find the need.
>
> Reaching out, I open doors,
>
> Remembering what's gone before.

Repeat the chant three times, and pay attention to who springs to mind. Give the person a call or send an e-mail, and catch up, for the memory of all the good times you've shared. If it's a relationship that's been bumpy, you might get some help (from divination or a wise friend) about how to handle the past more smoothly. Don't focus on forgiving and forgetting; after all, the past is still part of us. Instead, reach out to create the connection you'd like in the future.

Jenett Silver

February 27

Wednesday

Color of the day: White
Incense of the day: Lilac

Throw Conflicts to the Wind

Conditions are perfect to release disputes, whether they're with ourselves, others, or life in general. This includes discordant mental chatter, ongoing verbal conflicts, and any other challenges to harmony that involve thoughts and words. If a condition like this comes to mind, grab a notebook and pen. Write four pages without stopping, letting the words of the conflict spill out. If it's a conflict with yourself or the world, write down your inner monologue. If the conflict is with another person or group of people, write down the dialogue to the best of your ability. Then pull out the notebook pages that you wrote on, and safely burn them in a cauldron or pot. Light a cone of India Temple incense, and place the cone on the ashes. Once it has burned, mix the ashes together, then take them outside and throw them to the wind. If there's no wind, blow them away.

Tess Whitehurst

February 28

Thursday

Color of the day: Purple
Incense of the day: Clove

Amburbium Spell

To the Romans, Amburbium was a holiday of protection for body, mind, and spirit. They circled their homes, chanting and praying, offering sacrifices to ensure their safety from evil spirits.

Sprinkle salt in a large circle as you say:

*Within this circle I am safe
from all things.*

Inside the circle place three bowls: one with salt, one with red wine, and one with milk. Sprinkle some salt into the red wine while saying:

My body is safe and whole.

Sprinkle some salt into the milk and say:

My mind is safe and sound.

Finally, pour the red wine and the milk into the bowl of salt and say:

My spirit is safe and free.

When completed, sweep up the circle and place in the bowl with the rest of the sacrifice and say:

*I am safe, body, mind, and
spirit.*

Pour the sacrifice down the drain.

Patti Larsen

February Moon Table

Date	Sign	Element	Nature	Phase
1 Fri	Libra	Air	Semi-fruitful	3rd
2 Sat 7:02 am	Scorpio	Water	Fruitful	3rd
3 Sun	Scorpio	Water	Fruitful	4th 8:56 am
4 Mon 10:45 am	Sagittarius	Fire	Barren	4th
5 Tue	Sagittarius	Fire	Barren	4th
6 Wed 12:55 pm	Capricorn	Earth	Semi-fruitful	4th
7 Thu	Capricorn	Earth	Semi-fruitful	4th
8 Fri 2:16 pm	Aquarius	Air	Barren	4th
9 Sat	Aquarius	Air	Barren	4th
10 Sun 4:20 pm	Pisces	Water	Fruitful	New 2:20 am
11 Mon	Pisces	Water	Fruitful	1st
12 Tue 8:51 pm	Aries	Fire	Barren	1st
13 Wed	Aries	Fire	Barren	1st
14 Thu	Aries	Fire	Barren	1st
15 Fri 5:08 am	Taurus	Earth	Semi-fruitful	1st
16 Sat	Taurus	Earth	Semi-fruitful	1st
17 Sun 4:50 pm	Gemini	Air	Barren	2nd 3:31 pm
18 Mon	Gemini	Air	Barren	2nd
19 Tue	Gemini	Air	Barren	2nd
20 Wed 5:45 am	Cancer	Water	Fruitful	2nd
21 Thu	Cancer	Water	Fruitful	2nd
22 Fri 5:12 pm	Leo	Fire	Barren	2nd
23 Sat	Leo	Fire	Barren	2nd
24 Sun	Leo	Fire	Barren	2nd
25 Mon 1:52 am	Virgo	Earth	Barren	Full 3:26 pm
26 Tue	Virgo	Earth	Barren	3rd
27 Wed 8:02 am	Libra	Air	Semi-fruitful	3rd
28 Thu	Libra	Air	Semi-fruitful	3rd

Times are in Eastern Time.

March

March is a time of the year when anything can and does happen. Some days are warm. You can soak up the sun and feel the promises of the summer stirring in your heart. Other days an icy wind can chill you and have you clutching a jacket close. It's enchanting to watch daffodils and crocuses push their way up, proving that once again, life has reclaimed the earth. It's an exciting time of change, heralding the vernal equinox. Trees have begun to produce small, smooth buds on their bare branches, and nature is really pushing those buds to swell and pop forth with blossoms of all kinds, showering the world with color. I always think of March as nature's last snooze under the warm blankets in the morning, and now she must rise and face the shining day! It's a month all about breaking inertia, new beginnings, and potential. Magically, this is the perfect time to begin a new project and to take advantage of all the new growth energy in the air. It's also a perfect time to cast a spell to clear out what no longer serves us. Use the March winds to blow away the old, dead leaves and reveal new life.

Mickie Mueller

March 1

Friday

Color of the day: Purple
Incense of the day: Rose

Getting a Good Night's Sleep

When you find yourself lying awake in the dark of the night …

Instead of worrying, think of eleven things for which you're grateful. #1: You're sleeping in a bed in your own home.

Program your mind to recite the mantra of or a prayer to the goddess or god to whom you're devoted. My mind in default mode goes to *OM TARE TUTARE TURE SOHA*.

Pet the cat or whoever shares your bed. Snuggle up.

In your head, start writing your novel. Write poetry or compose music. Tell yourself that if it's good, you'll remember it in the morning. If you've forgotten it, then it wasn't worth remembering. Promise yourself that you'll try again tomorrow night.

Begin an exhaustive mental lecture to yourself on the history of ceremonial magic or alchemy or some other highly esoteric topic. Include every petty detail you can think of. You'll bore yourself back to sleep.

Barbara Ardinger, Ph.D.

March 2

Saturday

Color of the day: Gray
Incense of the day: Patchouli

St. Chad's Day

St. Chad was an English bishop and founder of a monastery who died in 672. He was noted for his fondness of taking long walks.

Today, in honor of St. Chad's Day, take a walk. But don't just walk—use the journey as a kind of meditation to seek the natural world. Even if the weather isn't ideal for walking, go outside for a while anyway. Take a long look around you and contemplate everything you see. We often take our surroundings for granted. Keep an open mind and be willing to discover something new. Look beyond the obvious and use your imagination!

What do you see? Write about it in a journal. Here's a chant to ponder as you walk:

> Move my body, step by step,
>
> As I look around,
>
> Let me see beyond what's here,
>
> More than sky and ground.

Ember Grant

March 3

Sunday

Color of the day: Yellow
Incense of the day: Almond

Guardian Circle

Ash, the third moon of the Celtic year, begins today. A sacred Druidic tree, ash has protective qualities and supports inner-self magic.

Invoke ash energy, then draw a large circle on plain paper. At its center place a dot and write *Me*. Identify family, friends, neighbors, acquaintances, and coworkers, placing people in your life within your guardian circle with a dot and their name. Those who guard your spirit, support your soul, and honor your inner self are placed within the circle. The safer you feel with them, the closer to center they appear. Those you need to guard against are placed outside the circle's boundary. The nastier they are, the further out they are placed.

With a quick glance your guardian circle will remind you who is your guardian and whom you need to guard against. View it frequently to remind yourself of each person's right place in your universe.

Dallas Jennifer Cobb

March 4

Monday

Color of the day: Lavender
Incense of the day: Neroli

March Forth!

In addition to enjoying today's pun, why not make today the day you move forward in something that you've been waiting for or putting off for too long? Here are some ideas.

Clean at least one room in your home that's been needing attention, maybe even in preparation for a full-on spring cleaning.

If there's someone in your life you've been meaning to get in contact with, give it a shot today with an e-mail, phone call, or letter.

Let go of at least one long-held grudge. It's got to be heavy to carry around!

Try something new that you've been intending to test out, like a new recipe or place to explore.

Have you been thinking about writing a book or taking on another project? Today write your first hundred words, do research, or otherwise get your action underway.

Lupa

March 5

Tuesday

Color of the day: Gray
Incense of the day: Cinnamon

Isidis Navigatum: The Ship of Isis

Honor the spirit of this ancient festival of Isis by first recognizing the luxuries you have. Just as boats for the goddess were packed with gifts and prayers for good fortune, now is a time to do an inventory of all you have gained over this past year and be thankful. From this place of appreciation, you can work magic to create abundance in new ways that are meaningful for your ongoing well-being and success. One way to do this is to make and offer a gift infused with words of blessing and prosperity for someone in your life who could use a little boost. Present it with love, humility, and sincerity in order to open the path for your own riches to follow.

Chandra Alexandre

March 6

Wednesday

Color of the day: Topaz
Incense of the day: Honeysuckle

Psychic Housecleaning

The signs are everywhere. Crocuses are blooming, birdsong is becoming more melodic, and the garnet-colored buds of the maples are beginning to swell. There is a quickening—in nature and in us.

Now is the time to give our homes a good psychic housecleaning. Here is one way to do this. At night before you retire, place a gray taper candle upon your altar, but don't light it. Sprinkle purifying herbs around it. Rosemary, bay leaf, and parsley would work well. Charge the candle by saying:

Let all negative energy be drawn into this candle and made harmless.

The next day light the candle and let it burn out. Scatter the herbs randomly outside. Then cleanse your own psyche: brew a cup of chamomile tea, sweeten with honey, and sip slowly. Let a feeling of well-being spread from head to toe.

James Kambos

March 7

Thursday

Color of the day: Turquoise
Incense of the day: Carnation

Celebrate Your Name

The first full week of March is "Celebrate Your Name Week." Does your name honor a family member or friend? Is your name unique? Research the history and meaning of your name. Track down your name day, once believed to be more important than a birthday. Tap into social media and find your name twin. If you have not already done so, create your Wiccan name—many books and websites offer formulas. Concentrate on your strengths with a list of positive adjectives starting with the letters of your name. For example:

> Energetic
>
> Merry
>
> Youthful
>
> Magical
>
> Eclectic

Emyme

March 8

Friday

Color of the day: Rose
Incense of the day: Vanilla

You Are Goddess

Today is International Woman's Day; it's a great day to embrace your inner Goddess. Take some time to sit somewhere quietly. If the weather is nice, get outside for a bit. Close your eyes and breathe deeply. Visualize all of the strong women who have inspired you in your life. Imagine that they are all part of the Great Goddess, and so are you. Imagine that the Great Goddess wraps you in her arms, sharing the power and strength of all those strong women and awakening the power of every great thing you've ever done within you. When you feel all of that feminine energy reach its nexus around you, repeat three times:

> I am Goddess, I am strong.
>
> I awaken my power, hear my song.
>
> Spiritual sisters, we are one.
>
> As we share our strength this spell is spun.

Carry that strength within you in everything you do.

Mickie Mueller

March 9

Saturday

 Color of the day: Brown
Incense of the day: Rue

Poppets for Peace!

Poppets—small stuffed doll-effigies for magickal purpose—are a simple, powerful type of intentional magick. Craft a "peace poppet" to bring peace between you and someone you disagree with, or step it up and work a charm for peace throughout the world.

Cut out two matching fabric pieces shaped like a small, chunky figure—a gingerbread cookie cutter makes a great template. Sew the pieces together, stuffing as you go with a magickal "cleansing" or purifying material such as sage or cedar. You might add chips of quartz, too. Write the following on a paper scroll and place inside the poppet:

> May peace be the focus of every heart.
>
> May every soul seek the best for all.
>
> May forgiveness be felt in every word and deed.
>
> May understanding forge a common bond.

Sew the poppet closed and hang it where the sun bathes it. Pray for peace!

Susan Pesznecker

March 10

Sunday

 Color of the day: Orange
Incense of the day: Juniper

**Daylight Saving Time begins
at 2:00 a.m.**

Meditation Aid from Shiva

Today is the Hindu festival Maha Shivaratri, celebrating the god Shiva. Shiva is the master of meditation and is known to meditate high in the Himalayan mountains for years at a time. Because of this he is often referred to as the "King of All Yogis."

If you are having trouble developing a regular meditation practice, or you simply want to strengthen your existing meditation skills, today is the perfect day to pray to Lord Shiva and petition his assistance. Sit in a comfortable position and visualize Shiva while reciting this simple mantra to him:

> Om namah Shivaya!

Repeat the mantra 108 times (a sacred number in Hinduism). You may wish to use a prayer mala to keep track of your recitations. Allow yourself to enter a meditative state as you repetitively recite the prayer mantra and become more focused. When finished, bow in oblation of gratitude.

Blake Octavian Blair

March 11

Monday

Color of the day: White
Incense of the day: Lily

New Moon in Pisces

New Moon Growing Projects

Spring is just around the corner and new projects are in the planning. It's time to sit under the new moon, the dark night sky, and plot your next projects.

A small dark moon ritual to the goddess Hecate to point you in the right direction is always a good way to start. In a quiet, darkened place with a single candle lit, sit and discuss with Hecate what projects are before you and ask her guidance to figure out where to start. I like to put the projects on index cards and use a pendulum to point to the first one to tackle. When she has shown you where to start, write on that card what ideas come to mind. Hecate, the goddess of the crossroads, will offer suggestions if you listen. Afterward, leave some offering to Hecate outside your door, if possible, to say thanks.

Boudica

March 12

Tuesday

Color of the day: Black
Incense of the day: Bayberry

Demeter's Day

The month's twelfth day is dedicated to Demeter, goddess of grain, the harvest, and the earth. She is mother to Persephone, and mourns her daughter's loss to the underworld during the fallow time of winter.

As spring approaches, we ready ourselves for the return of Persephone from the underworld, to be reunited with her mother. Although it may still feel and look like winter where you are, you can prepare for the renewal of spring and energize yourself for the last late days of winter. Create an altar for Demeter and leave small offerings and gifts for her to welcome Persephone home. Your offerings may be anything that represents spring, warmth, and growth, or the joys of motherhood and youth: seeds, flowers, fruit, candy, or small toys. Once spring arrives, share these small gifts with your loved ones.

Peg Aloi

March 13
Wednesday

Color of the day: Brown
Incense of the day: Lavender

Las Fallas Fire Ritual

In Valencia, today is the first day of Las Fallas, the festival that involves generous amounts of food, drink, and firecrackers, as well as the creation of large float-like sculptures that are later burned. It may be thought of as fun way to burn up the slow-moving energy of winter and transmute it into fuel for a fresh, opportunity-filled springtime.

So, gather up all your paper clutter: old magazines, mail, notebooks, receipts, and so on. Alone or with others, use some of the paper to create one or more flammable pieces of art: a sculpture, drawing, mask, collage, or anything that speaks to your sense of silliness and fun. Then start a fire in a fireplace or pit and throw in your work of art, along with the rest of the paper. As it burns, play music and dance as you feel the formerly stuck energy transforming into joyful fuel for the beautiful springtime days ahead.

Tess Whitehurst

March 14
Thursday

Color of the day: Green
Incense of the day: Myrrh

The Clover Spell

When you desire a wish to be granted:

Go to a hill on which the four-leaved clover grows. Pluck five of them by their stems and hold them up to the sky, saying:

Lord of the Day,

Lady of the Night

May you smile upon my rite.

Then face north and, as you throw one clover in that direction, state your wish. Then repeat the procedure to the east, south, and west. When finished, face north again and eat the fifth clover. As it has become a part of you and your life, so too will your wish.

From Scott Cunningham's
Book of Shadows

March 15

Friday

Color of the day: Pink
Incense of the day: Yarrow

Life's Purpose Spell

This is a wonderful spell to attract what it is you most want to do in life. For those who already know, it will bring clarity for the next step. For those who do not, it will bring about the event or circumstance that will make your purpose crystal clear.

Mix incense using sandalwood, orange, and cinnamon. Sit in a quiet place, preferably in view of the outdoors, and light the incense. Close your eyes and breathe in, pulling the scent toward you with both hands. Do this three times, then sit back and repeat this mantra for ten minutes:

I am my purpose.

Pay attention to any ideas or thoughts that appear, especially those that make your stomach flutter and send a thrill of fear through you. Those are the ideas you must act on. When the meditation is through, write down your ideas and act on them immediately.

Patti Larsen

March 16

Saturday

Color of the day: Black
Incense of the day: Sandalwood

New Stages

Theater has the power to move us and shake our worlds. Today marks the start of the Greek Dionysia, a festival of theater and civic understanding. We can celebrate by taking time to watch a movie (or go to a play) that helps us see our world in a new way. Short on time today? Make a list of movies you'd like to watch when you have time, or check out listings for plays or other productions coming up soon in your area.

Shakespeare offers a lot of options, or check out dramas about a historical period or an important historical figure, such as *Elizabeth*, *Agora*, or many Kurosawa films. If you want to stretch this out over a longer period of time, TV series like *Babylon 5*, *Foyle's War*, and *Battlestar Galactica* all do a great job of examining how we interact with others in community.

Jenett Silver

March 17

Sunday

Color of the day: Gold
Incense of the day: Hyacinth

St. Patrick's Day

Shamrocks & Snakes

Pliny the Elder noted that snakes are never found near shamrocks. Hence, the plant has become known as a remedy for all sorts of venomous bites. With this in mind as a metaphor, today consider the most poisonous of bites in your life, whether a relationship, a sense of betrayal, a job, a living situation, or some other harmful circumstance. Now create a shamrock to cure the ill that plagues you. Onto a canvas of verdant green, draw, paint, or collage images that represent your highest ideal, your greatest good, your most whole self. Take a moment to meditate, inviting in the power of the snake to help transform your woes. Wave your creation like a wand to dispel and conquer your troubles, thereby kissing the wound so that you may heal and grow.

Chandra Alexandre

March 18

Monday

Color of the day: Gray
Incense of the day: Narcissus

Finding a Parking Space

I don't know about you, but in the city where I live there's no place to park. At least it seems that way. You can invoke Asphalta, who was invented by Morgan Grey and Julia Penelope in their 1988 book *Found Goddesses*:

Hail, Asphalta, full of grace:

Help me find a parking place.

But if Asphalta takes too long to reply, you can use the Parking Space Word: *Zzzaaaaazzz.*

As you turn the corner to your street, take a deep breath, say the Word, and be specific:

Zzzaaaaazzz. A parking space near my building, please.

As you circle through the parking lot, take a deep breath and say:

Zzzaaaaazzz. A space near the door, please.

A space will open up. It may not be quite where you want it, and it may take two or three passes, so keep your eyes open.

Remember to say thank you!

Barbara Ardinger, Ph.D.

March 19

Tuesday

Color of the day: Red
Incense of the day: Ylang-ylang

The Diviner

The Quinquatria (or Quinquatrus), the festival sacred to Minerva, was celebrated on March 19 in the ancient Roman religious tradition. Because Minerva invented numbers, Quinquatria was traditionally a day when women consulted fortunetellers and diviners, as numbers played an important role in the interpretation of divine patterns and occurrences, and predictions of the future.

While most of us like to do our own divination, today seek out someone who will "read" for you, such as a friend, someone from your sacred circle or coven, or a recommended (and trusted) professional. Whether the person uses runes, cards, coins, water, glass, pendulum, or mirror, ask Minerva to speak through the diviner. Meditate on one situation in your life for which you want guidance, holding it in your focus. Then ask your question and listen. Open yourself to Minerva's divine wisdom, symbols, and sacred numbers as they are channeled to you.

Dallas Jennifer Cobb

March 20

Wednesday

Color of the day: White
Incense of the day: Lilac

Ostara – Spring Equinox –
International Astrology Day

An Ostara Egg Spell

Ostara is the Pagan sabbat that celebrates the spring equinox. It was named for the Teutonic goddess Eostra, which eventually led to the Christian holiday of Easter. The main themes of Ostara are rebirth and fertility. Symbols for Ostara include rabbits, flowers, and eggs. Eggs, a symbol of fertility, are sacred to both Pagans and Christians. They've been decorated at springtime since the days of ancient Egypt and Persia. In ancient Egypt and today in the Eastern Orthodox Church, eggs are usually dyed red. Red is the color of the life force, the Sun, and Christ's blood. The egg is rich with symbolism. The shell can represent the Earth or Christ's tomb. The white is associated with the Heavens, and the yolk with the Sun.

To create a new beginning, perform this spell. Turn your altar toward the east and place three hard-boiled eggs dyed red upon it. Think of something you wish to begin, then gently press two of the eggs together until the shells crack.

This symbolizes a break with the past and a fresh start. Take the third egg outside and gently roll it in the grass to honor the increasing power of the Sun. End your ritual by eating a pastry garnished with almonds to represent fertility.

James Kambos

NOTES:

March 21

Thursday

Color of the day: Purple
Incense of the day: Balsam

Power of the Mind

Today is World Poetry Day, a great chance to get in touch with your inner wordsmith. Why not craft an affirmation for yourself? First pick a topic you care about and want to nurture in your life, such as health, creativity, strength, connection, love, compassion, abundance, communication, or many others.

Next create an affirmation for your goal. Here's an example:

I welcome health, wealth, and wisdom into my day.

To make it a little more poetic, pick your intention and spend the day looking for symbols or objects that remind you of that goal. Then create a simple poem to repeat each day, reminding you of your intention. Here's an example, in haiku form:

Health grows like a tree.

Abundance rains gently down.

Wisdom flowers now.

You could even make a drawing to illustrate your poem, and post it by your altar.

Jenett Silver

March 22

Friday

Color of the day: Coral
Incense of the day: Violet

Jewelry Talisman Spell

You can make any piece of jewelry you own into a protective talisman. Choose your favorite ring, necklace, earring, bracelet, or other jewelry item that you wear often.

First clean the item with whatever method is safest for that type of jewelry. If in doubt, use water and toothpaste. As you clean, imagine any negative energy associated with the item being cleared away.

Next charge the item by allowing it to sit in the sunlight for a day or the moonlight overnight, or simply visualize your specific need as you hold the item in your hand. Finish by chanting:

As my body I adorn

With this special charm,

Keep me safe as it is worn,

Protecting me from harm.

Ember Grant

March 23

Saturday

 Color of the day: Blue
Incense of the day: Ivy

Protection Spell for Private Use

If you feel that someone is direct-ing negative energy at you, call for peace from the quarters. You can do this with or without a wand.

The most generic way to achieve protection is to face east and say:

Let there be peace in the east.

Turn clockwise to the south, west, and north, repeating your call for peace. When you have called all the quarters, return to east and say:

Let peace surround me.

Or:

May there be peace throughout the world.

During peace meditations it is important not to let hard feelings or anger muddy your intentions. Protection spells will not work if you are agitated when you undertake them. If you are in an angry frame of mind, take three deep, grounding breaths before beginning.

This spell can be done indoors, preferably at an altar, or outside. Let your deities guide you as to location, and do not be influenced by the weather. Powerful work can be done when the elements are at their worst.

Anne Johnson

March 24

Sunday

 Color of the day: Amber
Incense of the day: Frankincense

Palm Sunday

Nondenominational Blessings

If you are not yet out of the broom closet, and do not see it happening in the near future, you may grow weary of family occasions where grace is said at meals. You sit through long-winded, rambling prayers that do not apply to you in the least.

You can take control of the situ-ation by saying the blessing. Call upon the Creator, and offer thanks for safety, loved ones, and the fruit of the earth. Remember those absent with a moment of silence. Request continued protection and good for-tune. And out of benevolence throw in an *Amen* for those who do not share your beliefs.

Emyme

March 25

Monday

Color of the day: Silver
Incense of the day: Rosemary

Houseplant Spell for Growth

Houseplants add a wonderful boost of constantly growing life force to one's living space. Here is a spell to lend your magickal helping hand to aid a plant's growth while connecting to the element of earth. The moon is waxing now, a perfect time for growth. Find a small, appropriate gemstone or crystal. I find that clear quartz, kyanite, and tree agate all work well. Hold the stone between your hands and recite the following incantation:

> Stone of earth, add your might
>
> To this houseplant, day and night.
>
> Lend your shining, energetic light
>
> To help this plant grow, healthy and bright.
>
> So mote it be!

Visualize the stone's energy glowing a bright white, blue, or violet around the plant. Place the stone on the surface of the dirt inside the plant's pot. Watch as your plant grows vibrantly with the added energy from the stone. Periodically recharge the stone as needed.

Blake Octavian Blair

March 26

Tuesday

Color of the day: Maroon
Incense of the day: Ginger

Passover begins

Prince Kuhio Day

This is the birthday of Prince Kuhio, a Hawaiian royal who rallied for the rights of his people in the early 1900s. He was an educated and dedicated man, serving jail time for his attempts to preserve the monarchy. He ended up serving in the U.S. Congress and was dubbed "Prince of the Citizens" for helping to secure land for his people. In Hawaii he is honored today with parades, dancing, and games. This is a good day to charge a protective item with the spirit and courage of one who acted in the best interest of others. Select a stone to use as a talisman and use this chant:

> Stone I hold and charge with might,
>
> Aid the battles that I fight.
>
> Stone I hold let me be strong,
>
> Serve what's right against what's wrong.

Ember Grant

March 27
Wednesday

 Color of the day: Yellow
Incense of the day: Marjoram

Full Moon in Libra

Spell for a Spring Body Cleanse

In winter we tend to put on weight, as we eat to keep warm and physical activity lessens. The full moon is a time when the body absorbs anything we take in more fully than at any other time; similarly, the new moon is the ultimate time for the body to detoxify. As the moon waxes and wanes, the body absorbs or detoxifies in equal measure.

To make the most of this spring full moon, try this spell for weight loss. Prepare a light, simple meal of healthy food. Sit where you can see the full moon through your window. As you eat, visualize your body being nourished. Eat slowly and be aware that you feel satisfied. Each night as the moon wanes, eat a light, healthy dinner, and picture your body growing smaller as the moon does. You can repeat this spell every moon cycle.

Peg Aloi

March 28
Thursday

 Color of the day: Green
Incense of the day: Nutmeg

Compassion Spell

We often think of compassion for others as important, but rarely do we consider the personal application of it. Finding compassion for oneself is the key to feeling it for others in a healthy and healing way. This meditation will assist you in finding your own inner understanding and forgiveness while opening you to receive the same from those around you.

Sit in a comfortable position with feet flat on the floor, back straight, and eyes closed. Set a timer for at least five minutes or up to fifteen if you are able. Close your eyes and breathe deeply three times from your diaphragm to the top of your lungs to cleanse the air in your body.

Next, while you breathe in, mentally repeat the following:

I love myself.

I forgive all I have done.

On the exhale, say:

Forgiveness heals me.

Love fills me up.

Continue until the time runs out.

Patti Larsen

March 29

Friday

Color of the day: White
Incense of the day: Orchid

Good Friday

Spring-Clean Your Office

Do you work in a cube, an office, your car? With Friday's focus on growth, it's time to do some spring-cleaning.

First clean up your work area. Start by sprinkling salt around your cube. The office cleaner will remove it all in a day or two, but that will allow all the old, spent energy to be drawn down. You can do the same with your car, but use a vacuum.

Next clean with pine, rose wash, or whatever you are not allergic to. Follow with an application of Success Oil. I use sunflower oil as a base and add my favorites: a few drops of sandalwood and orange oils and mint leaves in the mix for the final touch.

Finally, put a success box in your work area. This can be something simple with a piece of pyrite and a silver coin and a tiny bottle of honey to draw success and make it stick.

Boudica

March 30

Saturday

Color of the day: Indigo
Incense of the day: Pine

Festival of Salus

Today is the Festival of Salus, a Greek goddess who was often petitioned for protection of health and safety. She was the daughter of Asclepius, god of healing. Today is also a Saturday during a waning moon—what better time to break out some magic to protect your health and well-being?

First carve a snake on a green taper candle. Then fill a goblet or wine glass halfway with salt, and stand the candle in the salt. Light the candle and repeat the following charm:

> Lady Salus, hear my call.
>
> I hereby banish one and all
>
> Any obstacle to my well-being and health
>
> And replace it with vitality and wealth.
>
> I create a shield by salt, goblet, and snake,
>
> And release all adversity in my wake.

Allow the candle to burn out, and throw the salt and candle stump far away from your home.

Mickie Mueller

March 31

Sunday

Color of the day: Yellow
Incense of the day: Eucalyptus

Easter

Be a Kite!

Lift yourself in an air meditation by imagining yourself as a kite. Stand outdoors on a dry, breezy day. Ground and center, feeling your connections to the Earth as you focus your energies deep within. Now stretch your arms out, imaging them as the kite's crossarms, while your feet and legs are the kite's long arm and your head is its topmost extension. Lift your chin high, looking up into the sky, and imagine the breeze picking you up. Feel the air swirl around you as your feet lift free from the ground. Meditate on the feelings of weightlessness and freedom as you rise into the sky, unencumbered by earthly connections. Imagine that you can fly, dipping and swinging through the sky with arms outstretched. Feel the excitement and energy: anything is possible! Allow yourself to be returned safely to the ground, where you can begin planning your next flight.

Susan Pesznecker

NOTES:

March Moon Table

Date	Sign	Element	Nature	Phase
1 Fri 12:33 pm	Scorpio	Water	Fruitful	3rd
2 Sat	Scorpio	Water	Fruitful	3rd
3 Sun 4:11 pm	Sagittarius	Fire	Barren	3rd
4 Mon	Sagittarius	Fire	Barren	4th 4:53 pm
5 Tue 7:14 pm	Capricorn	Earth	Semi-fruitful	4th
6 Wed	Capricorn	Earth	Semi-fruitful	4th
7 Thu 10:01 pm	Aquarius	Air	Barren	4th
8 Fri	Aquarius	Air	Barren	4th
9 Sat	Aquarius	Air	Barren	4th
10 Sun 1:19 am	Pisces	Water	Fruitful	4th
11 Mon	Pisces	Water	Fruitful	New 3:51 pm
12 Tue 7:17 am	Aries	Fire	Barren	1st
13 Wed	Aries	Fire	Barren	1st
14 Thu 3:08 pm	Taurus	Earth	Semi-fruitful	1st
15 Fri	Taurus	Earth	Semi-fruitful	1st
16 Sat	Taurus	Earth	Semi-fruitful	1st
17 Sun 2:09 am	Gemini	Air	Barren	1st
18 Mon	Gemini	Air	Barren	1st
19 Tue 2:55 pm	Cancer	Water	Fruitful	2nd 1:27 pm
20 Wed	Cancer	Water	Fruitful	2nd
21 Thu	Cancer	Water	Fruitful	2nd
22 Fri 2:50 am	Leo	Fire	Barren	2nd
23 Sat	Leo	Fire	Barren	2nd
24 Sun 11:49 am	Virgo	Earth	Barren	2nd
25 Mon	Virgo	Earth	Barren	2nd
26 Tue 5:32 pm	Libra	Air	Semi-fruitful	2nd
27 Wed	Libra	Air	Semi-fruitful	Full 5:27 am
28 Thu 8:53 pm	Scorpio	Water	Fruitful	3rd
29 Fri	Scorpio	Water	Fruitful	3rd
30 Sat 11:13 pm	Sagittarius	Fire	Barren	3rd
31 Sun	Sagittarius	Fire	Barren	3rd

Times are in Eastern Time.

April

There is so much going on in the month of April! There is April Fool's Day, and it's National Poetry Month. It's also the anniversary of the sinking of the Titanic and the opening of the first McDonald's. We celebrate the birthdays of Hans Christian Andersen, Leonardo da Vinci, Sherlock Holmes, and Daffy Duck. But what is April really all about? What is it that makes April special? April marks the real end of winter. Daffodils pop open and nod their yellow heads. Grass starts to recover from its frozen cover of snow. Trees bud, forsythia shows its yellow cloak, tulips display their lips, and the small animals—chipmunks, squirrels, rabbits, and other animals—wake up from their winter sleep. The promise of renewal is realized as the sun removes the icy chill from the air. Rain soaks the earth, prompting growth and preparing the flowers of the season. And we find ourselves shedding our winter coats on the first warm spring day. This is April!

Boudica

April 1

Monday

Color of the day: White
Incense of the day: Lily

April Fools' Day

New Views

April Fools' Day gives us a chance to look at the world from a different point of view. Like the Hanged Man in the tarot, turning ourselves around (and letting go of our dignity) can bring us surprising answers and insights. Pick a book at random, and flip through it without looking until you feel like you've found the right place. Look at the fourth sentence on the page, and see what it suggests to you.

Does this sentence bring a person to mind? A situation? What is the completely opposite way to think about the sentence? How might it apply to your life? What does it suggest about something you might be clinging tightly to, even though it no longer works for you? What could you do that would bring that energy into your life? If that sentence really doesn't work, try flipping through again, or use a different book.

Jenett Silver

April 2

Tuesday

Color of the day: Black
Incense of the day: Geranium

Passover ends

Light It Up Blue for Autism

It's World Autism Awareness Day and the second day of "Light It Up Blue," during which many businesses and organizations replace their normal lights with blue ones in order to promote worldwide awareness of autism. In honor of these objectives, and to support the unique challenges of people with autism and those who love them, you might light a blue candle today. Sit comfortably and take some deep breaths. Close your eyes, and mentally surround our planet Earth in bright blue light. See this light amplifying our understanding of autism and perfectly supporting those to whom it poses special challenges. Think or say something like this:

> I now call on the blue ray of understanding and communication. With gratitude, I see it increasing our understanding of autism so that we can work with it rather than against it and so that the blessings it contains can fully blossom and bless the world.

Tess Whitehurst

April 3

Wednesday

Color of the day: Yellow
Incense of the day: Bay laurel

Gratitude: Learning hard Lessons

We know we need to keep an attitude of gratitude, but how do we feel grateful when something lousy happens? I don't mean when your team loses or your favorite reality show is canceled. How can we feel grateful when we're laid off? When someone crashes into our car? When our e-mail is hacked? When our computer is attacked by a virus?

When something rotten happens, it's an Educational Experience. How to be grateful? "Well, at least I'm still breathing." "I got decent severance pay and I have transferable skills." "It wasn't my fault." "No one was hurt." "I've got good insurance." "My geeky friend will come and fix my computer tonight."

Worse things can happen, true catastrophes for which we'll need powerful magic, plus practical help from physicians or lawyers. But for the Educational Experience? "Thank you, Goddess. This is no fun, but I can learn something here. And I'm still breathing."

Barbara Ardinger, Ph.D.

April 4

Thursday

Color of the day: Crimson
Incense of the day: Jasmine

Festival of Cybele: The Megalesia

The Romans called her Magna Mater, bringing mother goddess Cybele from Anatolia when the Sibyls prophesied the time was right. Appealed to for a great many things, Cybele was also arbiter of moral and ethical dilemmas. Utilize the opportunity under her watchful gaze to divine the truth about (and a response to) a situation that is irksome or troubling to you. Take a bowl of water and drop three leaves onto the surface, having formulated a question for which a yes/no response will be useful. Three leaves face up is a yes. Two leaves up and one down is a yes with qualifications. Three leaves face down is a no. Two leaves down and one up is a no with qualifications. To ascertain the meaning or nature of the qualifications, crumble the leaves into the water, let them settle, and drain the bowl. Look for your fullest answer in the images you find left in the remaining leaves.

Chandra Alexandre

April 5

Friday

 Color of the day: Rose
Incense of the day: Thyme

Self-Love and Beauty Spell

The Romans held Fridays sacred to Venus, goddess of love and beauty. The Greeks believed Friday was Aphrodite's day. This is the day for a love and beauty spell—not "outside" love but rather "inside" love, self-love. Gather your favorite clothes, a piece of meaningful jewelry (magically charged, if possible), a hairbrush, and an anointing oil (jasmine or rose, for full love effect). Stand in front of a mirror and gaze at yourself, intoning:

> *I love myself as I am,*
> *beautiful inside and out.*

Apply scented oil.

> *I'm anointed by love's sacred*
> *care.*

Lovingly brush your hair.

> *I stroke my strong spirit.*

Put on your favorite clothes.

> *Cloaked in love's protection,*
> *I glow.*

Add jewelry.

> *Magic is mine, within and*
> *without.*

Fully anointed and dressed up, go out and enjoy yourself, knowing that self-love is more important than other love, and true beauty comes from within.

Dallas Jennifer Cobb

NOTES:

April 6

Saturday

Color of the day: Blue
Incense of the day: Magnolia

Thank Mother Earth

Before you plant your garden this spring, take time to thank Mother Earth. Begin by thinking about the blessings Mother Earth bestows upon us. We abuse and poison her, but still she sustains us. After your garden is plowed, kneel directly on the freshly plowed earth in simple ritual. Let your knees sink into the earth. Crumble the soil with your fingers; let it fall to the ground. You've done more than just prepare the seedbed, and you've done more than connect with the earth. You're connecting with the Wheel of the Year and the rhythm of the seasons. In an act of purification, sprinkle the soil with a few drops of vinegar. And now, my fellow gardener, you've learned one of the secrets only a gardener knows: We don't control the earth; we are partners with the earth.

James Kambos

April 7

Sunday

Color of the day: Orange
Incense of the day: Heliotrope

Be Flexible!

Change is a constant occurrence in our lives. Sometimes it's tough to deal with, especially when we're used to a particular routine or set of expectations. One thing that may help is a little bit of totemic Coyote energy. This isn't the potentially volatile trickster god, but the totem who embodies all the qualities of the physical, very adaptable animal.

Why Coyote? Because coyotes are one of the few animals that have broadened their range with the increase in human population. They've taken the ultimate bad situation—drastic change of environment and food source—and turned it to their favor. Coyote, the totem, overlooks this process.

As with any totem, approach with respect and perhaps a small offering. Ask Coyote for help with being more adaptable and flexible, and carry a small reminder, such as a stone fetish, to help invite that energy in when you need it.

Lupa

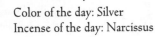

April 8
Monday

Color of the day: Silver
Incense of the day: Narcissus

The hanged Man Spell

The Hanged Man in tarot is about sacrifice and letting go. Today is a fantastic opportunity to release old anger or resentment, or to let go of a relationship that harmed you.

You will need something representing the cause of the injury as well as a token representing you. Bind them together with red yarn or thread, but be sure to leave part of both items exposed to the air. Tie off the yarn with a strong knot, leaving extra length on the tails. Take the bundle outside to a tree or bush, preferably the one closest to your bedroom, and tie onto a branch with the loose ends. Let the bundle hang, but fasten it securely. Then say:

> I release resistance.
>
> I let go of control.
>
> I allow this to be.

Let the bundle hang for nine days. This will return you to harmony. Then remove it from the tree and throw away.

Patti Larsen

April 9
Tuesday

Color of the day: Maroon
Incense of the day: Bayberry

Trash to Treasure

Yard sales! For many, April heralds the season of decluttering. Household items, once needed and loved, are to be found in driveways and garages almost every weekend. Consider repurposing a bench for a garden altar or a fireproof container for candle spells. You may find a metal bowl for kitchen witchery or books on the art of feng shui. In order to protect against negative energy, and before you have the opportunity to perform a thorough cleansing, recite this simple spell as you gently breathe on the item:

> From thine to mine
>
> This object be.
>
> My breath removes
>
> Stale energy.

Emyme

April 10

Wednesday

Color of the day: White
Incense of the day: Honeysuckle

New Moon in Aries

Spell for Guidance

The new moon is a traditional time for introspection. In the dark, moonless night we see most clearly, for we must look within and find our inner light. Use this time to meditate on your spirit—what you need to feel complete. You may not know what this is.

Find a quiet, dark place to sit, and light a single candle. Use whatever meditation techniques you prefer. Imagine the candle illuminating your innermost desires, thoughts, and needs. Visualize these deep feelings rising to your conscious mind, manifesting in you, true needs being met. Use this chant:

Inner light, be my guide.

Bring to sight what I hide.

In the dark I impart

What I hold in my heart.

What I need comes to me,

As I will, it shall be.

Ember Grant

April 11

Thursday

Color of the day: Purple
Incense of the day: Apricot

Bay Leaf for Prosperity

There are times when all of us could use a few extra dollars in our wallets. With Thursday having the prosperous influence of Jupiter, here is a simple spell to help you attract that bit of extra cash. The spell is best performed at the beginning of a waxing moon cycle to allow it to connect with the growth energies provided by the lunar phase.

Bay leaves are known to attract money and prosperity. Take a bay leaf and a one dollar bill. Create a packet by wrapping the bay leaf in the dollar bill, folding the bill into thirds. While doing so, recite:

Power of bay leaf, I ask thee,
Through methods fair and just,
Bring abundant prosperity.

Through the folds,
Three times three,
Bring abundant prosperity.

Tuck the packet into the billfold section of your wallet. Periodically repeat and replace the bay leaf as necessary.

Blake Octavian Blair

April 12

Friday

 Color of the day: Pink
Incense of the day: Alder

Send Love Rippling Out

We think of love spells as being personal, but the power of love can be a catalyst for positive change in the world. Find a quiet place to sit, and hold a rose quartz in your hands. Feel the warm, gentle energy it exudes and say:

Universal love fills me.

Allow it to fill your body. Let it ripple out and fill your house. Say:

Universal love fills my home.

Once you visualize your house full of light, allow it to pour out of your house, filling your neighborhood. Say:

Universal love fills my neighborhood.

Continue with this method, visualizing the warm rose-quartz light filling your town or city, then your county, your state, nation, continent, and then the whole earth, adding the affirmation as you go. When you have finished, sit quietly and enjoy the feeling of sharing love with the whole world. Take a moment to ground and center.

Mickie Mueller

April 13

Saturday

Color of the day: Brown
Incense of the day: Rue

Refresh Your Protection

Saturday afternoons can be times of reflection and a good time to reinforce the protection in your home. You should do a major working annually to protect your home and family. Reinforce your home protection spells at least once a month.

Make sure the mirrors on your windows that reflect negative energy away from your home are clean. Make sure the pentacles you drew in chalk on your windows and doors are reinforced. A special protection mix can be made with dragon's blood and mugwort mixed in some olive oil. Add a clove of garlic to the mix if the smell doesn't bother you—it is a strong mix! Dip your finger in the mix and make the pentagram on the doors and windows. My preference is to call for protection from a strong warrior god or goddess. I rather like Athena. She guards the door in my home.

Boudica

April 14

Sunday

Color of the day: Gold
Incense of the day: Juniper

April Showers Spell

*April is the cruelest month,
breeding*

*Lilacs out of the dead land,
mixing*

Memory and desire, stirring

Dull roots with spring rain...

—T. S. Eliot, "The Waste Land"

On a rainy day in April, look out
your window. Note as many details
as you can. How hard is it raining?
Is it dark? Windy? What colors can
you see? Now open your front door,
standing in the threshold. Imagine
how it will feel to walk into this
rain. Cold? Exhilarating? What does
it smell like? Open your senses and
let the weather's power affect you;
feel how it changes from moment to
moment. As you go through your
day, note how your mood and physical energy shift, and note how the
weather changes, too. The goal is to
try to attune with the weather, to see
how it affects your body and psyche.
You may be surprised to experience a
newfound sensitivity and awareness.

Peg Aloi

NOTES:

Page 81

April 15

Monday

Color of the day: Lavender

Incense of the day: Clary sage

Belili's Blessing

Monday, or Moonday, is a wonderful day for doing magical work. And with today being the start of the Celtic tree month of Willow, the fifth moon of the Celtic year, there is added magical energy to employ. Summon Belili, the Sumerian goddess of trees, as you incant this blessing upon yourself or others:

> Belili, bless me that I might be like the trees,
>
> My feet, firmly rooted in sacred earth, my roots long and connected,
>
> My arms reaching for airy skies, open wide, embracing,
>
> My fiery spirit soaring, light energy, clear and true.
>
> And like the sacred willow, the Witch's tree, let me drink from the waters of the world.
>
> Earth, air, fire, and water fill me,
>
> So that like the trees, I may long dance on this sacred earth.
>
> With limbs reaching long, I invoke Belili's green wisdom,
>
> Giving thanks for the goodness of trees.
>
> Blessed be, Belili.

Dallas Jennifer Cobb

NOTES:

April 16

Tuesday

Color of the day: White
Incense of the day: Ginger

Magical Window Cleaning

Tuesday's planetary ruler is Mars, so this is a good day to give your windows a magical spring-cleaning. It was once believed that a passerby could unknowingly cast the evil eye through a window simply by glancing at a house. For this reason, glass globes known as Witch balls were placed in front of windows to deflect any bad energy and prevent it from entering the home. To remove any trapped negativity from your windows, try this ritual. First thoroughly clean your windows, outside and inside. Then, in a spray bottle, mix warm water and three tablespoons of vinegar. Next wipe your windows with this mixture, wiping in a counterclockwise direction to banish bad energy. Then spray again, but wipe in a clockwise, circular motion to seal in the positive energy. Your home will smell fresh, and you'll feel the positive vibrations you've created.

James Kambos

April 17

Wednesday

Color of the day: Topaz
Incense of the day: Marjoram

Symbols on a Page

Many people use a physical altar to focus their intentions and ideas, but a physical altar isn't always convenient. Today take some time to draw a representation of what you want your life to become more like. You might include images of home, work, time with friends, your spiritual community, or your loved ones. Stick figures are just fine—you don't need to be a great artist!

You might draw scenes, or you might draw symbols (hearts, stars, spirals, waves, clouds, musical notes, lines and circles) connecting individual figures or shapes. Whatever you choose, include colors that make these things feel real to you and that help you connect them to you and the life you're creating.

When you're done, spend a few minutes imagining yourself walking through what you've drawn, interacting with each symbol, image, or figure. Finish by breathing softly across the paper, giving life to the intent.

Jenett Silver

April 18

Thursday

 Color of the day: Turquoise
Incense of the day: Clove

A Feast for the Ancestors

April 18 is my grandmother's birthday, and I often remember her with a special dinner. Treat your dearly departed to a special evening, featuring a glorious table, a bountiful feast, and this poem:

> A place at the table, a hallowed meal,
> The sideboard groans with our repast.
> We set a place with favorite foods
> And wait for the old ones to come at last.
>
> With cauldron filled and candles lit,
> We revel in the passing hours.
> As minutes pass and mists arise,
> We open to the old ones' powers.
>
> The hours strike, the time is come—
> The night falls dark and quiet and still.
> A whispered touch, a puff of wind…
> The old ones come to work their will.

> They leave as softly as they have come,
> Fading back into the veil.
> The feast for them, a magick night!
> We sit and share the old ones' tales.

Susan Pesznecker

NOTES:

April 19
Friday

Color of the day: Purple
Incense of the day: Rose

Taming the Minotaur

As the sun moves into Taurus, try this guided visualization. In the myth, the hero joins the group to be sacrificed to the Minotaur and sails to the magical island. He meets the princess. She gives him a ball of thread to guide him back out of the labyrinth after he has gone to the center and slain the monster.

What's the worst thing that could happen to you? An act of god? A personal disaster? In your meditation, personalize it. See an earthquake, for example, as Poseidon. See your boss as Loki. But don't be like Theseus and attack with a sword. Make your weapon (your Ariadne's thread) metaphorical—get CERT (Community Emergency Response Team) training so you're prepared in case of natural disaster. Adopt wisdom, reasonableness, and a friendly attitude on the job. Bring these metaphorical weapons to your daily life.

In your meditation, visualize your weapon as a practical symbol and step into your labyrinth. You can already hear the Minotaur roaring. When you arrive in the center, don't attack. Be cautious. Be polite. Try to reason with the monster. If that's not possible (there's no reasoning with destructive winds), ask for advice or guidance.

If it's good advice, follow it. Be guided by your inner wisdom. Give thanks that you've met the monster and tamed it.

Barbara Ardinger, Ph.D.

NOTES:

April 20

Saturday

Color of the day: Black
Incense of the day: Pine

Transformation Spell

On April 20, 1939, Billie Holiday recorded the civil rights song "Strange Fruit" about the racially motivated hangings of black men in the South, so today is a day to do a transformation spell. The herb rosemary is used ritually for many things, including grieving, healing, memory, protection, release, rituals for the dead, and transformation. Make a batch of simple biscuits, sprinkling the tops with rosemary and a pinch of sea salt. As they bake, meditate on worldwide civil rights violations of race, gender, class, and faith. Remember. Grieve. Pull warm buns from the oven. Slather one in butter, and as it melts and disappears, let go. Affirm:

> I remember and I grieve,
> I release and I retrieve,
>
> The sanctity of transformation,
> Ancient magic, heal this nation.

Savor the taste of healing rosemary, purifying salt, and blessed butter, and move on into a future filled with harmony, equity, and inclusivity.

Dallas Jennifer Cobb

April 21

Sunday

Color of the day: Amber
Incense of the day: Marigold

St. Anselm's Day

The writings of St. Anselm of Canterbury, while not always popular among "the powers that were" during his lifetime, are philosophically relevant to this day. In fact, he formulated what's known as "the ontological argument," debatably the most respected and logically sound argument in favor of the existence of a divine being. So, with the moon in Mercury-ruled and detail-oriented Virgo, this is a great time to perform a ritual for honing your powers of reason and persuasion so you can organize and articulate your thoughts in an ideal way. (This is helpful for things like debates, speeches, writing assignments, and philosophy tests.)

Anoint a yellow candle with essential oil of rosemary (or place fresh rosemary sprigs around its base). Light the candle and say:

> St. Anselm, please help me to think clearly, to speak effectively, and to see deeply into the inner workings of the universe. Thank you.

Tess Whitehurst

April 22

Monday

Color of the day: Gray
Incense of the day: Hyssop

Earth Day

Celebrating Earth Day

While many of us celebrate Earth Day every day, this is a good opportunity to make it even more special. One thing you can do is give an extra magical kick to letters written to elected officials about environmental matters.

Gather your letters and the envelopes you'll be putting them in. As you fold each letter and put it in its envelope, say:

> Words of power, words of will,
> May your receiver my desire fulfill!

Seal each envelope (using a wax seal as an additional flourish, if you like), saying:

> Carry my words safely on their way,
> So they may receive a resounding yea!

Place a stamp on each envelope while saying:

> I've paid my price, my part is done,
> May the battle I fight be mine and won!

Lupa

April 23

Tuesday

Color of the day: Red
Incense of the day: Basil

Temperance Spell

The Temperance card in tarot represents balance, health, and harmony in body, mind, and spirit. Fill two clay or ceramic cups halfway with water. In the first cup add three drops of orange oil and swirl, saying:

> I welcome harmony into my life.

In the second cup add three drops of lavender oil and swirl, saying:

> I dispel disharmony from my life.

Hold one cup in each hand and slowly pour the orange water into the lavender, saying:

> I choose balance and health.

Reverse the pour into the empty vessel and say:

> I release worry, concern, and stress.

Continue pouring two more times, repeating the above. When complete, pour half into the second cup so you are in two again. Go outside and pour the first cup on the left of your front walk. Pour the other on the right. Harmony will bless you every time you enter or exit.

Patti Larsen

April 24

Wednesday

Color of the day: White
Incense of the day: Lavender

healing from the News

On this day in 1704, the first-ever regular newspaper in the United States, *The Boston News-Letter*, was published in Massachusetts. Today we take our easy access to regular news and information for granted; however, on this day take a moment to remember that it wasn't always so easy to receive information about current events, even in our own city.

Today find a copy of your local newspaper or visit it online. Find a local news story about an event or situation that has occurred in your area that could use the benefit of some good energy and healing. Cut or print out the story and find a purple candle. Infuse the candle with your intent to help and send energy to all those involved in the situation, then set the candle in a holder on top of the article. Light the candle and visualize the healing energy and light surrounding those in need.

Blake Octavian Blair

April 25

Thursday

Color of the day: Green
Incense of the day: Mulberry

full Moon/Lunar Eclipse in Scorpio

A Benign Sacrifice

Robigalia is the ancient feast day for the protection of crops. Unfortunately some rituals for this day (and many others) have fallen out of favor due to the unsavory inclusion of animal sacrifice. Tonight's full moon adds to the power of rituals performed for a healthy growing season. For those with home gardens, or farms of any size, who choose to include Robigus in today's castings, consider this substitute: animal crackers. Add these tasty cookies in the shape(s) of the animal(s) of your choice to your cakes and ale, safe in the knowledge you have harmed none.

Emyme

April 26

Friday

Color of the day: Coral
Incense of the day: Cypress

Lilac Faerie Beauty Spell

Call upon the queen of the Fae to bring out your inner beauty with this lovely lilac spell.

If the lilacs are in bloom in your area, place fresh lilacs in a vase; otherwise a lilac-scented candle will work fine. Settle down and smell the scent of lilacs as you invite the presence of the faerie kingdom to join you.

Lady Tatiana, beautiful fae,

I ask a boon this April day.

Awaken my beauty from within

And let it glow upon my skin.

Visualize a sparkling glow growing inside of your chest; allow it to spread throughout your body, finally sparkling upon the surface of your skin. Enjoy the feeling as long as you wish. Remind yourself that you can carry your inner beauty on the outside anytime you wish. Later be sure to honor the faeries with a small dish of milk and honey left outside.

Mickie Mueller

April 27

Saturday

Color of the day: Indigo
Incense of the day: Patchouli

Saint Zita's Day

Saint Zita is the patron saint of housewives. Goddess equivalents include Vesta and Hestia, goddesses of the hearth and home. This is the day to honor your inner housewife. Reclaim this word for its positive meanings. The wife of the house is in control: she helps keep the home's inhabitants fed, clothed, clean, and healthy. She is the life force of the household. If you live alone, reflect on the ways you nurture and care for yourself: how could you improve on this? If you care for others, consider how you feel about this: do you need more help or think you deserve more respect and appreciation? How can you make changes to create a happier household? Try to make some small changes today: buy a new plant, clear out a cluttered drawer, or get your spouse or kids to make dinner or do the laundry.

Peg Aloi

April 28

Sunday

 Color of the day: Yellow
Incense of the day: Frankincense

Floralia

Flora was a Roman goddess of flowers—and sensuality. Some say she may have also been viewed as a goddess of springtime. Her celebration lasted until May 3 and could be the origin of May Day celebrations that came later. Flora is also rumored to be the original "May Queen" figure. Floralia was celebrated with decorative flower garlands, plays, games, feasting, drinking, and dancing. Today, in honor of Flora, decorate with as many flowers as you can find—put them everywhere. You can even dress in a floral pattern, if you'd like. Celebrate this season of abundant flowers and honor the goddess within you. Use this chant for a garden blessing:

> Flowers trained and flowers wild,
>
> Gardens growing lush or mild—
>
> Exotic or domestic,
>
> Every bloom majestic—
>
> On the world, goddess Flora smiles.

Ember Grant

April 29

Monday

Color of the day: Ivory
Incense of the day: Neroli

Taking Care of our Fin/Fur/Feather Friends

Make today a special day to groom and treat your pet friends with special care. Whether they are in a fishbowl or are your fine feathered friend, make sure they are well groomed and tended. Take your dog to the groomer for a scrub, clipping, and prettying-up. Cats can use a good combing to get out winter's old growth. Make sure they have all their shots and vitamins. Cages, tanks, and litter boxes should be scrubbed out, with fresh material in place. And always make sure they have fresh water!

Try to make Monday that special day to make time for your pets. Give them the attention they need and the special care they deserve.

Boudica

April 30

Tuesday

Color of the day: Gray
Incense of the day: Geranium

Blessing of the Seeds

In this world of increasingly geo-manufactured Frankenseeds, every one of us magickal types should be growing some of our own food and herbs, even if it's a single plant in a single pot. Every little bit helps, and everything you grow will make you happier and healthier.

Get a jump-start on the upcoming planting season by selecting and blessing your seeds. Use the Web to order several seed catalogs, and enjoy poring through them to make your selections.

Once your seed packets arrive, carry out the following ritual. First carry the packets into your yard and set them on the earth, incanting:

> May the bounteous Mother
> Earth nurture these seeds that
> they may take root!

Hold the seeds skyward, facing the sun, and incant:

> May Father Sun's energies raise
> these seeds to brilliant heights!

Then place the packets on your altar to charge with energy until planting time.

Susan Pesznecker

April Moon Table

Date	Sign	Element	Nature	Phase
1 Mon	Sagittarius	Fire	Barren	3rd
2 Tue 1:35 am	Capricorn	Earth	Semi-fruitful	3rd
3 Wed	Capricorn	Earth	Semi-fruitful	4th 12:37 am
4 Thu 4:41 am	Aquarius	Air	Barren	4th
5 Fri	Aquarius	Air	Barren	4th
6 Sat 9:00 am	Pisces	Water	Fruitful	4th
7 Sun	Pisces	Water	Fruitful	4th
8 Mon 3:02 pm	Aries	Fire	Barren	4th
9 Tue	Aries	Fire	Barren	4th
10 Wed 11:22 pm	Taurus	Earth	Semi-fruitful	New 5:35 am
11 Thu	Taurus	Earth	Semi-fruitful	1st
12 Fri	Taurus	Earth	Semi-fruitful	1st
13 Sat 10:13 am	Gemini	Air	Barren	1st
14 Sun	Gemini	Air	Barren	1st
15 Mon 10:49 pm	Cancer	Water	Fruitful	1st
16 Tue	Cancer	Water	Fruitful	1st
17 Wed	Cancer	Water	Fruitful	1st
18 Thu 11:13 am	Leo	Fire	Barren	2nd 8:31 am
19 Fri	Leo	Fire	Barren	2nd
20 Sat 9:08 pm	Virgo	Earth	Barren	2nd
21 Sun	Virgo	Earth	Barren	2nd
22 Mon	Virgo	Earth	Barren	2nd
23 Tue 3:25 am	Libra	Air	Semi-fruitful	2nd
24 Wed	Libra	Air	Semi-fruitful	2nd
25 Thu 6:25 am	Scorpio	Water	Fruitful	Full 3:57 pm
26 Fri	Scorpio	Water	Fruitful	3rd
27 Sat 7:32 am	Sagittarius	Fire	Barren	3rd
28 Sun	Sagittarius	Fire	Barren	3rd
29 Mon 8:21 am	Capricorn	Earth	Semi-fruitful	3rd
30 Tue	Capricorn	Earth	Semi-fruitful	3rd

Times are in Eastern Time.

May

For Witches and Pagans, May marks the "height" of the year, as we see with the Beltane sabbat. This Celtic holiday is the precise opposite of Samhain (Halloween) on the Wiccan Wheel of the Year. While the beginning of November marks a descent into darkness, the beginning of May marks an ascent into light. This is a month of fertility and frivolity, sensuality and human connection, making it a good idea to reflect on sex and sexuality. What is your relationship with sex? Do you overuse or neglect your sexuality? What is your view on orientation? What are your sexual imprints from childhood? Meditating on and studying both sex and sexuality in a cross-cultural context can help you develop a more realistic, balanced, and healthy understanding of this human force of pleasure and reproduction. All too often people choose to ignore or shut off their sexuality or overindulge in their urges. Certainly, either side of the equation is imbalanced. This month is bright, illuminating, celebratory, and sexual. We all have the option and opportunity to positively embrace our relationship with sexuality, and May is the ideal time for it!

Raven Digitalis

May 1

Wednesday

Color of the day: Brown
Incense of the day: Lilac

Beltane

Celebrating Beltane

Today is all about joy in the world, everything coming into flower, bursting with life. To celebrate Beltane, take a few minutes to find some food or drink you particularly love, that makes you feel alive and vibrant. Set it on your altar or somewhere in your home where you feel comfortable and at ease. Alternate taking a bite or sip with saying one of the sentences below. You can alternate what you say or repeat, depending on what moves you.

Here is delight.

I love my body.

Joy fills every moment of my life.

I am renewed in joy.

Beauty, joy, and plenty surround me.

I am creative, inspired by the world around me.

My life is abundant and flourishing.

(Or whatever other sentence moves you.)

When you are done, spend a few moments in reflection: what can you do today that will delight you, make you laugh like a child? See if you can find time to do that soon. It's also a great day to do gentle acts of self-care, such as eating a favorite food, using a wonderfully scented soap, or taking a leisurely walk through a favorite outdoor space. If you're in a romantic relationship, today is a great day to spend some time sharing your love and celebrating your connection.

Jenett Silver

NOTES:

May 2

Thursday

Color of the day: Turquoise
Incense of the day: Clove

Agathos Daimon: The Good Spirit

What if you really believed that you were protected by a guardian angel at all times? Hold on to that thought, at least for today. Good fortune is ripe for the taking, and you would be wise to offer a libation, preferably at the start of your day, to the spirit that portends abundant blessings. This could be the Greek Agathos Daimon, the Hindu Lakshmi, or the Roman Fortuna. Pour wine and offer prayers in thanksgiving to the Good Spirit for what you have and that which you will receive. If you wish to get a special boon, then make your libation three times, placing a coin so that it is washed over with the liquid. Then take the coin, saying:

Good Spirit of mine, I place in you my trust.

Keep the coin on your person and allow magic to unfold throughout the day.

Chandra Alexandre

May 3

Friday

Color of the day: White
Incense of the day: Mint

Orthodox Good Friday

Manipulating Energy

When you want to draw something into your life, it often helps to "stir the pot." Think about what you want, and draw sunwise circles or spirals with the index finger of your projective hand. Your circle will be tiny, so you can do this nearly anywhere. Keep drawing that little circle until it feels right to stop. Do it as often as necessary. I've stirred the pot for intentions that range from bringing in more business to speeding up traffic.

You can also unwind a situation by drawing moonwise circles with the same finger. I've done this to bring boring meetings to a swifter close and to quiet noisy neighbors.

Stirring and unwinding are effective, but not always obviously and not always right away. These techniques work best when you repeat them at regular intervals. Combine these techniques with other ways you know to manipulate energy.

Barbara Ardinger, Ph.D.

May 4

Saturday

Color of the day: Gray
Incense of the day: Ivy

A Stability Spell

If your energy seems scattered or you lack motivation, this spell will help ground you. You'll need a piece of brown fabric or a piece of burlap at least twelve inches square. You'll also need a small rock that appeals to you and some moist garden soil.

Spread some garden soil onto the fabric and place the rock in the center. Begin packing the soil around the rock, adding more soil if needed. As you do this, feel yourself connecting with the earth. Enjoy the sensation of working with the soil, just as you did when you made mud pies as a child. Tie up the ball of soil in the fabric. Say these words:

> Eternal cycle of birth, death, rebirth,
>
> I am one with the Earth.
>
> Now, I'm hard as bone,
>
> Now, I'm strong as stone.

Save your bundle and touch it when you feel weak.

James Kambos

May 5

Sunday

Color of the day: Gold
Incense of the day: Eucalyptus

Cinco de Mayo – Orthodox Easter

Celebrating Cultural Diversity

Today is Cinco de Mayo, the day on which those of Mexican descent celebrate the outnumbered Mexican army's defeat of the French at the Battle of Puebla. In the United States the holiday is largely celebrated as a day honoring heritage and pride in the Mexican culture.

Many of us live in multicultural communities, and an understanding of our different cultures is important. Many instances of intolerance, whether related to religion, ethnicity, or sexual orientation, stem from lack of understanding. Knowledge is indeed power and that is certainly true magick!

The Virgin of Guadalupe is seen not only as a patroness of Mexican culture but in addition it is thought that she is a modernized manifestation of Aztec mother goddess Tonantzin. Today make an effort to learn more about Mexican culture. You can say a prayer or light a candle as an offering to Guadalupe for her guidance during your studies.

Blake Octavian Blair

May 6

Monday

Color of the day: Gray
Incense of the day: Narcissus

Charm for Sleep

Having trouble sleeping? This seems to be a growing issue in today's fast-moving world. Try this nighttime routine. Take a warm bath, dress in soft, clean pajamas, sip chamomile tea, and repeat this charm over and over:

> My own bedroom window
> looks into the sky
>
> As the moon and the stars and
> the heavens go by.
>
> Through the black night sky
> they seem to barely creep,
>
> Yet they vanish each evening
> when I go to sleep.
>
> And yet, I still watch them,
> almost every night,
>
> Hoping always to catch their
> mysterious flight.
>
> But I soon fall asleep and with
> morning's sunrise,
>
> They've once again vanished …
> in front of my eyes.

As the charm becomes familiar, try to close your eyes as you repeat one verse, then open them again and look out your window at the night sky while continuing to repeat. Eventually, your eyes will stay closed. Sweet dreams!

Susan Pesznecker

NOTES:

May 7
Tuesday

Color of the day: White
Incense of the day: Cinnamon

Promote harmony in Relationships

Every relationship, whether with a family member, partner, friend, or coworker, has the potential for conflict. To bring peaceful energy into your relationships, think about any disagreements or other issues you're currently dealing with. Then, holding the image of those people involved in your mind, recite this:

> May I always speak from my heart as well as my mind.
>
> May I speak without judgment.
>
> May I listen with compassion for myself and for others.
>
> May I not be quick to react.
>
> May I remember that I cannot control others, only myself.
>
> May I treat others as I would like to be treated.
>
> May I know when to stay and when to walk away.
>
> May I remember that even when my peace is rejected, it still matters that I offered it.

Carry the feeling of peace and compassion with you when you interact with these people.

Lupa

May 8
Wednesday

Color of the day: Topaz
Incense of the day: Honeysuckle

Mental Clarity

You don't have to be a member of Mensa (the International High IQ Society) to tap into your own mental ability. Today is the Festival Day of Mens, the Roman goddess of the mind for which Mensa was named. If you have a situation about which you need some mental clarity, bring things into focus with this eye-opening spell. Write down the puzzling condition on a yellow piece of paper, then fold it three times. Light honeysuckle incense and hold the paper in the incense smoke. Use these words to focus your intent:

> Bring my vision into focus.
>
> Let smoke disperse all hocus pocus.
>
> The situation becomes quite clear
>
> As I see right through the false veneer.

Sit quietly, focusing your mind and allowing it to work through the problem. If an answer doesn't come, leave the paper under your pillow. When you awake, the situation should become crystal clear.

Mickie Mueller

May 9

Thursday

Color of the day: Purple
Incense of the day: Apricot

New Moon/Solar Eclipse in Taurus

New Beginnings Spell

Today is about new beginnings. The new moon in conjunction with a solar eclipse heralds the entrance of wild cards into your life that will force you to a new level. Embrace it while you can. This is a very special time and is perfect for moving ahead with projects and plans or even for triggering epiphanies. But be prepared: these days can be disruptive. To open yourself to the benefits, go outside at the time of the eclipse (please be careful not to look at the sun without proper protection) and recite the following incantation:

> Bright to dark, sun to moon,
> With open heart I beg a boon.
>
> Guide my path with goodwill,
> Through this change and hold me still,
>
> In your spirit and free of dread,
> On this road I choose to tread.

Repeat three times. Sit in quiet meditation, focused on your goals and the path laid out before you.

Patti Larsen

May 10

Friday

Color of the day: Coral
Incense of the day: Vanilla

May Feast

Ten days into the lusty month of May, a new moon heralds the waxing of energies. This is also a Friday—the day of Venus, goddess of love and friendship. Call upon your dearest friends or special loved one and enjoy a May celebration. Feast on strawberries in May wine; fruit and cheese; fresh, crusty breads; chocolate. Light yellow and green candles for sun and earth, or pink and red for romance and power. Ground and center, honor the elements and directions, and call upon Venus to bless the feast—enjoy! Leave a portion of the feast outdoors for the goddess, and in the morning bury any remains.

Emyme

May 11

Saturday

 Color of the day: Indigo
Incense of the day: Sage

The Lemuralia: Festival of Ghosts

Dedicate this day to bonds of love. Traditionally the Roman Lemuralia was the occasion when malevolent spirits were exorcised from the home with the sprinkling of black beans and banging of pots. But the ghosts of the dearly departed were also said to walk among the living, so now is your opportunity to reconnect with expressions of healing, hope, compassion, forgiveness, gratitude, and then release.

To honor a shared spirit of love this day, take a handful of white beans and place them on a red cloth. Utter the following as you turn each bean over:

> White bean, ghost of days
> gone by,
>
> Love once held in arms;
>
> Take this gift of mine today,
>
> A token and a charm.

Finally, tie up the little bundle and bury it. Your loves both near and far will have peace.

Chandra Alexandre

May 12

Sunday

 Color of the day: Orange
Incense of the day: Heliotrope

Mother's Day

Every Day Is Mother's Day

Most countries have some equivalent of Mother's Day. Traditionally we show our appreciation for our mothers with cards, gifts, breakfast in bed, or maybe a nice restaurant meal.

On this day we can go beyond honoring our own mothers: we can honor anyone who has nurtured us, including siblings, aunts or uncles, friends, teachers, or even our own children. Try giving a card or some flowers to someone who has nurtured you.

Those who follow earth-based spiritual paths can honor the Great Mother in all of her forms and names: Mother Nature, Mother Earth, the Horned God's Consort, Athena, Hera, Hecate, Cerridwen, Demeter, Ceres. Which mother goddess inspires you or makes you feel whole? Maybe you connect with the Earth itself as a mother. Place a reminder of your mother on your altar: a photo, a piece of jewelry or other keepsake, or a small globe to remind you of your Mother the Earth.

Peg Aloi

May 13
Monday

Color of the day: White
Incense of the day: Lily

Pilgrimage

Every year on May 13, hundreds of thousands of people make a pilgrimage to Fatima in honor of the Virgin Mary. Today make a symbolic pilgrimage to honor a special person or place by creating a shrine. You can do this for a god or goddess, or a sacred place you've visited or would like to visit. Use photos, statues, an so on. Take a symbolic pilgrimage in your mind, visualizing a journey. Consider the spiritual motivation behind this type of excursion. If you can't immediately think of a special place you would like to visit or a person you would want to honor, explore the idea. Use this chant for meditation:

Sacred places on the land

Far beyond the sea or sand,

Special people, honored souls,

Guide us as we seek our goals.

Ember Grant

May 14
Tuesday

Color of the day: Gray
Incense of the day: Ylang-ylang

Ignite Your Dreams

With the moon in emotional, inward-gazing Cancer on a fiery, Mars-ruled Tuesday, it's a lovely time to interweave your dreamy inner truth with passion-filled action by taking at least one concrete step toward manifesting your career-related desires.

So pull out a notebook, set a timer for five minutes, and write *I'd love to [fill in the blank]* over and over without stopping or censoring yourself. When the timer dings, review your entries and see if you can allow a vision for your most delightful future to mentally coalesce. If you notice your inner critic trying to tell you "that's just not possible" or some such nonsense, don't believe it. Set the timer for five minutes again, and brainstorm steps you can take in the physical world toward your goal; for example, enroll in a class, conduct research, start a website, and so on. Vow to take at least one step (even a small one!) today.

Tess Whitehurst

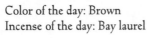

May 15
Wednesday

Color of the day: Brown
Incense of the day: Bay laurel

Shavuot

Energizing Floor Wash

Does the energy in your home need a boost? Does the vibe just feel stagnant or thick? Even after a good physical cleaning and organization, even the most serene and happy home can sometimes suffer from a case of the energetic blahs. Try this simple version of an energizing floor wash designed to raise and uplift the vibrations of your home environment.

In a full bucket of water, place three stones in any combination of citrine, sunstone, or carnelian. Allow their energies to infuse the water for an hour or so. Then add to the water 9 to 15 drops of any citrus essential oil or alternatively one tablespoon of lemon juice. Citrus fruits and their oils are known to have an energizing and uplifting vibration. Proceed to mop the floors and especially the entryway of your home with the freshly energized water.

Blake Octavian Blair

May 16
Thursday

Color of the day: Crimson
Incense of the day: Jasmine

Keep Your Luck Magic Wreath

Take a simple grapevine wreath and weave a long piece of red ribbon or yarn to form a five-pointed star in the middle. Then tuck sprigs of herbs into the wreath for good luck. Use chamomile, thyme, sage, clover flowers, rosemary, mint, yarrow, or any of your favorite good luck herbs. You can hot-glue star anise all around the wreath, if you wish. Feel free to dangle any of your favorite good luck charms, such as a small horseshoe, crescent moon, dragon, Chinese coins, and so on.

Once the wreath is complete, go outside and hang it on your front door. With the door closed, enchant it with the following charm:

Magical wreath, circle round,

Send bad luck into the ground.

Hold all good luck behind this door,

Peace, love, and prosperity evermore.

The wreath will deflect bad luck and hold the good luck in your home.

Mickie Mueller

May 17

Friday

Color of the day: Rose
Incense of the day: Yarrow

Green Man Invocation

The abundant green growth of spring is all around. Take time today to walk in the woods and give praise to Pan, Greek god of the woodlands, fertility, wild animals, music, nature spirits, and dance. If you live in a city, find a park where you can safely walk. If you live in the country, go to a favorite spot. Slow down enough to notice the abundant springing of life and, marveling in it, commune with the Green Man of spring:

In the riot of spring's wild surge,

We summon Pan with these words.

Horned god, dance throughout the trees,

Summon the beasts, and command the bees.

Sprouts and shoots, plants and vines,

Green magic energy now entwines.

Play your pipes and celebrate,

Great Pan, we invoke you on this date.

Later, as you walk toward your home, hum or sing and spread the spirit of Pan throughout the land.

Dallas Jennifer Cobb

NOTES:

May 18
Saturday

 Color of the day: Black
Incense of the day: Sandalwood

A home for Inspiration

Today is International Museum Day. The word *museum* originally meant "the seat of the Muses," a home for inspiration. Today, why not create an altar or space in your home that inspires you? Create a physical altar by cutting out (or printing) images that inspire you and arranging them in a pleasing way. You could attach them to a piece of poster board, a bulletin board, or your wall. Include words, symbols, and colors that connect the images or remind you of your major creative goals, such as the image of a pencil or the words *I love writing*.

You can also create a digital version by collecting online images and using them in a screensaver program or as a rotating desktop image. This can be a great way to keep some inspiration in your life during the workday—just pick images that fit your workplace culture.

Jenett Silver

May 19
Sunday

 Color of the day: Amber
Incense of the day: Almond

Planting a Garden of Friends

By mid-May, our gardens are growing nicely. We weed and water them and talk to the flowers and veggies we've planted. We begin gathering bouquets and good food.

We need to take the same care with our relationships. Add fertilizer and water, so to speak, with regular phone calls and genuine conversations. Be alert for little buggy things (a misspoken word, a forgotten event) that can wilt a friendship. Weed toxic people out of your personal garden and prune away power and jealousy issues.

Just as you spend time in the sun in your garden, create a sunny atmosphere when you spend time with your friends. Be generous. Share the bounty of your garden with both real and metaphorical flowers and veggies—compliments and little gifts, nourishing words and encouragement in time of need. Just as your real garden will flourish when you're a good gardener, so will your relationships.

Barbara Ardinger, Ph.D.

May 20

Monday

Color of the day: Silver
Incense of the day: Rosemary

The Witching Wand

Willow has a wild array of medicinal and magical powers. The tree of the Moon Goddess, willow has been favored by Witches for centuries, used to make magical wands and for witching or dowsing for water. Willow protects against evil and can avert danger. It aids healing, protection, and fertility spells and can enhance intuition and sacred knowledge. If asked nicely, willow will also grant wishes. While willow is growing rapidly, filled with excited water energy, harvest some for your own magical use. Sit under a willow tree and cast a protective circle. Meditate, connecting with willow energy, Moon Goddess intuition, and water-finding abilities. Ask for permission to remove an 18- to 36-inch tapering branch filled with witching magic. Holding the willow mindfully in both hands, chant:

> A witching wand for this Witch,
>
> Finding water I am rich,
>
> A magic wand for working good,
>
> I am blessed by willow wood.

Jennifer Cobb

May 21

Tuesday

Color of the day: Black
Incense of the day: Cedar

Back to Normal Spell

If you've gone through a stressful period and you're anxious for things to get back to normal, perform this spell. This ritual is based on an old Greek saying my mother used to say: "I was, I am, and I will be!" What this means is that you're affirming your strength and you'll stay on a steady path.

For this spell you'll need two identical violet or purple candles. Violet is a color associated with balance and is used to help realign energies. The candles may be scented, if you wish. Place the candles before a mirror and light them. Look at yourself intently in the mirror. Think of your situation and how you'll return things to normal. Begin the chant:

> I was, I am, and I will be!

Repeat the words as often as you wish. The transformation has begun.

James Kambos

May 22

Wednesday

 Color of the day: White
Incense of the day: Lavender

Totemic Diversity

Sometimes we forget that every animal or plant has a totem, and instead work primarily with the totems of charismatic beings like Wolf, Bear, and Eagle, or Redwood, Oak, and Rowan.

So today, try reaching out to a totem you wouldn't ordinarily connect with. For example, if you've only ever worked with animal totems, try exploring plant totems instead. Or if you usually work with mammals or trees, try going for the smaller, hidden totems in the underbrush—or who are the underbrush!

If you've never contacted a totem before, today is a good time to try. One easy way to do this is to visualize going through a tunnel in the ground, and then coming out in a natural place where you may find the animal or plant totem. Explore the place until you find the totem, and then respectfully start a conversation.

Lupa

May 23

Thursday

 Color of the day: Green
Incense of the day: Nutmeg

Achievement Spell

Today is about completion. Taking pride in your achievements has never been so important. By recognizing the things you have accomplished, you welcome more success. Without that understanding and recognition, it is difficult to move forward. If you take the time to acknowledge what you have done, the universe will give you more of what makes you happy.

On a plain piece of paper, list all the things you are proud of. If this is the first time, you may need a couple pieces because you will be going far back into your childhood. Try to uncover as many accomplishments as you can. Get into the happy feeling of success. No accomplishment is too small. When finished, fold the pages and place inside your pillowcase, closest to the mattress. Sleep on it. More accomplishments will come to you. When they do, write those down, too, and continue the practice daily.

Patti Larsen

May 24

Friday

Color of the day: Pink
Incense of the day: Orchid

The Comfort of home

Sometimes we just need a break to restore us. This tea is a great way to relax with some warming herbs to brighten your day. You can make this with water, but it's even better with apple cider or apple juice.

For each cup of liquid, tie up the following in a tea strainer or bit of cheesecloth:

> 1 teaspoon cinnamon (or one stick)
>
> 1 teaspoon nutmeg (fresh ground is best)
>
> 1 teaspoon allspice
>
> 1 teaspoon cardamom (or 5-8 cardamom pods)

Heat the water (or juice/cider) to near boiling. Float the spices (in a tea strainer or bit of cheesecloth) in the water for 5 to 10 minutes. You can add 1 tablespoon lemon juice and honey to taste.

Drink, taking in the blessings and restorative warmth. These herbs all have strong associations with health, prosperity, and well-being.

Jenett Silver

May 25

Saturday

 Color of the day: Brown
Incense of the day: Magnolia

**Full Moon/Lunar Eclipse
in Sagittarius**

Isis and Horus Full Moon of Protection

There may be times when a mother feels the need for protection for herself and her baby. Do this little ritual in a place where you feel you are the safest. Use a white candle for Isis and a red candle for Horus. Use water mixed with some salt to represent earth, and water with a black stone sitting in the mix as a center for protection. Sprinkle the water/salt mix around your circle. Create your circle, calling Isis as the Goddess and Horus as the God. When you are all prepared, hold your baby and the stone taken out of the salt/water mix and say this little prayer—it is easy to learn and can be repeated until you feel the secure touch of the Goddess:

> Lady Isis,
> hear my plea.
>
> Protect my baby
> and protect me.
>
> As Horus sits
> safely on your knee,
>
> Keep us safe
> and trouble free.

When you are done, have some milk and a cookie. Thank Isis and Horus and ask that they stay to keep you feeling safe till the troubles pass. If you find you are still troubled, make sure you have taken care of the mundane reasons for your insecurity first ... and then repeat this prayer/ritual as needed.

Boudica

NOTES:

May 26

Sunday

 Color of the day: Yellow
Incense of the day: Hyacinth

Minimum Spell

The school year is winding down, spring cleaning needs to be completed (or started), and the yard and gardens need tending. This weekend is the unofficial beginning of summer. You have parades and barbecues to attend, food to prepare, family to visit. Sometimes it is all you can do to get through a day of activity—forget about creating and casting a spell.

Take a few minutes of your private time in the morning to light a candle and offer up your spirit to the elements. Ask for strength and stamina, and give gratitude for your blessings. Taking just a little time to ground and center will smooth the day. (Remember to extinguish the candle!)

Emyme

May 27

Monday

Color of the day: Ivory
Incense of the day: Hyssop

Memorial Day (observed)

Gratitude Basket

The words *memory* and *remember* both spring from common Latin roots meaning "to be mindful" or "to call something to mind." Use this idea of intentional recall to start a gratitude basket. Find an attractive lidded basket, box, or other container. Cut long, thin strips of paper, each about ½ x 6 inches. Every day date one of the strips and either write something on it that you're grateful for or write a short gratitude charm. (For wonderfully aesthetic results, work with pretty papers and brilliantly colored inks.) Twist the strip around a pencil until it forms a coil, then add the coiled paper strip to your gratitude basket.

From time to time, or whenever you need a spiritual boost, take a strip from the basket, unroll it, and read, replacing it when done. May these bursts of grateful memory inspire your mood and lift your spirits!

Susan Pesznecker

May 28

Tuesday

Color of the day: Maroon
Incense of the day: Geranium

Spell of the Silver Bough

The apple tree is a powerful symbol of love, abundance, and contentment. This spell can help you become more open to the blessings of life and the beauty of your surroundings.

You will need a branch of apple blossoms, which you can obtain from the woods or a local orchard at this time (or you may use a branch from a craft store if apple trees don't grow in your area). Lay the branch upon your altar and light three votive candles in front of it. As you gaze at the branch, think of all the positive aspects of your life, all that you have: your loved ones, your health, your home, your work, your skills and talents. Visualize these blessings as blossoms on an apple tree. Feel the warm candle flames illuminating your blessed life, and see the branch's blossoms as proof that life's abundance is always renewing itself.

Peg Aloi

May 29

Wednesday

Color of the day: Topaz
Incense of the day: Honeysuckle

Oak Apple Day

Oak apples, while they sound attractive, are actually galls on oak trees caused by the larvae of parasites. You may have seen these balls on trees in your area. This day is called Oak Apple Day (or Royal Oak Day) in Britain due to a celebration established in 1660 in honor of King Charles II taking back the throne of England after he had been exiled. The oak imagery comes from the folklore of oak representing good luck: during the English Civil War, Charles hid in the branches of an oak tree. Use acorns, oak leaves, or an oak apple to create a talisman:

Mighty oak, protective tree,

Let good fortune come to me.

Ember Grant

May 30

Thursday

Color of the day: Turquoise
Incense of the day: Balsam

Flush Your Prosperity Blocks

Our abundance-manifesting endeavors can sometimes be thwarted by old, limiting beliefs or vows we made in prior lifetimes. Today the conditions are perfect for rewriting these old programs so we can unite with the constant flow of affluence that is our true nature.

Light a white candle and say:

Gods and goddesses of wealth, please reveal the old mental programs that may be blocking my flow of abundance.

Then, on a length of toilet paper, make a list of everything that pops into your mind, such as "People with money aren't happy," "Spiritual people don't care about money," or vows of poverty you made in old lifetimes. Next spend time with each item on your list, finding ways that it isn't true or doesn't have to be true. Then flush the old beliefs and vows down the toilet, saying something like:

Thank you, but I don't need you anymore! Goodbye!

Tess Whitehurst

May 31

Friday

Color of the day: Purple
Incense of the day: Vanilla

Tarot for Abundance

Tarot spells for increasing wealth and abundance require focus and concentration but are powerful tools for getting what you want. Always approach tarot spellcasting with the purest of intentions to ensure the reward has no strings attached.

Place a plain, black tablecloth on a small table. Hold a piece of citrine in your right hand while your left hand places the following cards on the table in this exact order:

In the center, place the Fool, for innocence.

On the right, the Empress, for power over life.

On the left, the Chariot, for energy and confidence.

Directly below, the World, for a sense of completeness when the task is done.

Directly above, the Sun, reflecting happiness and contentment as well as success.

Then place the citrine on the Fool card. The power of this Sun crystal will center your desire for abundance and draw it to you. Leave in place for twenty-four hours.

Patti Larsen

NOTES:

May Moon Table

Date	Sign	Element	Nature	Phase
1 Wed 10:20 am	Aquarius	Air	Barren	3rd
2 Thu	Aquarius	Air	Barren	4th 7:14 am
3 Fri 2:25 pm	Pisces	Water	Fruitful	4th
4 Sat	Pisces	Water	Fruitful	4th
5 Sun 9:03 pm	Aries	Fire	Barren	4th
6 Mon	Aries	Fire	Barren	4th
7 Tue	Aries	Fire	Barren	4th
8 Wed 6:09 am	Taurus	Earth	Semi-fruitful	4th
9 Thu	Taurus	Earth	Semi-fruitful	New 8:28 pm
10 Fri 5:21 pm	Gemini	Air	Barren	1st
11 Sat	Gemini	Air	Barren	1st
12 Sun	Gemini	Air	Barren	1st
13 Mon 5:57 am	Cancer	Water	Fruitful	1st
14 Tue	Cancer	Water	Fruitful	1st
15 Wed 6:38 pm	Leo	Fire	Barren	1st
16 Thu	Leo	Fire	Barren	1st
17 Fri	Leo	Fire	Barren	1st
18 Sat 5:33 am	Virgo	Earth	Barren	2nd 12:35 am
19 Sun	Virgo	Earth	Barren	2nd
20 Mon 1:07 pm	Libra	Air	Semi-fruitful	2nd
21 Tue	Libra	Air	Semi-fruitful	2nd
22 Wed 4:55 pm	Scorpio	Water	Fruitful	2nd
23 Thu	Scorpio	Water	Fruitful	2nd
24 Fri 5:49 pm	Sagittarius	Fire	Barren	2nd
25 Sat	Sagittarius	Fire	Barren	Full 12:25 am
26 Sun 5:28 pm	Capricorn	Earth	Semi-fruitful	3rd
27 Mon	Capricorn	Earth	Semi-fruitful	3rd
28 Tue 5:48 pm	Aquarius	Air	Barren	3rd
29 Wed	Aquarius	Air	Barren	3rd
30 Thu 8:30 pm	Pisces	Water	Fruitful	3rd
31 Fri	Pisces	Water	Fruitful	4th 2:58 pm

Times are in Eastern Time.

June

The Roman poet Ovid provides two etymologies for June's name in his poem "The Fasti." The first is that the month is named after the Roman goddess Juno, wife of Jupiter and the patroness of weddings and marriage. That's a nice tie-in, because June is known as the month for weddings. The second is that the name comes from the Latin word *iuniores*, meaning "younger ones," as opposed to *maiores*, meaning "elders," for which May is named. The birthstone is the pearl, or sometimes alexandrite or moonstone. The flower associated with the month is the rose, and roses tend to be abundant and blooming in June in the Northern Hemisphere. The summer solstice, usually on June 21 or 22, is also referred to as Midsummer. In the Northern Hemisphere, the beginning of the meteorological summer is June 1; in the Southern Hemisphere, June 1 is the beginning of the meteorological winter.

Magenta

June 1
Saturday

Color of the day: Brown
Incense of the day: Rue

Spell for Love

Witches know that the first rule of love spells is to use them on ourselves first. We can't make another person happy if we're unhappy with our own lives. This spell involves taking a self-inventory and embarking upon transformation.

Light a pink seven-day candle. Take a sheet of paper and write down the qualities about yourself that you think people find lovable. These may be physical attributes (your eyes, your hair) or your personality (your generosity, your humor). Then, on the other side, list those qualities that need improving. Don't be too harsh, but be honest.

Place the paper on your altar, with the positive list facing up, and place the candle over it. When that candle has burned down, replace it with a yellow candle (for new beginnings), and flip the paper over. Reread the paper every few days to remind yourself of your goals.

Peg Aloi

June 2
Sunday

Color of the day: Amber
Incense of the day: Frankincense

Rice Offering for Abundance

Today is the Malaysian festival of Gawai Dayak in celebration of the rice harvest. When the last grains are gathered through the collective efforts of the community, festivities begin, including prayers for protection and luck. Rice is a staple grain in many areas of the world and represents blessings of prosperity and abundance.

In honor of this cultural day and to give thanks for your own abundance, leave an offering of uncooked rice on your household altar or dining room table. Try cooking a meal with rice as an ingredient and share it with loved ones, if possible. Before and/or during the meal, go around the dinner table one at a time, allowing all those in attendance to offer their own recitations of prayers and blessings of gratitude, luck, abundance, and protection. So mote it be!

Blake Octavian Blair

June 3
Monday

 Color of the day: Lavender
Incense of the day: Neroli

Bellona's Sword

Sometimes we all get silenced. We lose our voice, don't speak out when a wrong has happened, get overpowered by someone speaking far too loudly, or just can't find the words to say how we feel. Today let Bellona, an ancient Roman war goddess, help you to fight the war against silence, because sometimes silence is complicity. Wielding a sword and wearing a helmet, Bellona is armed with a spear and torch. Her festival was held every year on June 3. Let Bellona help you speak out against wrongdoing. Chant:

> With Bellona's sword I cut the silence, I speak out.
>
> Against violence, evil, and all wrongdoing, hear me as I shout.
>
> With Bellona's spear I stand guard, speaking strong and sure,
>
> Her torch brings fiery clarity, my words are true and pure.
>
> I wear Bellona's helmet to protect my deepest intent,
>
> Let Bellona's blessing be upon me, and let silence relent.

Dallas Jennifer Cobb

June 4
Tuesday

Color of the day: Scarlet
Incense of the day: Basil

Break a Negative Spell

Negative spells usually come about when we find ourselves doing self-destructive acts. We say something we really shouldn't have said, or do something we shouldn't have done. Sometimes it can be because of something you did to yourself, and sometimes it is the work of others.

The act of breaking a negative spell is called an *uncrossing*. To achieve this, start with a self-cleansing. Take a soaking bath in specially chosen oils: a few drops of lavender, lemon, mugwort, and rose. These oils encourage self-cleansing and calm and thereby reverse the spell with protection and forgiveness, because nothing reverses a negative spell better than a return to sender (even to yourself) of peace and love. And forgiveness is always at the center of healing negativity. Work on transforming the source from hate to forgiveness.

Boudica

June 5
Wednesday

Color of the day: Yellow
Incense of the day: Bay laurel

In God We Trust

As today is a day of loyalty, honesty, and oaths inspired by the Roman festival of Semo Sancus, god of trust, we would be wise to harness these energies to make a meaningful vow. Take some time to meditate on your spiritual quest and soul's yearning. What is most sacred to you in connection with the Divine? What steps do you want and need to take to fulfill your heart's calling? Search within for answers and come to a place of calm commitment. Here, utter a vow that will take you ever more deeply into the Mystery. Utter it once that it may gain strength within you; utter it twice that it may find a hold in the ethers; utter it thrice that you may have the support you need each day.

Chandra Alexandre

June 6
Thursday

Color of the day: Green
Incense of the day: Myrrh

Butterfly Magic and Lore

Butterflies begin to appear more frequently now in gardens. The butterfly has been a symbol of happiness, rebirth, and transformation in many magical traditions since ancient times. It is also believed that they represent the human soul after death. Butterfly designs were carved into wood and stone statues by ancient Mexican civilizations.

Here is a magical exercise using butterfly imagery. Cover your altar with brilliantly colored fabric such as red, yellow, or orange. Quietly sit before your altar, and in your mind's eye see a butterfly hovering over flowers in a garden. Let the butterfly represent something you'd like to change in your life. Eventually see the butterfly flying gracefully higher and higher in the sky—then disappearing. That is a sign your wish has been received by the Unseen Realm. To attract butterflies to your garden, plant flowers such as coneflowers, lantana, and zinnias.

James Kambos

June 7
Friday

Color of the day: Pink
Incense of the day: Rose

Spirals of Protection

This protection spell is both simple and effective, making a fine addition to your magickal repertoire. The spell consecrates and protects one's personal space, meaning the charm moves with you. This makes it perfect for travel.

Close your eyes briefly and use the index finger of your dominant hand to trace deosil (sun-wise) spirals in the air around you. Turn deosil in a circle as you make them, casting a shell of spirals around your body. Trace some directly overhead and underfoot, too. As you work, incant:

> Wrapped I am in Spirals Light
>
> No harm or hurt may come to me.
>
> Whether day or whether night,
>
> Cloaked in safety I shall be.

Visualize the protection surrounding you like a web of safety. Note: Although one's finger works fine, the spell could also be done with wand, athame, or whatever is at hand.

Susan Pesznecker

June 8
Saturday

Color of the day: Gray
Incense of the day: Ivy

New Moon in Gemini

Embrace the Darkness

We're hardwired to want light. Light helps us see, and in more dangerous times it could be the crucial factor in getting home safely without attack or accident. However, darkness has its value as well. It's restful, when we feel safe enough, and we can cultivate darkness as a quiet place for magic and meditation.

Spend some time in the dark tonight. Go to a quiet room, and shut out as much of the light as you can. If you're comfortable, go into a closet, or blindfold yourself. Then simply sit in the darkness and see how it changes your perception.

How comfortable do you feel in the dark? Do you notice your other senses more? How does the darkness affect your ability to focus? Try a meditation or other magical activity that you normally would do in the light (provided it's safe to do without being able to see!).

Lupa

June 9
Sunday

Color of the day: Yellow
Incense of the day: Eucalyptus

A Simple hearth

Today is the festival of Vestalia, the celebration of Vesta's flame in Rome. We can bring Vesta, goddess of hearth and home, into our own homes by tending to our hearths.

Choose a candle to represent your hearth. This works best with a pillar, but any candle will do. On the candle, carve symbols of a safe and welcoming home, and, if you wish, anoint it with oils that fit your idea of a welcoming home (orange for good cheer, cinnamon and nutmeg for prosperity, rosemary or lavender for health and balance).

Each time you tend your home by doing chores, light the candle and repeat a simple blessing for your home, such as:

Here is hearth, here is home.

Blessings on all within.

When you're done, extinguish the candle, letting the smoke carry the blessing through your home. Create a new candle as needed.

Jenett Silver

June 10
Monday

Color of the day: Ivory
Incense of the day: Clary sage

Clerihew for Vesta

June 7–15 is the festival of Vesta, goddess of hearth and home. Her temple in Rome was tended by virgins, taking their cue from the goddess—also a virgin.

A clerihew is a four-line, humorous, biographical poem, created by E. C. Bentley, a twentieth-century English humorist. The form of these whimsical poems lends itself to spells in its brevity and may be used to honor our gods and goddesses.

The goddess Vesta

Often knew best, a

Virgin protector.

Bless my home sector.

You may wish to try your hand at writing a clerihew for your personal deity.

Emyme

June 11
Tuesday

Color of the day: Black
Incense of the day: Cinnamon

Courage

Draw on your inner strength today to build courage. Consider things you are afraid of and face them head-on. To remind you of your strength, dedicate a special piece of jewelry or other keepsake to carry with you. Alternately you can simply use a piece of red ribbon. Tie a knot in the center to symbolize a bond of strength. Place the item in a circle of red or white candles. Visualize the strong flames charging the item with energy. Say:

> There is no fear that I can't conquer.
>
> There is no task I can't complete.
>
> I have courage that I need
>
> To accomplish any feat.

Let the candles burn out. Wear or carry your talisman whenever you need a boost of courage.

Ember Grant

June 12
Wednesday

Color of the day: White
Incense of the day: Marjoram

The Sun Spell

In tarot, the Sun is the most powerful and positive card in the deck. For this spell you will need a dandelion. They are powerful plants, filled with positive sun energy. Also, they are well known to increase psychic abilities and connection to spirit. In a small glass bowl, crush the petals with a spoon. Go outside and sit in a sunny spot, and dip your fingers into the mixture. Apply to the backs of both hands. Place your hands over your heart, with the essence exposed, and repeat the following as you breathe slowly and deeply, face turned up toward the sun:

> Thank you for sharing your power.
>
> Thank you for sharing your warmth.
>
> Thank you for sharing your light.
>
> Thank you for sharing your joy.

Repeat the mantra three times. Leave the dandelion essence on your hands for as long as you can, and breathe it in when you think of it.

Patti Larsen

June 13
Thursday

Color of the day: Purple
Incense of the day: Carnation

Epona's Feast Day

Epona is a Celtic goddess whose name comes from Gaul; she is also known as Macha in Ireland, and Rhiannon in Wales. She is the protector of horses, who were a central part of life in the British Isles. The White Horse at Uffington (near Banbury) is the most famous chalk hill figure in England, and dates from the Neolithic era. The nursery rhyme "Ride a cock horse to Banbury Cross, to see a fine lady upon a white horse" may be a reference to pilgrims who journeyed to honor Epona there. English poet G. K. Chesterton also wrote about the horse in his 1911 poem "The Ballad of the White Horse":

> Before the gods that made the gods
>
> Had seen their sunrise pass,
>
> The White Horse of the White Horse Vale
>
> Was cut out of the grass.

To honor Epona and the majestic animals she protects, place a basket of apples (a horse's favorite food and one native to England) on your altar.

Peg Aloi

June 14
Friday

Color of the day: Rose
Incense of the day: Yarrow

Flag Day

Invite New Friendship Spell

On this day in 1959, the United States welcomed Hawaii as a state. If you would like to welcome a new friend into your life, use the energies of this Friday during the waxing moon and a Hawaiian symbol of friendship, the pineapple, to attract a friend of like mind. Cut up a fresh pineapple and eat some. Then wrap a piece of the leaf in a piece of pink fabric and tie with a yellow ribbon. Charm your pineapple pouch:

> Pineapple, sweet and bright,
>
> A kindred spirit I seek to invite.
>
> I seek a friendship of like mind,
>
> With open heart and a spirit kind.

Carry the pouch with you in your purse or pocket when you go out into the world. Remember, you have to be a friend to have a friend. Remain open and friendly with people you meet, and see what the day brings you.

Mickie Mueller

June 15
Saturday

Color of the day: Indigo
Incense of the day: Pine

The Naked Truth

Today the ancient Teutons celebrated St. Vitus's Day with fires honoring the sun. These fires, called *need-fires*, were built by youthful firemakers who were often required to work naked. In honor of this tradition, get naked in the sun, safely. Choose a spot in your home where the sun shines where you can lie naked, undisturbed, for a period of time. Spread a cloth, remove your clothing, and lie down. Close your eyes and see the sun's fiery red glow through your eyelids. Feel the energy of the sun soaking into your skin.

This solar energy that fuels plant growth also feeds you. Ask yourself *What does my spirit need?* and listen intently for the answer. What do you need to feel safe and happy? Harvest the energy of the bright sun, and envision it feeding, fueling, and growing all that is "needed" in your life. Feed your needs.

Dallas Jennifer Cobb

June 16
Sunday

Color of the day: Gold
Incense of the day: Almond

Father's Day

Fatherly Forgiveness

Just as each moment and situation can be seen as the perfect trigger for your soul's most ideal unfolding, there is no way your father can be anything other than the perfect father for you. So, regardless of the nature of your relationship on the surface level (whether you know him or not, whether you get along or don't, whether he's living or dead, and so on), the following exercise will bring healing blessings to you, your father, and the world.

Close your eyes and connect with the part of you that completely forgives and is completely forgiven. Then connect with this same aspect of your father. See both your hearts glowing with light. See this light expand to fill and surround both of you. Remember that love is the only truth, and allow everything else— just for the moment—to fall away.

Tess Whitehurst

June 17
Monday

Color of the day: Gray
Incense of the day: Lily

Soft Mead Recipe

For a small amount of non-alcoholic mead, take one quart spring water, one cup honey, one lemon cut into slices, and a half teaspoon nutmeg. Boil in a non-metallic pot, removing the scum as it rises with a wooden spoon. Add a pinch of salt and the juice of half a lemon. Strain and cool. Drink in place of alcoholic mead, wine, etc.

From Scott Cunningham's
Book of Shadows

June 18
Tuesday

Color of the day: Red
Incense of the day: Bayberry

Tears of Isis

The goddess Isis cried and the Nile flooded. Before her search for the pieces of Osiris, she sat and wept. Crying brings release and, with that, the strength to venture forth anew, cleansed of old wounds and sorrows. Withholding tears leaves the land dry and barren. It darkens the heart.

Drawing on the powers of water, find time today for a meditative bath, a relaxing swim, or a trip to the seashore to help move you into awareness of grief or sadness. Find your tears, or, if you prefer, place a pot of salt water on your altar to honor that which has been mourned and allow for cleansing. Anoint your heart and offer this prayer to Isis:

> Overflowing with tears inside
> I come to you
> Ready to release my pain and
> suffering.
>
> Goddess, take my heart
> And wash it clean with your
> love
> That I might start again.

Chandra Alexandre

June 19
Wednesday

Color of the day: Brown
Incense of the day: Lilac

Staging a Pagan Jewelry Race

Start celebrating summer by staging a Pagan jewelry race with your circle or coven. First find a venue. This can be a track or a driveway, but it should not (for reasons made obvious below) be longer than the typical city block. Invite everyone you know and tell them to bring *all* their Pagan jewelry—amulets, rings, necklaces, earrings … every bit of jewelry they ever wear to a ritual, meet-up, or gathering.

At the starting line, tell your racers to put on all that jewelry. Shout, "Go!" The first person to stagger or crawl across the finish line is the winner.

Give the winner a nice prize, though preferably not another necklace of magical stones. Find ways to give nice prizes (preferably not more jewelry) to the other racers. (Copies of this book are good.) After the awards, shed the jewelry, put it away somewhere safe, and have a feast.

Barbara Ardinger, Ph.D.

June 20
Thursday

Color of the day: Turquoise
Incense of the day: Mulberry

Where's My Focus?

As we reach toward the summer solstice tomorrow, it's a great time to take stock of what's going on in our lives. What's flourishing and growing? What's still in shadow? A simple divination reading might illuminate things for you. The following method will work with tarot cards, runes, or any similar divination method (stones, oracle cards, etc.).

Shuffle as you normally would. Lay out two cards/runes/stones in a horizontal row. Place the third in the middle, closer to you, to make an arrow. The first shows the aspects of the situation that you're currently seeing. The second shows the aspects you have not been noticing, for whatever reason. The third shows what you can do to move forward toward your goals. Take time to reflect on what you've learned, and brainstorm a few specific actions to add to your to-do list.

Jenett Silver

June 21

Friday

Color of the day: White
Incense of the day: Cypress

Litha – Summer Solstice

Divine Masculine Invocation

Today is the summer solstice (Midsummer) and the longest day of the year! No matter what our gender, we all have masculine and feminine aspects to ourselves. To maintain a healthy balance, we must both honor and recognize these dual aspects.

Today, with the sun at the peak of its power, is the perfect time to honor our relationship with the divine masculine that resides within all of us. Here is a simple Midsummer-themed invocation you can recite today in recognition and honor of your ever-present divine masculine:

Midsummer Day! Solar rays radiating bright,
Bathing us in your divine masculine light!

Illuminating our divine masculine within,
Balancing the sacred inner feminine.

Power of the god without and within,
Always with us even as now the light shall grow thin.

Wisdom of the sage and of the sun,
So shall it remain as the waning of the light has now begun.

So mote it be!

Blake Octavian Blair

NOTES:

June 22
Saturday

 Color of the day: Blue
Incense of the day: Magnolia

Conscious Cooking

Kitchen witchery is all about food and its preparation, and using that for one's manifesting intent. However, before you can make that magic happen, you need to know what you're working with.

Prepare a meal that is made from as many locally grown, organic, and free-range ingredients as you can get and afford. If you go to a farmers' market, talk to the farmers about how the animals were raised and killed, and how the plants were cultivated. Ask at the grocery store where the food you buy comes from; some stores will list the state (or country!) of origin.

As you're preparing the meal, think about the physical places the food came from, the pastures and fields and orchards. Remind yourself, as you eat, that you are eating the soil of the places the plants and animals came from.

Lupa

June 23
Sunday

Color of the day: Orange
Incense of the day: Hyacinth

Full Moon in Capricorn

Full Moon for Prosperity

Prosperity can cover health, wealth, and opportunity. When working your full moon this month, here are some thoughts to focus on when you step into your circle with your deities:

Family Health—We all know the cost of health care, and asking for good health is not a bad idea. Ask your deities that insurance always cover all your medical needs, and that you will never be without it. If you do not have health insurance, ask your deities that your medical needs always be met without strain on your personal finances. Focus on green for health.

Wealth—We can always use a raise or a better job ... or we may need a job to begin with. Work with your deities on getting a good job, keeping a good job, getting a well-deserved raise, or being offered a better position with more money. Focus on yellow for success.

Opportunity—Always ask for the opportunity to make your life better, and never pass up an opportunity to improve your life. Work with your deities to gain that special opportunity that will open doors to a new kind of prosperity, one that you will find interesting, fun, and profitable. Focus on orange for opportunity.

Never doubt yourself or what you can do with the aid of your deities.

Boudica

NOTES:

June 24
Monday

Color of the day: White
Incense of the day: Narcissus

Midsummer's healing herb

This is the festival of San Juan, or John the Baptist, believed to have been born six months before Jesus. As with many Christian feast days, its origins are pagan.

At Midsummer, the herb known as St. John's wort is blooming with bright yellow flowers. The herb has many uses in healing and is effective for mild depression in capsule and tincture form. There is some risk of blood pressure spiking if these forms are combined with certain foods, but drinking an infusion of St. John's wort is beneficial and has no side effects.

Country folk in Europe believed that picking the herb on this day made its healing powers more potent. Try to pick your St. John's wort in the morning, just after the dew has dried. You may use it fresh, but it's more potent after it has been dried, which may be done on a cookie sheet in a warm oven (preheat to 200, then turn off heat).

Peg Aloi

June 25
Tuesday

Color of the day: Gray
Incense of the day: Ylang-ylang

GLBT Month

Two years ago today, New York became the sixth state to legalize same-sex marriage. Many consider it no coincidence that this occurred during Gay, Lesbian, Bisexual, and Transgender Month. The Pagan community is no stranger to discrimination similar to the GLBT experience, and celebrates this milestone. During your evening ritual, light a candle and say a few words of gratitude for the continued and increasing tolerance for all beliefs and orientations.

Emyme

June 26
Wednesday

Color of the day: Topaz
Incense of the day: Lavender

Personal Power hand Wash

To boost your personal power, brew a cup of Earl Grey tea and include a slice of fresh ginger and a sprig of sage. While the tea steeps, draw a pentagram in the air above the cup and charge it with the following charm:

Tea and bergamot bring success,

As I go forth I shall impress.

Powerful ginger and sage be clever,

As I stand strong in each endeavor.

Allow the tea to cool. Strain it through a coffee filter, and store in a glass jar in the refrigerator. Pour some tea onto your hands before big meetings or important engagements. Rub it all over and allow it to air-dry; do not wash off. Once it has dried, the power remains with you all day even if you have to wash your hands later on in the day. Brew a fresh batch as needed.

Mickie Mueller

June 27
Thursday

Color of the day: Crimson
Incense of the day: Jasmine

Debt Relief

Financial burdens can cause so much pain and stress in our lives. If you are trying to resolve a difficult financial situation, use this spell to help you remain centered and calm. Keep your perspective: yes, this is an important issue, but remember to focus on the meaningful aspects of your life and don't get bogged down with worry.

To begin, decorate your altar with symbols of the most meaningful things in your life, things money can't buy: family, friends, and so on. Burn some incense, relax, and use this chant:

Through the swamp of debt I crawl,
Moving slowly through the mire,
I'm not alone in this shortfall—
Some face needs more dire.

One step at a time, break free,
Rise and once again stand tall,
Eventually I will succeed—
It's only money, after all!

Ember Grant

June 28
Friday

Color of the day: Coral
Incense of the day: Violet

Yemaya Relationship Cleanse

Today is perfect for releasing wounds and/or energetic cords related to old romantic involvements, from this life or a former one. This can be helpful because wounds and cords such as these can resurface in our present life and keep us from experiencing the love we desire.

This traditional ritual involves calling on Yemaya, the orisha and mother goddess of the sea. Say a simple prayer asking her to cleanse and heal you of these old emotional/energetic conditions. Offer her seven white roses or the rose petals from one white rose. If you can get to the ocean or another safely swimmable body of water, place the rose or petals in the water and then completely immerse yourself in the water seven times. If you can't get to a moving body of water, place the roses or petals on your altar and then immerse yourself in a sea salt bath seven times.

Tess Whitehurst

June 29
Saturday

Color of the day: Brown
Incense of the day: Sage

Uncrossing Vinegar

It's Saturday and a waning moon, as well as East Anglian Herb Harvesting Day, so it's the perfect time to make herbal uncrossing vinegar you can use all year long. In a decorative jar or bottle, place 3 garlic cloves, 3 peppercorns, sprigs of rosemary, sage, and thyme, and a pinch of sea salt. Close the lid and seal it with melted wax. Hold it in your hands and charge it with the following:

> Vinegar strong and herbs of power,
>
> I charge you now within this hour.
>
> Uncross, uncross, with powers imbue,
>
> I charge you now, uncrossing brew.

Leave the vinegar to sit undisturbed for one month, then break the seal and use it for uncrossing spells. Pour some over your doorstep to protect you from negative vibes. Write down your troubles and cover the list in the vinegar. Mix a little with water for a floor wash. Get creative.

Mickie Mueller

June 30

Sunday

Color of the day: Yellow
Incense of the day: Heliotrope

Day of Aestas Spell

The Roman goddess Aestas was the corn goddess of summer. She is represented by the tarot card the Empress and symbolizes all things surrounding material prosperity, powerful sexual energy, and radiant health.

To honor Aestas, place a white candle in the center of the table. Place a small wooden plate on the table, and rub the edges of the plate with ginseng oil as a sexual enhancer. Next sprinkle the plate with dill for its healing properties. Now drizzle the plate with a mix of olive oil and garlic. Tear off a chunk of cornbread with your fingers. Warm the bread over the candle for three or four seconds, then dip in the oil on the plate. Eat the cornbread while repeating mentally:

Wealth, money,
health, abundance.

All these are mine.

Patti Larsen

June Moon Table

Date	Sign	Element	Nature	Phase
1 Sat	Pisces	Water	Fruitful	4th
2 Sun 2:33 am	Aries	Fire	Barren	4th
3 Mon	Aries	Fire	Barren	4th
4 Tue 11:53 am	Taurus	Earth	Semi-fruitful	4th
5 Wed	Taurus	Earth	Semi-fruitful	4th
6 Thu 11:32 pm	Gemini	Air	Barren	4th
7 Fri	Gemini	Air	Barren	4th
8 Sat	Gemini	Air	Barren	New 11:56 am
9 Sun 12:16 pm	Cancer	Water	Fruitful	1st
10 Mon	Cancer	Water	Fruitful	1st
11 Tue	Cancer	Water	Fruitful	1st
12 Wed 12:58 am	Leo	Fire	Barren	1st
13 Thu	Leo	Fire	Barren	1st
14 Fri 12:26 pm	Virgo	Earth	Barren	1st
15 Sat	Virgo	Earth	Barren	1st
16 Sun 9:19 pm	Libra	Air	Semi-fruitful	2nd 1:24 pm
17 Mon	Libra	Air	Semi-fruitful	2nd
18 Tue	Libra	Air	Semi-fruitful	2nd
19 Wed 2:38 am	Scorpio	Water	Fruitful	2nd
20 Thu	Scorpio	Water	Fruitful	2nd
21 Fri 4:31 am	Sagittarius	Fire	Barren	2nd
22 Sat	Sagittarius	Fire	Barren	2nd
23 Sun 4:08 am	Capricorn	Earth	Semi-fruitful	Full 7:32 am
24 Mon	Capricorn	Earth	Semi-fruitful	3rd
25 Tue 3:27 am	Aquarius	Air	Barren	3rd
26 Wed	Aquarius	Air	Barren	3rd
27 Thu 4:32 am	Pisces	Water	Fruitful	3rd
28 Fri	Pisces	Water	Fruitful	3rd
29 Sat 9:07 am	Aries	Fire	Barren	3rd
30 Sun	Aries	Fire	Barren	4th 12:54 am

Times are in Eastern Time.

July

Juty is the hope of April, the lushness of May, and the growth of June all brought to fulfillment. Now, flower beds are splashed with color, garden-fresh produce appears at roadside stands, and the Grain Goddess watches over ripening crops. The mornings are dewy, and there's a sweetness in the air. On July 4, we pause to remember a special July morning years ago in Philadelphia, when statesmen gathered to declare that a young, struggling nation was free and independent. In colonial times the full moon of July was called the Blessing Moon. Independence Day is the main holiday of the month, celebrated with parades and barbecues. It's also a good day to declare magical goals to free ourselves from bad habits and patterns. With the sun in the water sign Cancer, cleansing and fertility magic of all kinds are appropriate. Simply taking a swim will cleanse your body, mind, and spirit. More than anything, July dazzles us. July is an awesome thunderstorm on a hot afternoon. It's a meadow turned white with Queen Anne's lace, and it's firefly nights. July is summer's song being sung. Sweet July—it's the high note of the year.

James Kambos

July 1
Monday

Color of the day: Silver
Incense of the day: Hyssop

Melting Obstacles

We all have obstacles in our lives. This charm will help melt them away. Gather an ice cube and a towel. Plain water is great for the ice cube, but you can also freeze an infusion of herbs related to your goal (rosemary for health, basil or spices for prosperity, etc.). Small ice cubes work especially well, but larger ones are fine.

Hold the ice cube in your hands, thinking hard about what you want to melt away from your life. Perhaps it's a barrier to your creativity or your health. Maybe you're frustrated by old habits or patterns. Whatever your need, keep your mind focused on it. Let the heat from your hands melt the ice, and as the ice melts, let the obstacle flow away and dissolve. When all the ice is melted, wash your hands with some nice soap and move forward more freely into your day.

Jenett Silver

July 2
Tuesday

Color of the day: White
Incense of the day: Ginger

Renewing Your Intention of Gratitude

It's been six months since you wrote your list of nine things for which you're grateful and held them to your heart. If you still have your list, get it out and study it. If you want to make changes, do so. Or write a new list.

Become quiet and hold the revised list to your heart again and see each thing for which you're grateful written there in beautiful calligraphic script.

When you're ready, set an indigo candle on a fireproof surface. As you light the candle, invoke a goddess or god important to you, perhaps a Great Mother or Father. Read each item aloud, saying, "Thank you, [goddess or god]." Tell why you are grateful.

Finally burn the list in the flame of the indigo candle. Let the candle burn down, then bury the wax and the ashes of the list in your garden or a potted plant.

Barbara Ardinger, Ph.D.

July 3
Wednesday

Color of the day: Yellow
Incense of the day: Lilac

Midweek Energetic housekeeping

We've reached the midpoint of the week and, being situated in the thick of things, Wednesdays often seem to have a bit of energetic anxiety and clutter. Sometimes despite our best efforts we end up bringing some of that stress home with us, and if left unattended it can accumulate.

Time for some midweek energetic housekeeping! To work in harmony with the today's energy boost from Mercury, gather any of the following herbs with Mercurial correspondences: lavender, mint, parsley, fennel, lemongrass, or dill. Combine into a loose incense and burn on an incense charcoal. Fan the smoke with your hand or a feather throughout your home to neutralize any collected stress or anxiety and to elevate the energetic vibration inside your home. Be sure to fan the smoke into the corners, coat closets, laundry room, and other often overlooked places where energy may stagnate and accumulate.

Blake Octavian Blair

July 4
Thursday

Color of the day: Green
Incense of the day: Balsam

Independence Day

Prosperity Firework Spell

In the United States July 4 is Independence Day, something of a national fire festival. The day also has historical references as a fire festival celebrating "Old Midsummer Eve," where balefires were lit as the sun went down. This spell programs the power of fireworks with your magical intent. Use this spell when lighting your own fireworks or watching a professional display. As each firework soars into the air, watch it, focusing intently on your goal. Visualize yourself wealthy, with all of your needs met. Use only positive thoughts. As the firework explodes, repeat this phrase in your mind:

> By the power of fire,
> I send it out higher.

You may repeat this with every firework you see, as often as you wish. Your power builds with every explosion. At the end of the finale add this phrase:

> For my greatest good and with harm to none, so mote it be.

Mickie Mueller

July 5
Friday

Color of the day: Purple
Incense of the day: Mint

healing and Purification Weaving

Get some wool or other natural-fiber yarn or string. Cut three equal strands, at least twelve inches long, and knot them together at one end. Then braid the strands together tightly. Visualize any illnesses, injuries, or other impurities you would like to remove from yourself or your home flowing through your hands and being bound into the braid. As you do so, say the following:

> Woven fibers, strong and true,
>
> Wrapping round the trouble here.
>
> Pain and anguish, illness, fear,
>
> In this binding shall accrue.

Then take the weaving to an isolated place, such as far out in the wilderness or at the top of a building (without trespassing!). Tie the weaving to a branch, pole, or other object, and let the elements slowly wear away the fibers and the impurities over time.

Lupa

July 6
Saturday

Color of the day: Black
Incense of the day: Patchouli

harmony with Electronics

With Mercury in retrograde, we are back in a time when electronics and communications devices may foul up at every given opportunity. In addition to making sure your batteries are fully charged at all times, and making sure your prized equipment is unplugged during storms that generate lightning (which can travel back on telephone and power lines and blow out our equipment), I recommend asking Mercury, the god of communications, to protect your equipment and improve your communications during this period of retrograde:

> Lord Mercury, hear my prayer
>
> And keep my equipment in good repair.
>
> Keep it free from static and power surge
>
> And any other electrical scourge.
>
> Help me keep communication clear,
>
> For what I mean is what they hear.

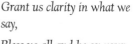

Grant us clarity in what we say,

Bless us all and be on your way.

Boudica

NOTES:

July 7
Sunday

Color of the day: Gold
Incense of the day: Juniper

A Water Scrying Spell

This is the seventh day of the seventh month. Seven is the most mystical of all numbers. The seventh son of a seventh son was considered to have enormous spellcasting powers. The seventh daughter of a seventh daughter was frequently thought to possess great powers of prophecy.

Since this day falls in the water sign of Cancer, water scrying would be especially effective today. Begin your scrying session after dark using a bowl of water, a birdbath, or a pond. Stir the water seven times using your power hand, then speak this charm:

Ancient Ones, I call upon the power of the ancient way.

I call upon the power of this, the seventh day.

I call upon the power of the seven seas.

Bring me the gift of prophecy.

As the ripples in the water subside, scry deeply into the water without thinking of anything specific.

James Kambos

July 8
Monday

Color of the day: Gray
Incense of the day: Neroli

New Moon in Cancer

Keeping hope Alive Spell

This spell is intended to help you or someone you love deal with a chronic illness.

Buy a bouquet of flowers at the grocery store or a flower arrangement from a florist. As the flowers begin to wilt, take the arrangement apart and put the flowers that are freshest into a different vase. While those are still in your home, look for other flowers (wild or bought) to add to the arrangement. Try not to throw out the whole arrangement—ever! Just keep modifying it.

As you freshen your flower arrangement, say:

I am keeping hope alive.

May all around me grow and thrive.

The ways of life, we cannot know,

So flowers come and flowers go.

This spell will remind you that chronic conditions ebb and flow, so we should live in the moment and enjoy whatever beauty comes our way.

Anne Johnson

July 9
Tuesday

Color of the day: Black
Incense of the day: Cedar

Ramadan begins

Our Lady of Peace

Make invocation this day to the spiraling forces of peace that unite heaven and earth. Bring balance to your life not by trying to equalize work and play but by fleshing out resentments and dealing with them. Set boundaries around the ways you wish to spend your precious time, and be clear in your articulation of them to others. Enlist friends, colleagues, and family in supporting you in what is most important to you. Create harmony by selflessly putting yourself first. In other words, just like an oxygen mask on a plane, you are advised to take care of yourself and so you are then best able to care for others. Call to the Goddess as Mary, Eyasha, Eirene, or Tara to bring about the desired result.

Chandra Alexandre

July 10
Wednesday

Color of the day: White
Incense of the day: Bay laurel

Lady Godiva Day

Protection spells crafted today (Wednesday) hold double power when dedicated to Lady Godiva, with a touch of Wodin. Legend has it Lady G rode naked on her horse down the main street of town in order to convince her husband to be less harsh in the collection of taxes.

Be mindfully generous and wise in your thoughts, words, and deeds today. Include a white candle for purity and a red candle for power at your personal evening ritual, at which you may choose to be skyclad to further honor Lady G.

Emyme

July 11
Thursday

Color of the day: Crimson
Incense of the day: Myrrh

Wild Water Magic

Make a vow: *I will not walk by wild water.* It's still early in the summer and chances are you will visit water in its natural state, be it a river, pond, ocean, stream, lake, or waterfall. When you do, do not walk by. Instead, squat down at the shore, dip your hands in the water, and whisper:

Sacred mother of emotion and psychic intuition, I greet you.

Look for signs of danger or pollution, and if you see them, heed the warning. But if you can, shed your clothes and enter the water. Wash your arms, legs, and torso, saying:

Mother, cleanse, heal, and nourish me.

Relax into the embrace of the water:

*Cradle me as I float in the waters of your womb.
Buoy me up and support me.*

Now dip under, letting the water cover the crown of your head. Then resurface, feeling reborn, fresh and new, restored and sanctified by the mother.

Dallas Jennifer Cobb

July 12
Friday

Color of the day: Rose
Incense of the day: Alder

Smell the Roses

The summer night is like a
perfection of thought.

—Wallace Stevens, "The House
Was Quiet and the World Was
Calm"

Julius Caesar was born on this day,
and gives his name to the month of
July. The Anglo-Saxon names for
July are Heymonath and Maed mon-
ath, which refer to haymaking and
flowering meadows.

Summer's bounty of flowers can
be a balm to the soul. If you don't
have your own garden, visit a public
one or one at a friend's house, and
enjoy the sensory gifts of nature.
Be sure to smell them! The healing
powers of flowers are the basis of
many aromatherapy cures, in particular rose, lavender, and geranium.

If you're inspired to begin gardening, start with something simple
like flowering annuals, which are
plentiful at garden shops in summer.
Petunias, pansies, mums, and impa-
tiens are particularly colorful and
long-blooming. Place pots of them
near your front door to bless your
home and all its visitors. Choose colors that make you feel energized.

Peg Aloi

July 13
Saturday

Color of the day: Brown
Incense of the day: Rue

Feast of Santa Rosalia

This three-day festival celebrates
Rosalia, a saint and hermit
whose spirit is believed to have
rid Palermo of the Black Plague.
In honor of this festival, spend
some time today doing things to
clear away physical or emotional
clutter and rejuvenate your spirit.
This can be as simple as cleaning
something— a closet, a drawer, or
even your car. Is there an area of
your home, yard, or work environment that you've been neglecting? Is
there a book you've been meaning to
start or finish? Maybe you've been
thinking of getting a new haircut
or a manicure—do it! Or start that
exercise or diet program you've been
putting off. Use this chant to charge
your effort:

Refresh, renew, take part—

Today I will restart

To clean and clear, begin

To make my way again.

A new event or deed,

Today I will proceed.

Ember Grant

July 14
Sunday

Color of the day: Yellow
Incense of the day: Marigold

Feast to the Graces Spell

The Romans celebrated this day with a Feast to the Graces, the old goddesses of beneficence. It was thought that honoring them welcomed beauty, charm, and goodness and also brought joy for the rest of the year. This spell is also excellent for creativity and art inspiration, as the Graces were known to guide and assist those in creative fields.

Place a pure-white napkin on the table and assemble the following ingredients: dark chocolate, red wine, whole grain bread, real butter, nuts or seeds of your choice, a slice of pear, and a slice of cooked beef or chicken. (Note: If you are vegetarian, another protein source will suffice.) Sample from each food, sipping wine in between and chewing slowly, saying:

Thank you for your gifts to me.

Thank you for my creativity.

I honor you in word and deed.

I make use of every seed.

Patti Larsen

July 15
Monday

Color of the day: White
Incense of the day: Clary sage

Simple Balance Ritual

The only constant is change. One of the aims of magic is staying awake to this change as it plays out in our lives, so we can maintain holistic balance and harmony in all life areas. Today is an excellent day to do just that.

Write down your balance-related goals in present tense, as if they're already true; for example: "I always have plenty of time," "I exercise moderation in my caffeine intake," "My energy level is steady and strong," and so on. Place your list face up on a plate.

Then carve the word *BALANCE* into a purple candle. Hold the candle in both hands, close your eyes, and take some deep breaths. Conjure up a feeling of deep well-being and divine equilibrium, and direct this feeling into the candle. Set the candle on top of the list and light it. Sprinkle dried chamomile and rosemary on the list around the candle's base.

Tess Whitehurst

July 16
Tuesday

 Color of the day: Red
Incense of the day: Bayberry

Sky Skrying

Tuesday—named for the Norse god Tyr, the Old English god Tiu, and the Germanic god Twia—is associated with the rune Tiwaz, a glyph of an arrow pointing straight up. Tyr is associated with justice and sacrifice, especially sacrificing individual wants for the good of the community. A spiritual warrior, Tyr exemplified honor and righteousness. Take direction from Tiwaz today, look to where the rune points—up.

Lie on your back in a safe, private spot, outdoors. Gaze up into the sky, and breathe deeply, invoking Tyr. Pulling from the sky, inhale Tyr's faith, loyalty, and commitment to the collective. Exhale, releasing selfishness, isolation, and false pride into the earth below. Continue exchanging energy, letting go of fear, doubt, and rigidity and breathing faith into your magical community, friends, and family. Feel Tyr and Tiwaz filling you with the power, strength, and longevity of collectivity and supportive community.

Dallas Jennifer Cobb

July 17
Wednesday

Color of the day: Topaz
Incense of the day: Marjoram

Birth of Nephthys

A goddess often associated with death, Nephthys was also nurse-mother to Horus and one invoked during childbirth. In her, the principles of creation, preservation, and destruction come alive.

Use this awareness today to create a sacred totem that captures all the potency, nourishment, and dynamic tension of your reality. Conjure up your skills in arts and crafts; tour nature for stones, feathers, and shells; and begin putting together a magickal tool that you can use daily to help you through tough spots or sweeten already magical moments. Place it on your altar for charging overnight and use in the morning. Allow Nephthys and all she holds in relationship to the cycle of life to be your inspiration this day.

Chandra Alexandre

July 18
Thursday

Color of the day: Green
Incense of the day: Mulberry

Knowing That All Is Well

There's no way the fourteenth-century English mystic and anchorite Dame Julian of Norwich could be considered a Pagan, but we Pagans can take to heart something she wrote following her visions of Jesus: "All things shall be well. All manner of things shall be well."

What a wonderful promise this is! It's a basic truth of existence, and it also shows how the followers of different spiritual paths can come together and find common ground.

Let's augment Dame Julian's promise:

> All is well. All manner of
> things shall be well. All can
> only be well.

Believe it! These words are the screensaver of your head and heart. They're your favorite app.

Let these words be the first words you speak aloud when you awaken in the morning and the last words you speak before you go to sleep at night.

Barbara Ardinger, Ph.D.

July 19
Friday

Color of the day: Coral
Incense of the day: Thyme

Long Day Delight

The long days of sun are upon us. Take time to celebrate and observe these long days, before they shorten too much. Set your alarm for a few minutes earlier than sunrise. When you wake, go outside and watch the sun rise, and mindfully delight. Appreciate the quiet, privacy, and sanctity of early morning. Walk in your neighborhood, weed your garden, or sit and watch the sun's gradual climb into the sky. Say:

> Long days, short nights,
> summer sun, in you we delight,
>
> Strong rays, blessing bright,
> radiant, life-giving light.

Throughout the day, pause frequently and note the position of the sun and the quality of its light. In those moments, mindfully delight. At dusk, return to where you greeted the sun this morning and give thanks:

> You've lightened, and brightened,
> and rose overhead,
>
> Now glorious sun, it's time
> for bed.
>
> Sun, good night, in this long
> day, I do delight.

Dallas Jennifer Cobb

July 20
Saturday

Color of the day: Gray
Incense of the day: Sandalwood

Worry-Me-Not

Summer can be especially challenging for many people. There's so much to do, and our normal habits and schedules can be chaotic due to vacations and other expectations. Take a little time to create a smooth worry stone, into which you can put all your stress and jangly uncertainty.

During a walk outside, pick a stone that feels good in your hand. River stones are particularly good, but any smooth stone that fits your hand is fine. (You may also have a polished stone or crystal at home you'd like to use.) Roll the stone around in your hand, getting familiar with every curve and dip. When you're ready, roll it between your hands, directing energy into the stone, and repeat the following chant:

> Old rock, strong and sure.
>
> I create my worry's cure.
>
> Old rock, bring me calm.
>
> Be now my healing balm.

Carry the stone with you as needed.

Jenett Silver

July 21
Sunday

Color of the day: Amber
Incense of the day: Almond

Feed Our Children

Schools that run from September to June provide children with subsidized meals. Four months from now the community food banks will be collecting food for the November and December holidays. Right now, in the "center of summer," children may be going hungry. Drawing from a theme of generosity, organize a food drive with your family, coven, or neighborhood. Collect child-friendly, healthy beverages and snacks. Through a local charity you may choose to "adopt" a family or families for the summer. Or one day a week until September, deliver your goods to a local food bank. Bless your donations with this very simple spell:

> To those who lack,
>
> From those who have.

Emyme

July 22
Monday

Color of the day: Lavender
Incense of the day: Rosemary

Full Moon in Aquarius

Wishing Spell

For this spell you will need a bowl or cup of water, a small piece of paper, and a pen or pencil. Place the bowl so the moon's reflection is caught in the water. If it's cloudy or you can't see the moon, visualize it. Focus on a desire you have, and write that wish on the paper. Then drop the paper into the water. Chant. Visualize your wish being accepted by the universe. Because it is a heartfelt desire, you deserve it. Allow to sit overnight so the writing dissolves and the paper softens. Pour the water onto the ground and bury the paper. Say:

> Moonlight, charge this wishing spell,
>
> Keep this secret that I tell.
>
> Moonlight, my desire fulfill,
>
> I place this in your care until...
>
> I offer it unto the Earth—
>
> To guard my wish, protect its worth.

Ember Grant

July 23
Tuesday

Color of the day: Gray
Incense of the day: Ylang-ylang

Neptunalia

In ancient Rome, honoring Neptune on this, his sacred feast day, was believed to ensure rainfall and prevent drought from damaging crops. The Romans celebrated this wonderful watery god by having a picnic.

You can enjoy your own Neptunalia outside for lunch or dinner on this day. Brew an infusion made from spring water and three bay leaves. Bless it under the summer sun and sprinkle it over your garden. Say:

> Mighty Neptune, your triton held high,
>
> Protect my garden, in this season so dry.
>
> Keep your water flowing to every good root,
>
> And in your honor shall it render its fruit.

Enjoy a meal outside in honor of Neptune. If you decide to grill, make sure to drop a small portion into the fire as a sacrifice. Drink spring water or wine, if you choose. Before the sun goes down, give your garden a good soak from the hose.

Mickie Mueller

July 24
Wednesday

Color of the day: Brown
Incense of the day: Honeysuckle

Running horse Spell

Summer is a good time to start an exercise routine. The weather's nice (though, depending on how hot it is, you may want to wait until later in the evening or early in the morning when it's cooler). Plus there are more options for buying exercise gear as well as finding partners to help keep motivated.

You can ask the totem Horse for help with your new program, as horses are some of the most athletic animals. Start with your shoes. Using a permanent marker, draw a symbol of Horse on the soles of your exercise shoes. This can be as simple as a horseshoe, but you can be as elaborate as you like.

Then, before you exercise, ask Horse for strength and endurance in your workout, as well as health and safety. You may even visualize that you are putting on strong horse's hooves.

Lupa

July 25
Thursday

Color of the day: Purple
Incense of the day: Apricot

To See If Rain has Stopped

To see if the rain has stopped for good, look to the sky. If you see birds, it's a good sign that the rain has finished. However, to be sure, watch the birds in flight. Say aloud:

> Birds of the air,
>
> Fly without care.
>
> Will it rain here?
>
> Will it rain there?

If the birds fly off, stop chanting and look closely at the direction they fly. Say:

> To the east, 'twill be clear.
>
> To the south, storm you'll hear.
>
> To the west, never end.
>
> To the north, Sun descend.

**From Scott Cunningham's
Book of Shadows**

July 26
Friday

Color of the day: Pink
Incense of the day: Rose

Count Your Blessings Spell

In July the Goddess blesses us with abundance. Gardens begin to yield fruits and vegetables; flower gardens are a tapestry of color. When you affirm that you're grateful for what you've been blessed with, you open yourself up to receive even more.

This spell will send out good karma and increase your chances to receive abundance. Decorate your altar or a table with the seasons' bounty—vegetables or bouquets of flowers are nice. Begin by facing east. Raise your arms in gratitude and say:

Thank you for all that I have.

Turn north and silently forgive anyone who has hurt you. Then turn south and say:

Thank you for sending me everything I need.

Close the ritual by inhaling and exhaling deeply. Be prepared to receive unexpected good fortune from the cosmos.

James Kambos

July 27
Saturday

Color of the day: Indigo
Incense of the day: Pine

Green Corn Ceremony

This Native American ceremony, held during the time of the Big Ripening Moon in late July/August, is a time of forgiveness and renewal, to awaken a sense of the sacredness of life. The Green Corn Dance or Ceremony was observed by many indigenous peoples, most notably the Cherokee or Tsalagi, and including the Creek, Seminole, and Chicksaw tribes. Traditionally all wrongdoing was forgiven at this time, and sacred objects, such as medicine bundles, were renewed and displayed.

The more festive part of the ceremony included singing and dancing, and was known as a *puskita*, although this eventually changed to *busk* in English. The busk was meant to show gratitude for the ripening corn and for the first harvest, and celebrated the community as they ate the first of the crop together. The late July moon is the perfect time to give thanks for the first harvest as we approach the Pagan festival of Lammas.

Peg Aloi

July 28
Sunday

Color of the day: Orange
Incense of the day: Frankincense

A Personal Shield

Design a personal shield to be used in magickal practice or as an altar adornment. Begin by choosing a shape: circle, triangle, shield-shaped, and so on. Working with a paper pattern, divide your shield into a number of sections, each of which will feature a key component. You might include sections devoted to family, a specific magickal practice, one or more elements, astrological information, your magickal name or training, or whatever else seems appropriate to your shield. For protection, include symbols, runes, or other instruments of shielding or defense.

Transfer your pattern to fabric using fabric paint markers, appliqué, fabric glue, ribbons, buttons, trim, or other media to create the design. Or transfer the pattern to wood, leather, metal, or some other durable material, and decorate appropriately. Magickally empowered, your shield will protect you, enliven your magicks, and maybe even beautify your sanctum sanctorum.

Susan Pesznecker

July 29
Monday

Color of the day: White
Incense of the day: Narcissus

Freedom Spell

We all carry things that do not serve us and only poison our spirits. Today it's time to cleanse the toxins from mind and body.

On a small table, drape a small black cloth. In the center, place visual representations of your slavery to those guilts holding you captive. Place them side by side, overlapping if necessary. As you do, repeat the following:

I gave you my power.

When you are done placing items, observe them for a moment, breathing deeply and focusing on the emotions these items represent. Then take salt and make a circle around the items, saying:

You have no power over me any longer.

When done, observe the items again. Absorb the truth of your freedom. Breathe deeply, exhaling all the toxins from your system. Now gather the cloth at the corners and tie off the bundle with a red string, and throw it in the trash.

Patti Larsen

July 30
Tuesday

Color of the day: Black
Incense of the day: Geranium

Exploring the Mother

When we give birth to an idea, or acquire a child, or care for someone who needs our help, we find ourselves calling upon the Mother within.

The Mother is not just a caregiver of children. She is the teacher of life experiences; she is the provider. Her inner warrior will fight for everything that her child (or charge or project or dream) needs. Each of her creations will be nurtured till it is mature, then it will be allowed to go on its own.

We return to the Mother when we need healing, loving, or nurturing. She will kiss the boo-boos and hold us till we stop shaking.

We need the Mother as much as we find we need to be mothers. We live to care, and we care to be loved. Embrace the Mother within and find out what caring is all about.

Boudica

July 31
Wednesday

Color of the day: Yellow
Incense of the day: Lilac

Bathe Away Your Worries

Today's a great time to quiet our minds and banish excess worrisome and/or obsessive thought patterns so we can experience deeper clarity and peace. With that in mind, light a stick of frankincense incense and soak in a warm bath into which you have dissolved one cup sea salt and 20 drops white chestnut essence (one of the Bach flower remedies). Keep plenty of drinking water on hand into which you have placed 2 to 4 drops of white chestnut essence.

As you soak, allow your thoughts and worries to do what they will, but periodically remember to consciously relax your body and feel the frenetic energy of your thoughts dissolving and being neutralized by the water. Allow yourself to release the hold these thought patterns have over you. Whenever you notice them arising, simply say, "Thank you for sharing," and let them go. Repeat again and again if necessary.

Tess Whitehurst

July Moon Table

Date	Sign	Element	Nature	Phase
1 Mon 5:43 pm	Taurus	Earth	Semi-fruitful	4th
2 Tue	Taurus	Earth	Semi-fruitful	4th
3 Wed	Taurus	Earth	Semi-fruitful	4th
4 Thu 5:21 am	Gemini	Air	Barren	4th
5 Fri	Gemini	Air	Barren	4th
6 Sat 6:14 pm	Cancer	Water	Fruitful	4th
7 Sun	Cancer	Water	Fruitful	4th
8 Mon	Cancer	Water	Fruitful	New 3:14 am
9 Tue 6:48 am	Leo	Fire	Barren	1st
10 Wed	Leo	Fire	Barren	1st
11 Thu 6:12 pm	Virgo	Earth	Barren	1st
12 Fri	Virgo	Earth	Barren	1st
13 Sat	Virgo	Earth	Barren	1st
14 Sun 3:41 am	Libra	Air	Semi-fruitful	1st
15 Mon	Libra	Air	Semi-fruitful	2nd 11:18 pm
16 Tue 10:24 am	Scorpio	Water	Fruitful	2nd
17 Wed	Scorpio	Water	Fruitful	2nd
18 Thu 1:54 pm	Sagittarius	Fire	Barren	2nd
19 Fri	Sagittarius	Fire	Barren	2nd
20 Sat 2:39 pm	Capricorn	Earth	Semi-fruitful	2nd
21 Sun	Capricorn	Earth	Semi-fruitful	2nd
22 Mon 2:07 pm	Aquarius	Air	Barren	Full 2:16 pm
23 Tue	Aquarius	Air	Barren	3rd
24 Wed 2:22 pm	Pisces	Water	Fruitful	3rd
25 Thu	Pisces	Water	Fruitful	3rd
26 Fri 5:29 pm	Aries	Fire	Barren	3rd
27 Sat	Aries	Fire	Barren	3rd
28 Sun	Aries	Fire	Barren	3rd
29 Mon 12:43 am	Taurus	Earth	Semi-fruitful	4th 1:43 pm
30 Tue	Taurus	Earth	Semi-fruitful	4th
31 Wed 11:42 am	Gemini	Air	Barren	4th

Times are in Eastern Time.

August

Named for Roman Emperor Augustus Caesar, August means "regal, dignified, or grand." It calls to mind the celebrations of late summer and golden fields of tall, nodding stalks of grain. It also begins the bounty of autumn. To draw the power of August into your spellcasting, use its correspondences. Its herbs include angelica, bay, chamomile, fennel, marigold, St. John's wort, and sunflower. Add grains such as barley, corn, rye, or wheat. For stones, use carnelian or jasper. Burn heliotrope or frankincense. General colors are yellow, gold, and deep green. Most deities associated with August have a certain dignity. Diana, goddess of woods and hunting, has a temple holiday on August 13. Thoth, god of writing and the moon, oversees several feasts. Then there is Lugh, a trickster and Jack-of-all-trades. Lugh celebrates this month with games and competitions. With those associations, what kind of spellcraft can you work in August? Try rituals about gathering, harvesting, or preserving. Spells for health and vitality get a boost from the strong solar energy. On a more personal note, turn to appreciation and friendship, the natural counterpoint to the love and fertility focus of spring and summer.

Elizabeth Barrette

August 1

Thursday

Color of the day: Purple
Incense of the day: Nutmeg

Lammas

First Garden harvest

Lammas: the first of the three harvest sabbats. Offer blessings to Lugh and collect petals from the flowers in your yard and garden for drying. No doubt you have planted flowers that have special meaning for you; for example, marigolds and sunflowers for the sun and roses for love. Consult almanacs to see what gatherings are best done at night.

After complete drying, place the petals in airtight, clearly marked and dated glass containers. A local craft shop can help if you are unsure of the drying process. Store the petals in a cool, dry place. Throughout the year you will find these ingredients have great power, being from your own soil and prepared by your own hand.

Emyme

August 2

Friday

Color of the day: White
Incense of the day: Violet

Undoing habits

Choose a habit you'd like to give up. Take a piece of string (embroidery floss, yarn, whatever you can both tie and untie easily) in a color that fits with your habit (black or white are great neutrals). Tie four knots, as below, focusing on each intention as you tie that knot.

Knot 1: Mental aspects of this habit (why it appeals to you, reasons you've kept it).

Knot 2: Actions related to this habit (things you do).

Knot 3: How you feel about this habit, your emotions and concerns about giving it up.

Knot 4: The practical aspects of this habit.

Starting tomorrow, untie one knot each day, releasing the last one on the new moon on August 6. As you untie each knot, release those thoughts, actions, emotions, and practical aspects from you. Destroy the cord when done. To strengthen, add a chant when you create the charm.

Jenett Silver

August 3

Saturday

Color of the day: Black
Incense of the day: Sage

harvesting Blessings and Prosperity

This simple daily practice will bring blessings and prosperity into your life and send blessings and prosperity into the world.

Whenever you see a penny (or other coin) on the sidewalk, pick it up. Most people are careless with pennies and think they have no value. But we know that tiny things can add up to big things. We also know that copper is sacred to Aphrodite, the Great Creatrix. We're not careless with tiny things.

Pick up the penny with your receptive hand (your left hand, if you're right-handed) and say aloud:

> For those in need.

Tuck the penny into your pocket. Carry it around for a few days, then lay it on one of your home altars.

I lay coins on my Dame Fortuna altar. I have piled up so many pennies, I had to buy a little bank. It's filled with blessings for and of prosperity.

Barbara Ardinger, Ph.D.

August 4

Sunday

Color of the day: Gold
Incense of the day: Eucalyptus

Spell to Remove Barriers

Sometimes we hit roadblocks that seem to get in the way of our goals. This can happen at work or in our personal lives. Use this spell to remove obstacles that are preventing you from moving forward.

Burn a yellow or gold candle, chant, and focus on a clear road toward your destination. If you sense anything blocking your way, visualize the object dissolving harmlessly. Say:

> Clear the path,
>
> Pave the way.
>
> Nothing keeps
>
> Success at bay.

Ember Grant

August 5

Monday

Color of the day: Silver
Incense of the day: Hyssop

Aura Cleansing

Take some time away from the summer heat to get rid of some of the astral junk from your aura. Fill a tub with warm water and dissolve a handful of sea salt. Add a few drops of lavender oil or some lavender buds, plus a large, tumbled quartz crystal. Place your hands over the tub and charge the water with the following chant nine times:

> *Water, salt, and flowers dear,*
>
> *Cleanse my aura, make it clear.*

Close your eyes and visualize the water glowing. Play some relaxing music and give yourself some time to connect with your inner self while you soak in the tub. Make sure you immerse your whole body in the water during the bath. Once you're finished, and you're thoroughly pruned and relaxed, drain the tub and proclaim:

> *Astral junk and negativity bane,*
>
> *I banish you right down the drain.*

Mickie Mueller

August 6

Tuesday

Color of the day: Red
Incense of the day: Cedar

New Moon in Leo

Harvest Blessings

Many Pagans observe the four major cross-quarter festivals over an extended period of time, to correspond with the astrological activity taking place. This new moon is perfectly positioned for the observation of Lammas, the festival of harvest. Even if you celebrated with a ritual at the weekend, use the powerful moon energy to your advantage and perform a ritual for a new endeavor.

Lammas is the very beginning of the harvest season, and a time to consider what we will harvest in the days and weeks to come. Do you want a new job, a new lover, a new home, a new approach to a problem? The new moon is the perfect moment to perform workings for bringing new opportunities into our lives. The night sky devoid of moonlight is a blank slate: what will you write on it?

Peg Aloi

August 7

Wednesday

Color of the day: White
Incense of the day: Honeysuckle

Ramadan ends

Swimming with Sea Serpents

Of all the cryptozoological beasties, one of the best known is Nessie, the Loch Ness Monster. Whether you believe water monsters, anomalous hairy hominids, and other cryptids exist, there's no denying the compelling power of the mythos surrounding them. Try creating your own cryptid, just for fun. Here are some things to consider:

- What does it look like? Is it a variation on a known animal or something entirely unique?

- Where is it found? What environment does it live in?

- Who has seen it, and under what circumstances?

- Is it dangerous? Does it have any strange powers or abilities?

- What else makes it stand out?

Then try creating stories, mock news articles, artwork, and other supporting "evidence." If you really want to get things going, invite your friends to participate in the process and see how far you can get the mythos to spread!

Lupa

August 8

Thursday

Color of the day: Turquoise
Incense of the day: Carnation

Beat the heat Enchantment

In Japanese culture today is the second day of Doyo, or "the dog days." Many of us in the Northern Hemisphere are feeling the effects of some of the hottest days of the summer season. This makes for a perfect time to commune with the cooling and revitalizing element of water while also helping you to remember to maintain a healthy level of hydration! Pour yourself a tall glass of ice water and then charge the water by holding the glass between your hands and speaking the following enchantment into the top of the glass:

Water flowing, water blue,
Water to cool, water to renew.

Water so nurturing,
Water so sustaining.

From head to toe, your powers
shall flow,
Your revitalizing benefits
I shall sow!

So mote it be!

Blake Octavian Blair

August 9

Friday

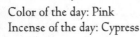

Color of the day: Pink
Incense of the day: Cypress

Inspired Texting

In 1892 Thomas Edison received a patent for the two-way telegraph. One hundred and twenty years later, the telegraph has been replaced by the smart phone, and the dots and dashes of Morse code have been supplanted by texting and leetspeak.

Today's phone texting, because of its brevity, is often devoid of much emotion, let alone magick. You can add magickal oomph to your e-communications by creating an electronic sigil to add to your messages. You needn't explain the symbol to others; just knowing it's there will let you know you're giving your messages of love and friendship a magickal boost as they fly across the ether. Use keystrokes to create a sigil, or perhaps just add something as ultra simple as ending every message with three dots or a lunar parenthesis. It will make you feel happy and magickal every time you push <send>.

Susan Pesznecker

August 10

Saturday

Color of the day: Indigo
Incense of the day: Rue

Opalia Spell

The Romans celebrated this day as a holiday of the growing of seeds. With this spell you will take that celebration one step further by using nature's power to grow an idea with the seed.

Take a small clay pot and fill with organic potting soil. Plant mint seeds in the pot. Mint represents abundance of money, love, and protection, all ideal properties to feed your plans. As you plant the seeds, whisper over them three times:

As with the seed, so with the idea.

Take good care of your mint as it grows, whispering the same mantra over the seeds every morning. As the plant emerges, so will your idea. As the mint grows, your idea will also.

Patti Larsen

August 11

Sunday

Color of the day: Yellow
Incense of the day: Hyacinth

Take Control

Stress seems to be a constant companion with the demands of job, family, and friends. Sometimes we can get too stressed out, and we need to stop and take care of ourselves.

Each day we should make time for ourselves. Some quiet time should be an essential part of our daily routine, as it does help us keep in good health. Many find relief in a bath with essential oils that promote relaxation, like lavender and rose, and soft candlelight. Others will close the door to their bedroom and relax with some soft music or a good book. You may like a walk to enjoy a touch of nature.

No matter what you do, each day should include at least some quiet time for yourself. I recommend at least half an hour a day. Make it part of your routine.

Boudica

August 12

Monday

Color of the day: White
Incense of the day: Neroli

Wish upon a Star

About now, the Perseids meteor shower will peak, and tonight the sky will be filled with more shooting stars. Once again it's time to "wish upon a star." For centuries the Perseids have inspired magic and legends for numerous civilizations. There is one thing, however, that most of these magical traditions have in common: a shooting star is a sign of change. So this is a good time to work magic for any change you wish for in your life.

Tonight as you gaze at this cosmic show, hold one wish firmly in your mind. Keep this thought in mind as you sit in your ritual space. Drape your altar with a piece of deep blue fabric, and light one white candle. Extinguish the candle and watch the smoke as it spirals upward. The candle represents the stars, and the smoke symbolizes your wish being carried to the Divine.

James Kambos

August 13

Tuesday

Color of the day: Gray
Incense of the day: Ginger

Get Your Mojo Back

The sexy waxing Scorpio moon, when it falls on a passionate Tuesday, is an excellent time to work magic aimed at getting your mojo back, or enhancing your charisma and seductive allure. Place a garnet in a small red cloth bag along with some dried damiana. Tie the bag closed and anoint with your own cologne or perfume. Hold it in both hands, relax, close your eyes, and imagine that you are growing roots that are going deep into the earth. Visualize/imagine/feel these roots passing through layers of rock and water until they finally enter the earth's fiery core. Draw this molten energy up your roots and into your body. Connect with your mojo. Feel your potent sexual energy pulsating powerfully throughout your body and aura. Say:

Magnetic, charismatic, powerful and true,

My sexual power now shines through.

Keep the charm close for the rest of the moon cycle.

Tess Whitehurst

August 14

Wednesday

Color of the day: Topaz
Incense of the day: Lavender

Thirteen Goals of a Witch

Know yourself.

Know your Craft.

Learn.

Apply knowledge and wisdom.

Achieve balance.

Keep your words in good order.

Keep your thoughts in good order.

Celebrate life.

Attune to the cycles of the earth.

Breathe and eat correctly.

Exercise the body.

Meditate.

Honor the Goddess and God.

From Scott Cunningham's "Wicca: A Guide for the Solitary Practitioner"

August 15

Thursday

Color of the day: Green
Incense of the day: Clove

holy Day of Obligation

Consider your obligations today and find a way to make peace with them. We all have commitments on the spiritual path that guide and sustain us, but how often do we lament having yet another thing to do, no matter how important?

Today find inspiration in the mother goddesses who hold the intensity of life with grace, skill, and purposefulness. Invoke your favorite goddess or be open in the moment. Ask that she be a facilitator of your soul's longing in this world, specifically around all you have on your plate. Make an offering of three coins and ask that in return something to which you have committed is made less burdensome. Keep the coins on your altar for three days, and the spell will be done.

Chandra Alexandre

August 16

Friday

Color of the day: Purple
Incense of the day: Orchid

Beauty Spell

Charge a favorite piece of jewelry today to enhance your attractiveness. As you chant, hold the item in your projective hand and visualize it as a token of your best and most lovely qualities. Focus on building your self-confidence, allowing your inner beauty to radiate outward, enchanting everyone around you. Never question your beauty—know it. Live it. Keep in mind that the item is a tool, a reminder of the real, true beauty you possess as a human being. Say:

> Beauty that shines, glow from within,
>
> Beauty be mine, deeper than skin.
>
> Beauty divine, free me from doubt,
>
> Beauty be mine, within and without.

Ember Grant

August 17

Saturday

Color of the day: Brown
Incense of the day: Ivy

Sea Glass Spell

Sea glass is any piece of soda bottle or other broken glass that has been weathered by the actions of sand and water. For instance, shards of green bottles will become translucent, and the edges will be rounded and dull to the touch.

Sea glass can be found by beachcombing in areas that have concentrations of it. To locate a "sea glass beach" in your area, do an Internet search. Some beaches are famous for their sea glass, while others have none at all.

Since sea glass began as something sharp that is now smooth, it is a wonderful object for working away anger. Rub the edges of the sea glass and say:

Take my anger, sea and sand.
Make me like this glass.

Important: Craft stores sell "sea glass." This is manufactured—not the real thing. The spell works best when you claim your own piece of sea glass from a beach.

Anne Johnson

August 18

Sunday

Color of the day: Orange
Incense of the day: Marigold

Step Back Meditation

Sometimes a situation just gets overwhelming. One of the best ways to regain control is to take a step back and get a little distance as best you can.

When you first recognize that things are running away with you, simply acknowledge this fact. You can even say something like this, out loud if possible:

I'm feeling really overwhelmed
right now.

Next do your best to focus on your breathing and nothing else. Pay attention to the way the air feels going through your nose, throat, and lungs.

Once you feel a bit calmer, bring your attention back to the situation at hand. Then deliberately take a step back, physically. Imagine you are taking a step back from the situation, not leaving it behind entirely but just getting breathing room. Then look at the situation as objectively as you can, and go from there.

Lupa

August 19

Monday

Color of the day: Lavender
Incense of the day: Lily

Gratitude Feast

The Roman festival Vinalia Rustica was held today historically, and featured a ritual dedicated to the protection of vine crops and an abundant harvest.

Organize a Vinalia Rustica Feast. Invite neighbors, friends, and family. Make it a potluck, and request dishes featuring seasonal fruits and vegetables, locally produced where possible. Get several bottles of local wine. Set a table outdoors—on the deck, in the backyard, or on a balcony—under Jupiter's sky. Decorate with green and purple, the colors of grapes and garden flowers. Add four purple candles.

When guests arrive, gather around the table, light the candles, and call in the directions. Invoke Jupiter, god of the sky, and Venus, goddess of the garden and wine, asking for weather blessings and garden protection. Toast the wealth of the season gathered at the table, and drink in the abundant harvest of good food, friends, and community.

Dallas Jennifer Cobb

August 20

Tuesday

Color of the day: Black
Incense of the day: Cinnamon

Full Moon in Aquarius

Building an Altar to Dame Fortuna

Fortuna is a Latin goddess who carries a cornucopia of blessings and steers our lives with her rudder. It's good to have her for a friend.

Find a base for your altar. (I use a large orange platter.) Set a figure of Dame Fortuna in the center and give her jewelry to wear. Set a green candle in front of her. Here's the good part: surround Fortuna with every kind of symbol of good fortune you can find. Wishbones painted with glitter. Chocolate coins. Red origami cranes. Red and blue corn. Magical tokens, crystals, shells, beautiful beads. Charms you make yourself in bright colors. A magnet. Major arcana card X (the Wheel of Fortune). On this altar, clutter is good.

Light the candle, and maybe some good incense, and invoke the goddess:

Great Fortuna, you hold the course of my life in your hands.

Everyone has a place on your wheel. We go up, we go down, we go up again.

Dame Fortuna, bless me and watch over me as I journey through my life. Keep me safe in my place on your wheel, and when I'm down, help me remember that the wheel always turns and better fortune is always ahead.

Dame Fortuna, with your rudder and your cornucopia, inspire and lead me to success in all my endeavors.

Barbara Ardinger, Ph.D.

NOTES:

August 21

Wednesday

Color of the day: Yellow
Incense of the day: Marjoram

Music Makes It Better

There are many ills that follow us around and even some that have been with us for a lifetime. But nothing cures the mind, body, and spirit like penetrating song—rhythm and sound that take us to the depths of our emotional life.

Sing to yourself today, creating lyrics and a tune or using something tried and true to suit your mood and desire to offload some of the baggage you have been carrying. Let your song bring strength, courage, and resolve. Let it bring passion and inspiration. Let nothing stand in the way of fun and soulfulness as you sing. Explore a range of sounds and expressions; let yourself be increasingly uninhibited as you see what your voice can do. Allow the music to fill you—to be you and you it—until you naturally end the song. Channel the energy raised into personal healing, and return to your day uplifted and happy.

Chandra Alexandre

August 22

Thursday

Color of the day: Crimson
Incense of the day: Myrrh

Time for You Spell

When the sun is in Virgo, we are rushed and so wrapped up in doing that we don't take the time needed to enjoy what we have created. This is especially true of Virgos themselves. This spell will help you quiet your mind as well as take back the understanding that it is just as fine to admire your life as it is to advance it.

Place a small hourglass in front of you. When ready, turn the glass over and say out loud as fast as you can all the things on your to-do list. You only have until the glass runs out. When it does, stop. Now flip it over and say all the things you are grateful for. Repeat the process. Feel the difference. The things you rush about to do don't seem so important, do they? Finish with gratitude once again.

Patti Larsen

August 23

Friday

Color of the day: Rose
Incense of the day: Mint

An August Love Charm

Many plants that mature in August make superb ingredients for love charms, and since this is a Venus day, it's a good day to do a little love magic.

Here's what you'll need: A piece of pink fabric the size of a handkerchief, a leaf of Joe-Pye weed, a few leaves of valerian, and a teaspoon of cornmeal. As you think of your magical intent, crumble the ingredients in the center of the fabric. Tie up the corners of the cloth with pretty pink or white ribbon. Tie another piece of ribbon about three feet long around your bundle. Lay the charm on a table across from you. Without thinking of anyone specific, pull the bundle toward you. Visualize that you're drawing the perfect love into your life. Hide your charm and see what happens.

James Kambos

August 24

Saturday

Color of the day: Gray
Incense of the day: Magnolia

Blocking a Spell

Whether real or perceived, sometimes we think that someone may be sending us something we really do not want. Here are some suggestions to help block that unwanted energy:

Hang small pieces of mirror facing out in your windows. These reflect back whatever negativity may be coming your way.

Place smoky quartz pieces at all entrances to your home, doors, and windowsills to keep out unwanted presences. Black river stones work just as well.

Hang small wind chimes on your front and back porches to keep away annoying manifestations. The tinkling noise is said to annoy them more than they could annoy you.

Finally, do a self-check. Now that you are secure, what was it that made you think someone or something wants to send you something you don't want? Work on making right the wrong, or banish them from your life for good.

Boudica

August 25

Sunday

Color of the day: Amber
Incense of the day: Heliotrope

Spell for Right Livelihood

Too often we see our jobs as just a means to make money, but our work should also be satisfying. If you are seeking work that fulfills you on a deeper level, try this spell.

First take a dollar bill and tear it into four pieces. These pieces represent abundance and possibility. Place the four pieces in the four directions of your home: east, south, west, and north. Visualize opportunities coming from all directions. Write down five different jobs you'd love to have. These can be as outrageous as you wish and in no particular order. Place the list on your altar, then light a green candle to place beside them. As the flame burns, say:

All things are mine,

All things are thine,

All is one,

All is possible.

Repeat this ritual once a week as you embark on your job search, and explore the many options that await you.

Peg Aloi

August 26

Monday

Color of the day: Gray
Incense of the day: Clary sage

Create a Finger Labyrinth

Walking a labyrinth is known to provide space for inner examination, metaphorical journey, and even healing. Most of us don't have access to a full-scale labyrinth, but you can still benefit through finger-walking a portable version. Visit the website of The Labyrinth Society (http://labyrinthsociety.org/). Exploring the site will yield a number of printable labyrinths; print one, set it on a flat surface, and you're ready to begin. Breathe slowly, ground and center, and begin, moving your finger from the entrance and working toward the center. As you proceed, allow yourself to slip into a quiet, peaceful state in which you ponder your questions and await an answer. If you're looking for healing, focus on that as you "walk." Pause in the center, then make the journey back out. The site also features the option of finger-walking a cyber labyrinth on-screen. Enjoy!

Susan Pesznecker

August 27

Tuesday

Color of the day: White
Incense of the day: Basil

Tending Ourselves

The coming of the harvest season can bring a lot of challenges. It's easy to overwork and find ourselves exhausted, cranky, and struggling to keep up. So today, take a few minutes to take care of yourself.

Fill a bowl with water (you can add a drop of orange or lavender essential oil) and dip your hands in. Wash away your assumptions about what you "should" do or "must" do. Let your mind clear. Cup water in your hands and say:

Guide my hands.

Touch your forehead and say:

Bless my choices.

Finally place your hand over your heart and finish with these words:

My heart guides the work of my day.

As you move through your day, listen to your heart. See if you can hand off tasks to someone else, or do them in a way that requires less effort or that brings more joy.

Jenett Silver

August 28

Wednesday

Color of the day: Brown
Incense of the day: Bay laurel

Air Element Home Clearing

It's a perfect day to cleanse your home with the element of air. Assemble a naturally shed feather tied with string into a makeshift necklace, a handheld fan (made from paper is fine), a bell or chime(s), and a bundle of dried sage. Stand comfortably and breathe deeply. Call upon and consciously embody the energy of wind. Place the feather around your neck to symbolize your alignment with the air element as you say:

I am the fresh and cleansing wind.

Safely light the sage bundle, and as it smokes, hold the bundle and a small bowl in one hand while holding the fan in the other hand. Fan the smoke to distribute it around the room as you move in a counterclockwise direction through each room and area and repeat:

I powerfully cleanse this space and leave sparkling energy in my wake.

Finish by ringing the chime in each area.

Tess Whitehurst

August 29

Thursday

Color of the day: Purple
Incense of the day: Balsam

Get Out of Your Own Way

Do you have a goal that you just can't seem to reach no matter how hard you try? Could you be standing in your own way to success? This may be the time for some self-examination.

With a black pen, make a list of any fears you can think of relating to your goal. Think hard about it. Are you afraid that your success might bring more responsibility, challenges, or paperwork? Once your list is complete, write a positive response to every fear right over the top in red ink. Bury the list at a crossroads. As you walk away, toss a penny from your birth year over your left shoulder and say:

I banish fear, my truth is near.

Whenever you think of your fears regarding your goal, chase the thought away, replacing it with a positive. Go out there and make your dreams come true.

Mickie Mueller

August 30

Friday

Color of the day: Coral
Incense of the day: Thyme

Friday Attraction Spell

Friday is a great time for an attraction spell. Invoke Freya, the Teutonic goddess of love, beauty, and prolific creation. (You may want to be careful about the prolific creation bit, and take proper precautions.) Gather a candle (white for purity, red for passion, or pink for something in between), matches, and lavender essential oil. Anoint the candle with oil, and place it in a safe candle holder on your altar. Close your eyes, envisioning what or whom you want to attract. Imagine it in intense detail. Say:

I enlighten what I desire,
It warms to me with this fire.

Light the candle.

Lavender bring me peace of mind,
And makes what I desire mine.

Inhale deeply.

I do not struggle, fret or hurry,
It comes in Goddess' time, no worry.

Extinguish the candle. Keep it on the altar, and repeat this mini-spell regularly to draw your desires to you.

Dallas Jennifer Cobb

August 31

Saturday

Color of the day: Blue
Incense of the day: Patchouli

Ancient Prayer to herbs

U se this prayer while preparing herbal mixtures for healing purposes.

Now also I make intercession
to you, all ye powers and herbs,
and to your majesty: I beseech
you, whom Earth the universal
parent hath borne and given
as a medicine of health to all
peoples and hath put majesty
upon, be ye now of the most
benefit of humankind. This
I pray and beseech you: be
present here with your virtue,
for she who created you hath
herself undertaken that I may
call you with the good will of
him on whom the art of medi-
cine was bestowed; therefore
grant for health's sake good
medicine, by grace of these
powers aforesaid.

From Scott Cunninghman's
Book of Shadows

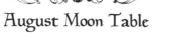

August Moon Table

Date	Sign	Element	Nature	Phase
1 Thu	Gemini	Air	Barren	4th
2 Fri	Gemini	Air	Barren	4th
3 Sat 12:29 am	Cancer	Water	Fruitful	4th
4 Sun	Cancer	Water	Fruitful	4th
5 Mon 12:58 pm	Leo	Fire	Barren	4th
6 Tue	Leo	Fire	Barren	New 5:51 pm
7 Wed 11:57 pm	Virgo	Earth	Barren	1st
8 Thu	Virgo	Earth	Barren	1st
9 Fri	Virgo	Earth	Barren	1st
10 Sat 9:08 am	Libra	Air	Semi-fruitful	1st
11 Sun	Libra	Air	Semi-fruitful	1st
12 Mon 4:18 pm	Scorpio	Water	Fruitful	1st
13 Tue	Scorpio	Water	Fruitful	1st
14 Wed 9:04 pm	Sagittarius	Fire	Barren	2nd 6:56 am
15 Thu	Sagittarius	Fire	Barren	2nd
16 Fri 11:25 pm	Capricorn	Earth	Semi-fruitful	2nd
17 Sat	Capricorn	Earth	Semi-fruitful	2nd
18 Sun	Capricorn	Earth	Semi-fruitful	2nd
19 Mon 12:07 am	Aquarius	Air	Barren	2nd
20 Tue	Aquarius	Air	Barren	Full 9:45 pm
21 Wed 12:43 am	Pisces	Water	Fruitful	3rd
22 Thu	Pisces	Water	Fruitful	3rd
23 Fri 3:13 am	Aries	Fire	Barren	3rd
24 Sat	Aries	Fire	Barren	3rd
25 Sun 9:13 am	Taurus	Earth	Semi-fruitful	3rd
26 Mon	Taurus	Earth	Semi-fruitful	3rd
27 Tue 7:08 pm	Gemini	Air	Barren	3rd
28 Wed	Gemini	Air	Barren	4th 5:35 am
29 Thu	Gemini	Air	Barren	4th
30 Fri 7:33 am	Cancer	Water	Fruitful	4th
31 Sat	Cancer	Water	Fruitful	4th

Times are in Eastern Time.

September

September takes its name from the Latin prefix *sept*, meaning "seven," because until 153 BCE it was the seventh month of the then ten-month calendar. Even when the calendar changed, September kept its proud name. September is also known as Muin or Vine, the Celtic tree month that goes from September 2 to 29. The magical associations of Vine month include fertility, prosperity, and binding. Just as vines can creep into everything and bind onto outside structures, September is a month in which we creep into new environments and bind onto structures. Kids of all ages pack up and go back to school this month, back to structure and learning, tests and scores. Parents shift gears, too, imposing more structure on their kids, with earlier bedtimes and functional routines, plus falling into routines of their own: packing lunches, reviewing homework, and reading together. Like a vine in September, we hold on to new structures, climb toward new goals, and enjoy the fertile fruits of our labors. Take time to celebrate your accomplishments. Identify what you have achieved over the summer and vow to hold tightly to the structures that can support wild creativity. September is a time for all this.

Dallas Jennifer Cobb

September 1

Sunday

Color of the day: Yellow
Incense of the day: Juniper

Greek New Year

This is the day when the Greeks celebrate their new year, symbolized by the start of the sowing season. Seeds are blessed and wreaths are made of seasonal plants, fruits, and nuts, while the old wreaths from the previous year are thrown into the sea. The new wreaths are dipped in seawater, and, in addition, water and stones are collected for protection; tradition says one should gather forty pebbles and water from forty waves.

While this may be harvest time in many areas, it's also a time to plan ahead for next year. Celebrate this cycle by making your own seasonal wreath, blessing seeds or bulbs to be planted now for spring bloom, or by gathering stones and water for protection. Use this chant:

Hope and promise future holds,

Seed to fruit, young to old.

Then we plant the seed again,

Circles, cycles, never end.

Ember Grant

September 2

Monday

Color of the day: Silver
Incense of the day: Rosemary

Labor Day

Peace at Work Spell

Since this is Labor Day, it's a good time to give thanks for not only our job but also our coworkers. In many instances we spend more time with our coworkers than our families. And in many ways our coworkers become family.

I developed this spell to help you maintain a peaceful relationship with the people you work with. You'll need a light blue candle, nine chopped pecans, a pinch of feverfew foliage, and a few green pine needles. Light the candle and scatter the pecans, feverfew, and pine needles around the candle. Think of what you enjoy about your coworkers. Release any work-related stress by letting the tension flow from your body, through your feet, and into the earth. Extinguish the candle. Scatter the spell ingredients outdoors in an area you find peaceful.

James Kambos

September 3

Tuesday

Color of the day: Scarlet
Incense of the day: Ginger

The Fool Spell

The Fool is the first of the tarot major arcana. Everything about this card is childlike and innocent, trusting the moment and leaping on instinct. Today is a wonderful opportunity to not only reconnect with your inner child but to reveal the next step in your path with clarity.

To be like a child, one must act childlike. Assemble the following: multi-colored construction paper, scissors, colored pencils and pens, glue, glitter, feathers, and anything else that appeals to you. Now create something magical with your supplies. Play. Explore your tools. Release judgment and just have fun. Don't have a plan—children rarely do. Look at what you have and trust in the process. When you are finished with your beautiful creation, be grateful for it and, as you would with a child's artwork, put it on your refrigerator for all to admire.

Patti Larsen

September 4

Wednesday

Color of the day: Topaz
Incense of the day: Marjoram

Invoking the Blessed Bees

You know how Witches are always saying "Blessed be"? Without knowing it, they're invoking our Found Power Animal, a magical insect that I wrote about in my book *Finding New Goddesses*. The Bees are shining golden insects that live in the Golden Hive and are attended by Melissa, their devoted beekeeper-priestess.

The Bees bring us sweet blessings with their honey, pollen, propolis, and beeswax, and sometimes they use their magic venom as "sting therapy" to teach us a lesson. Both the Blessed Bees and their relations in the mundane world have traditionally been seen as harmonious workers and bearers of peace and fertility. Their relatives include Spelling Bees and Quilting Bees, who bring us the blessings of literacy and homey comfort. Here's the invocation to the Blessed Bees:

Twinkle, twinkle, Blessed Bees,

As I ask you, grant it please.

Wisdom, health, abundancies—

As I will't, so mote it, Bees.

Barbara Ardinger, Ph.D.

September 5

Thursday

Color of the day: Crimson
Incense of the day: Jasmine

New Moon in Virgo –
Rosh hashanah

Jupiter Protection Spell

This new moon on Thursday aligns with the Roman god Jupiter, and today also happens to be one of his festivals, Jupiter Stator. This festival commemorates Jupiter's assistance to and protection of Romulus and the Roman army during a great battle when the odds were against them.

Call upon Jupiter during this new moon to bump up the protection around you and your home and family. Do a search online for the Third Pentacle of Jupiter, a seal that protects against physical and metaphysical threats. Alternately use the astrological symbol for Jupiter. Either print the seal on your computer printer or draw it accurately by hand, if you have the skill. Use a glue stick to affix the seal on a royal blue seven-day jar candle. Visualize a shield around your entire house, and call upon Jupiter for protection:

Jupiter, with your power and might,

I call upon you this new noon night,

Shield and protect us and our home.

Against threats of spirit or flesh and bone.

I surround my home with a circle of power,

And keep us all safe each day and each hour.

Burn your candle for one hour. You may refresh your magical shield in the future using the candle an hour at a time again, preferably on a Thursday or during a full moon.

Mickie Mueller

NOTES:

September 6
Friday

Color of the day: Coral
Incense of the day: Vanilla

Apple Seed Divination

Apples have long been associated with knowledge, love, and magick. Various world mythologies also tie apples to love goddesses, which we also often associate with Fridays. In celebration of the apple's symbolism with wisdom, try your hand at this apple seed divination.

Cut an apple crossways, creating top and bottom halves. Your cut should reveal the rough shape of a pentagram laid out by the seeds. Count the total number of visible seeds on the surfaces of the halves. This is the number you have divined. Use your favorite system of number magick/numerology to analyze the meaning of your divination. For example, the number two often represents partnerships, five is often understood to mean balance and protection, nine can be seen as abundance, and ten may mean completion and closure. When finished, you may offer the apple to your deity of choice or consume it as you feel appropriate.

Blake Octavian Blair

September 7
Saturday

Color of the day: Black
Incense of the day: Sandalwood

Car Protection Spell

Whether you own a car or are traveling in someone else's, you can use this simple spell to protect the car and its contents. Before you get in, circle four times around the car, clockwise, chanting:

*I call the earth, steadfast
and true, to protect this car
through and through.*

*I invoke air, sweet life and
health, bless this car and
carried wealth.*

*I call on fire, burning bright,
give this car reliable might.*

*I invoke water, flowing free,
bless this car, and bless me.*

When you get in the car and fasten your seatbelt, say:

*Goddess, hold this car in
your hands, deliver us to our
destination,*

*Guide and protect us evermore,
in this divine transportation.*

If you're leaving your car in a parking lot or on the street, you can use the first four lines again, to invoke protection around your car and its contents while it sits unattended.

Dallas Jennifer Cobb

September 8

Sunday

Color of the day: Gold
Incense of the day: Hyacinth

Dance with the Changes Meditation

Fall can be a riotous show of color in many parts of the world, one last burst of life and radiant beauty before the starkness of winter. Today take some time to bring a little of that abundant energy into your life by picking three (short) pieces of music and dancing to them, in whatever way helps you feel the beat and enjoy the music.

For the first, pick a song that reminds you of what you love now. It might remind you of the glory of summer, the power of the sun, a current goal. For the second piece, choose something that makes you think of transition, that space where anything is possible. For the third, choose a song that guides you toward a long-term goal, such as a creative project, time with family or friends, or a particular need in your life. Reflect on what comes up during this moving meditation.

Jenett Silver

September 9

Monday

Color of the day: White
Incense of the day: Neroli

Ganesha Chaturthi

Today begins the festival of Ganesha, the four-armed elephant Hindu god of wisdom and good fortune. Considered to be the god of "everybody," he is beloved and worshipped across many Hindu sects, and his festival is celebrated worldwide. Ganesha resides in the base chakra, a foundation and support for all other chakras.

Over the next ten days, dress your altar in red cloth and flowers, and place upon it a color picture of Ganesha in all his jeweled finery. Include him in your daily rituals and offer praise for his benevolence. If you wish, partake of foods containing coconut. Be on the lookout for positive change in your life.

Emyme

September 10

Tuesday

Color of the day: Red
Incense of the day: Bayberry

Physician, heal Thyself!

Was it yesterday you gossiped or said something not so nice about someone? Maybe nothing comes immediately to mind, but the point is, you may be wasting energy on the affairs of others when you could do a bit to clean up in your own house.

Start small, perhaps making a promise to listen more carefully. Then spend time reflecting on what sets you off or makes you afraid. Use this information to begin asking yourself probing questions and then giving honest answers. To aid your process, mix an elixir of honey, mint, lemon, and water. Speak over it the following words in order to be cleansed and released from old attachments:

> That my word be true, my deed be pure,
>
> I drink this drink, commitment sure;
>
> The sweet and sour, fresh and clear,
>
> All make it so; bind and adhere.

Now drink and take in the spell, giving yourself permission to release, grow, and open anew, seeking to create right relationships wherever you may go.

Chandra Alexandre

NOTES:

September 11

Wednesday

 Color of the day: Yellow
Incense of the day: Lavender

One-Minute Meditation

The word *meditate* comes from Latin roots meaning "to measure," and being successful with meditation means making regular (measured) time for it in one's daily schedule. But alas, in today's hyper-paced world, our personal meditation time is too often pushed to the back burner. A friend of mine avoids this with a one-minute meditation.

Set your smart phone, iPod, tablet, or laptop to alarm hourly, and select a gentle, pleasing sound for the alarm (my friend prefers a harp's soft chord). When the alarm sounds, pause, close your eyes, and engage in one minute of mindful, meditative calm as you slip into "other space." Breathe slowly and evenly, emptying your mind and relaxing as your cares drift away. Finish with end words like "Blessed be" or "I am restored" to close the session, allowing you to reenter "normal space." You'll experience a sense of calm, proving the effectiveness of these mini-meditations.

Susan Pesznecker

September 12

Thursday

 Color of the day: Green
Incense of the day: Mulberry

Scribble Scrying

Divination doesn't always have to have a prefabricated system of symbols or tools. Sometimes spontaneity is the best solution.

All you need is a big piece of paper and some crayons, colored pencils, or markers. Pick out one dark color and start scribbling with a long, single line all over the paper, looping and crisscrossing it. Then start looking for shapes in the scribbles, and color them in with other colors, even if they overlap. Do this until you feel you've brought out enough images.

Next meditate on the images, how they fit together, and what they mean to you. If you started out with a specific question, see how the images create an answer.

Lupa

September 13

Friday

Color of the day: Rose
Incense of the day: Alder

Epulum Jovis

Among Witches, Friday the 13th is often thought of as lucky. And what better way to enhance that luck than by celebrating Epulum Jovis, or "the God's Banquet," an ancient Roman festival on this date honoring Juno, Jupiter, and Minerva, the goddess of protection and wealth, the sky and thunder god, and the goddess of wisdom and worldly endeavors, respectively.

To curry the favor and receive the considerable blessings of these gods, place statues or pictures of them on the dinner table, set places for them, and cook a simple yet delicious dinner. Serve the deities food, and in all other ways treat them as honored guests. If you have any special requests, perhaps save them for tomorrow. For now, just dine and align your life with the goodwill of these powerful gods. When you've finished, return their meals to the earth or place them in a compost bin (don't eat them!).

Tess Whitehurst

September 14

Saturday

Color of the day: Gray
Incense of the day: Magnolia

Yom Kippur

Create a Spell Box

A long time ago a friend of mine said she had a "wish box." She would cut out magazine photos of the things she wished for, such as a new house and furniture, and place them in a pretty box.

Recognizing the magical significance of this, I created what I call a "spell box." All you need to do is get a box; shoe boxes and hat boxes work great. Give the box a spiritual cleansing, perhaps by smudging with sage. Then decorate the box as you wish and fill with photos of what you want most. Use these photos on your altar as you do spellwork to obtain your wishes. Keep your spell materials in the box as your spells are working. When your wishes manifest, remove old photos and spell materials from the spell box. Spiritually clean your box occasionally.

James Kambos

September 15

Sunday

Color of the day: Orange
Incense of the day: Marigold

A Charm for Prosperity

In today's times we're all search-ing for prosperity, and you can improve the odds of finding it by burying a charmed coin under your front porch (or close to your front door). Use a coin with as much silver as possible: pre-1965 dimes work well. Before burying the coin, bless the ground and coin with salt water or a cedar smudge. Use a small trowel to bury the coin at dawn (the time of growing, expanding ener-gies), on a Sunday (associated with prosperity and finances), and under a waxing moon (synonymous with burgeoning growth). As you cover up the coin, incant:

> Silver coin, now buried deep,
>
> Here beneath the earth you sleep.
>
> Multiply in Luna's arms
>
> Luck and coins exchanged for charms.

Finally, trace a solar symbol in the dirt over the coin, adding the sun's prosperous energies to the spell. So mote it be!

Susan Pesznecker

September 16

Monday

Color of the day: Lavender
Incense of the day: Clary sage

To Protect Children

Kids love things in their pockets. Black river rocks with some protection oil and a symbol or pic-ture painted on them can be carried in their pockets or purse. Have the child/ren work on it with you! Ask them if they have something they would like to paint on the stone. You will be surprised at what they come up with. A picture on the stone is just as good as a symbol. Help them work on it in a way that speaks to them. It will never be a secret stone, and you should always treat any-thing a child is going to have with openness. If you teach them to treat the stone with respect, and not to treat it as the only means of protec-tion, then it can help them feel safer at night, when away from home, or when the boogie man is at his worst.

Boudica

September 17

Tuesday

Color of the day: White
Incense of the day: Cedar

Magical Lists

Sure you make mundane lists, for groceries and chores, but why not make a magical list, to help you stay protected, empowered, and progressing?

If you keep a daily journal, make your magical list in the back of it, so you can review it daily. Use headings like *Wealth* instead of *Work*, *Learning* versus *School*, *Belonging* rather than *Home*, *Relationships* and not just *Family*, plus *Self-Care* and *Spirit*. Under each heading list the things, big and small, that need to be done to move forward. Under *Spirit*, identify the themes to meditate on, Goddess or God energy to invoke in your life, preparations needed for rituals, circles, and gatherings, and even reminders to clear the energy absorbed at certain meetings or events.

Each day review your magical list and do what is needed to clear and center yourself magically, enabling you to stay positive, creative, and magical, clearing anything that could impede you.

Dallas Jennifer Cobb

September 18

Wednesday

Color of the day: Brown
Incense of the day: Bay laurel

Sukkot begins

Ritual Bath

Vervain

Garden mint

Basil

Thyme

Fennel

Lavender

Rosemary

Hyssop

Valerian

Use slightly less valerian; otherwise, equal parts. Mix and put into bath bags during the moon's increase. Tie with a red drawstring and use one for every bath. Make several so you have a good stock on hand.

From Scott Cunningham's
Book of Shadows

September 19

Thursday

Color of the day: Purple
Incense of the day: Carnation

Full Moon in Pisces

Talk Like a Pirate Day

Avast, me hearties! More than ten years ago International Talk Like a Pirate Day was created. Today being a Thursday (expansion and generosity) and a full moon (prosperity), why not add some whimsy to the mix for a future free from pillaging?

In pirate speak, craft a spell to bring protection and abundance. Wrap the spell in a piece of red cloth. Place in a small glass jar, and add a penny, nickel, dime, quarter, and dollar coin or bill. By the light of the moon, bury your treasure. Be sure to mark the spot and your calendar. Next September 19, unearth the jar and review your request. Repeat annually as needed.

Emyme

September 20

Friday

Color of the day: Pink
Incense of the day: Yarrow

Coping with a Potentially Difficult Day

When you're facing One Of Those Days and don't know where to turn, try this quick tarot spell. Make a list of all the things you think you need to accomplish today, all the obstacles you'll probably face, and the possible rewards if you succeed.

Lay this list on a table and read it again as you shuffle your tarot deck. If a card falls out while you're shuffling, this is a jump card. Accept it as instant information or advice. Lay the deck on your list and ask for guidance. Now cut the deck three times. Lay three cards from left to right and label them *morning, noon,* and *afternoon or evening.*

Examine the cards. If you get a major arcana card, the tarot is probably shouting at you. Pay attention. Interpret each card and see what the potential for your day might be.

Barbara Ardinger, Ph.D.

September 21

Saturday

Color of the day: Brown
Incense of the day: Patchouli

U.N. International Day of Peace

Make Room for Abundance

The beginning of the harvest season is just around the corner; time to clear away the all the unnecessary stuff from your life to make room for all the new abundance the universe can offer you in the coming season.

Go through your closet and clear away old clothing, coats, and blankets. Sell or donate things you can't use. Discard stacks of old mail and files and even go through the junk drawer. Get rid of anything in your home that you no longer need. Nature abhors a vacuum; therefore emptying out things you don't need leaves space for good things to come into your life.

Once everything is cleared out, go around your house counterclockwise with a sage bundle and fan the smoke all around, using this blessing to clear the energy:

I cleared the clutter all away

And welcome abundance a place to stay.

Mickie Mueller

September 22

Sunday

Color of the day: Amber
Incense of the day: Frankincense

Mabon ~ Fall Equinox

Harvest Celebration

Adorn your home with all the traditional fall decorations, such as cornucopias, gourds and pumpkins, apples, nuts, corn, leaves, and mums. Add your own personal touches as well, with candles, stones, and so on. Pile everything in a basket or bowl or make a wreath.

Host a harvest dinner party with family and friends. Visit a local farmers' market. Celebrate with foods that are in season where you live, and enjoy some local wine. Use this chant when you sit down for your harvest feast:

Balance of the day and night,

Balance of the dark and light,

Celebrate the harvest time,

Raise a toast and sing this rhyme:

Welcome autumn, let us cheer,

Bounty for another year!

Pour some of your ritual or celebratory beverage in your garden or into a potted plant as an offering for the next growing season.

Ember Grant

September 23

Monday

Color of the day: Ivory
Incense of the day: Lily

Listening to Memory

In Buddhist thought, the entire week of the equinox is a bridge, a time when the dead travel between their far shore and our world, to be remembered on the equinox. In our own lives we can use this time to remember whom and what we've loved, and what we miss.

Lay out five cards (or runes or oracle cards) in a row, focusing on the question *What should I remember from those who've gone before?*

Position 1 reminds you of thoughts and ideas, things important to loved ones who've gone before.

Position 2 focuses on actions, the way you make choices in your life.

Position 3 looks at emotions and connections, and what matters to you.

Position 4 looks at the foundation of your life, the practical choices.

Position 5 ties these together and adds a layer of your spiritual life.

Reflect on what you've learned, and journal.

Jenett Silver

NOTES:

September 24

Tuesday

Color of the day: Gray
Incense of the day: Ylang-ylang

Break a Curse Spell

To break a curse, the curse's power must be bound, weakened, and destroyed. To break a suspected curse, never try to perform negative magic to harm the person who placed the curse; instead concentrate on destroying the curse's power. Here is one method.

You'll need a small grapevine wreath and jute garden twine. As you work this spell, concentrate on the idea that the curse has no power over you. Begin by wrapping a piece of the twine tightly around the wreath; feel as if you're choking the energy out of the curse. When you feel you've bound the curse's power, say this:

Round and round, this curse
is bound.

You have no power over me,

Now I'm free.

Bury the wreath away from your home as you speak these words:

I'm no longer your slave, now
rot, rot in this earthly grave.

Gradually the curse's power will diminish.

James Kambos

September 25

Wednesday

Color of the day: White
Incense of the day: Honeysuckle

Sukkot ends

Creativity Spell

Today is a wonderful chance to recharge your creative energy for the rest of the year. By staying in tune with your inventive side, you make it easier for the universe to communicate with you, and you open yourself to manifestation. This spell will help you access your creative energy, which also needs to be refreshed and rejuvenated.

You will need modeling clay (the type that air-dries) and peppermint oil. Burn a small amount of oil in a diffuser while you sculpt the clay, working it carefully in your hands until warm. It does not matter what you create as long as you focus on the connection between your hands (you) and the clay (your creativity). When you are happy with what you have made, allow the clay to harden. Once set, paint the surface with the oil to seal in the creativity for the year.

Patti Larsen

September 26

Thursday

Color of the day: Turquoise
Incense of the day: Apricot

Exploring the Crone

Welcome the Crone into your world and explore her attributes. The Crone is a wise woman, one who is smart enough to know that knowledge is good, and application of knowledge is better, but knowing when to apply the knowledge is the secret of living a long and healthy life. She is aware of the cycle of life, death, and rebirth and does not fear it.

The Crone takes care of herself; her age demands it. She cannot afford to be careless, as it may cause a physical or emotional injury from which she may never recover. She has to be quiet and peaceful, so that when needed, she can call upon the warrior that is she—her mettle has been tested and has proven strong in battle.

Embrace the Crone. She is not to be feared, but is someone you want on your side when you need her.

Boudica

September 27

Friday

Color of the day: Purple
Incense of the day: Mint

Make a Magickal Water Garden

Are you looking to embrace the water element? Would you like to add a peaceful corner to your garden for quiet meditation? You can accomplish both by creating a small water feature.

You'll need a medium-sized garden pot (with no hole in the bottom), a bag of river rocks, a small fountain pump, bubbler tubing, and electrical access. Decide where you want the pot to be located. Place the pump in the pot first; attach the bubbler tubing so it pokes out about two inches above the pot's upper edge. Fill the pot with river rocks and then with water. Plug in the pump, trimming the tubing as needed to create a gentle bubbling.

Sit quietly by the pot when you want a peaceful moment for meditation or magickal workings. Enjoy your miniature water garden. The birds will enjoy sipping from it, too, and your garden will thrive with the watery harmony in its midst.

Susan Pesznecker

September 28

Saturday

Color of the day: Indigo
Incense of the day: Pine

Emotional Cleansing

When the waning moon is in watery Cancer, we have a special opportunity to cleanse ourselves of old, lingering emotions—such as guilt, grief, and anger—so we can get our life and emotions flowing in the most ideal ways.

Today obtain a reusable water bottle that you love. Using a permanent marker and/or tape, put the words *Emotional Freedom* on the bottle. Fill it with drinking water. Hold it in both hands and visualize very bright white light coming down from above, entering the crown of your head, and going down to your heart and out your hands into the bottle. Say:

> Great Goddess, please infuse
> this water with vibrations of
> healing, purification, and love.

Drink at least half your body weight in ounces before the end of the day. Repeat the ritual whenever you refill. When feelings come up, feel them fully and then let them go.

Tess Whitehurst

September 29

Sunday

Color of the day: Yellow
Incense of the day: Heliotrope

Michaelmas Prosperity

Michaelmas is a Christian feast day marking the autumnal equinox, in honor of Saint Michael the archangel. But the entire autumn season in England is often referred to as Michaelmas. The Feast of Michaelmas held in medieval times included fairs and feasting. Roast goose, prepared elaborately and decorated with feathers to look as if it was still alive after being cooked, was the traditional dish, and the saying goes, "Eat a goose at Michaelmas, and you will not want for money all year." The traditional spice used in Michaelmas dishes is ginger, a plant with many health-giving properties. This was also the traditional time to sow wheat and rye for late winter crops.

To partake of the prosperous energy of the season, prepare a meal seasoned with ginger, drink some ginger beer, or make gingerbread from scratch.

Peg Aloi

September 30

Monday

Color of the day: Gray
Incense of the day: Rosemary

Create a Dream Journal

A dream journal is the perfect magical companion for your bedside table. It's the best way to learn more about your subconscious mind, obtain dream messages, and track prophetic dreams.

First find a blank book. If you wish, choose one with a lock on it so you can keep all your subconscious secrets safe. Decorate the outside with calming images. If the book is already decorated, you may want to add a personal touch to the inside cover.

On the first page, state the purpose of your dream journal, to track and record your dreams and to gain better insight from your subconscious mind. The statement only needs to be a paragraph long. Then press a leaf of catnip in the book and allow it to dry; this makes an excellent bookmark for a dream journal. Always record your dreams before you get out of bed. You'll remember more this way.

Mickie Mueller

September Moon Table

Date	Sign	Element	Nature	Phase
1 Sun 8:01 pm	Leo	Fire	Barren	4th
2 Mon	Leo	Fire	Barren	4th
3 Tue	Leo	Fire	Barren	4th
4 Wed 6:43 am	Virgo	Earth	Barren	4th
5 Thu	Virgo	Earth	Barren	New 7:36 am
6 Fri 3:12 pm	Libra	Air	Semi-fruitful	1st
7 Sat	Libra	Air	Semi-fruitful	1st
8 Sun 9:44 pm	Scorpio	Water	Fruitful	1st
9 Mon	Scorpio	Water	Fruitful	1st
10 Tue	Scorpio	Water	Fruitful	1st
11 Wed 2:36 am	Sagittarius	Fire	Barren	1st
12 Thu	Sagittarius	Fire	Barren	2nd 1:08 pm
13 Fri 5:56 am	Capricorn	Earth	Semi-fruitful	2nd
14 Sat	Capricorn	Earth	Semi-fruitful	2nd
15 Sun 8:05 am	Aquarius	Air	Barren	2nd
16 Mon	Aquarius	Air	Barren	2nd
17 Tue 9:58 am	Pisces	Water	Fruitful	2nd
18 Wed	Pisces	Water	Fruitful	2nd
19 Thu 12:58 pm	Aries	Fire	Barren	Full 7:13 am
20 Fri	Aries	Fire	Barren	3rd
21 Sat 6:33 pm	Taurus	Earth	Semi-fruitful	3rd
22 Sun	Taurus	Earth	Semi-fruitful	3rd
23 Mon	Taurus	Earth	Semi-fruitful	3rd
24 Tue 3:34 am	Gemini	Air	Barren	3rd
25 Wed	Gemini	Air	Barren	3rd
26 Thu 3:24 pm	Cancer	Water	Fruitful	4th 11:55 pm
27 Fri	Cancer	Water	Fruitful	4th
28 Sat	Cancer	Water	Fruitful	4th
29 Sun 3:57 am	Leo	Fire	Barren	4th
30 Mon	Leo	Fire	Barren	4th

Times are in Eastern Time.

October

"H alloweeeen, the witches riding high ... Have you seeeen their shadows in the sky?" So begins a rhyme I learned as a grade school student. Halloween then was October's crown, a magical time of mystery and excitement—and a time to fill a pillowcase with candy bars in an hours-long orgy of trick-or-treating. The magic of Halloween and Samhain is still with me; my love for the month of October grows stronger with each passing year. October is all about preparation—and change. The weather dampens, temperatures drop, days shorten, leaves fall, and everything ebbs as Earth slips inexorably toward winter's deep sleep. But even as Earth's energies seem to chill and settle, there remains much to do. It's time for wintering-in: to dress warm and light a fire on the hearth. Time to brew pots of tea and sink deep into books and study. Time to launch plans that will blossom in the spring. Magical tools begun during autumn and finished during winter and early spring will be heavy with accumulated power and intention. Divination studied throughout these months will tap deep into your psyche, leaving you with skills previously unimagined. Embrace the lessons of dark, wise October.

Susan Pesznecker

October 1

Tuesday

Color of the day: White
Incense of the day: Cinnamon

Retreat

According to Shinto belief, this is the time of year when the gods gather for a yearly convention. The gods leave their various shrines and come together in a kind of retreat. During this time all but one of the shrines in Japan are vacant—the one that is occupied is the place where the gods have gathered. At the end of the month, the gods are welcomed back.

This tradition reminds us that everyone needs to rest and take a break. Make today a kind of restful retreat in whatever way you can. This may simply mean taking time to do something nice for yourself. If you have trouble breaking away, use this chant:

Give me time, take a break,
Slowly calm this hurried pace.

Let me have some time for me
To renew my energy.

Ember Grant

October 2

Wednesday

Color of the day: Yellow
Incense of the day: Lilac

Hump Day Helper Spell

Wednesday is hump day, the day when we pass the middle mark of the work week. Sometimes the hump feels insurmountable. Today invoke the magical qualities of coffee to help get you through the slump of hump day. Mindfully fill the kettle, saying:

Water, let me flow like you.
Soon this day will be through.

Put the kettle on to boil:

Fire, as you burn bright,
I'm energized by your warmth
and light.

Standing in the kitchen, breathe deeply:

Air, inspire and uplift,
Fill me with your sacred gift.

Then, grounding energy through your feet, say:

Earth, your strength I call
upon.
Help me now to carry on.

Pour water, press plunger down on press to make coffee, and drink. With each sip, summon the culminating energies of the elements, so

you are suffused with the perseverance, patience, and strength of the universe. Now you can go climb that hump.

Dallas Jennifer Cobb

NOTES:

October 3

Thursday

Color of the day: Turquoise
Incense of the day: Clove

Our Devoted Friends

Today is a great opportunity to bless any pets in your household. Check out their food, water, and bed. Take a moment to cleanse them and bless them, as you would your bed. While visualizing your pet healthy and happy, say:

> Love, health, and all blessings
> on you.

Check their toys: have the toy mice disappeared under the couch or the chew toys been destroyed? Bring home a few new ones, and bless them for health and energy. Spend a little extra time grooming and making much of your pets. Listen to what they tell you through their energy and actions.

If you don't have pets at home, this is a great day to learn more about animal welfare issues. Consider volunteering at an animal shelter or visit a friend's pet for a while.

Jenett Silver

October 4

Friday

Color of the day: Coral
Incense of the day: Violet

New Moon in Libra

The Dark Justice of Nemesis

The new, or "dark," moon is known to be an ideal time for working spells of protection, binding, severing, and banishing. Nemesis is one of the ancient dark goddesses, a Kali-like force who balances justice with retribution and typically exacts revenge for acts of presumption or hubris. The word *nemesis* itself means "retribution" and comes from the late sixteenth-century Greek word *nemein*, meaning "give what is due."

Invite Nemesis to assist you in a ritual of banishing or when you wish to seek justice. For best results work when the moon is in an earth sign (Taurus, Virgo, or Capricorn); this is also an effective time to recover misplaced or misappropriated goods. To deal with the results of anger or hubris, work with the moon in a water sign (Cancer, Scorpio, Pisces). The new moon reaches peak height around noon—although it will be below the horizon and not visible.

On small pieces of black paper, use a silver pen to write about those issues that you wish to resolve so as to create a clean slate. Meditate silently on these, then feed them to a fire, saying:

> *From fire to ash, Nemesis, remove this burden, cleanse my soul, renew my intention, free me from malice, support my efforts to follow a path of justice. So shall it be.*

Susan Pesznecker

NOTES:

October 5

Saturday

Color of the day: Blue
Incense of the day: Rue

To Diana

Lovely goddess of the bow!

Lovely goddess of the arrows!

Of all the hounds and of all the hunting

Thou who wakest in starry heaven

When the Sun is sunk in slumber;

Thou with Moon upon thy forehead,

Who the chase by night preferrest unto hunting in the daylight,

With thy nymphs unto the music of the horn—

Thyself the huntress, and the most powerful;

I pray thee think, although but for an instant,

Upon we who pray unto you!

From Scott Cunningham's
Book of Shadows

October 6

Sunday

Color of the day: Gold
Incense of the day: Eucalyptus

Washing Blessings into Your Life

When you take a shower, think about the magical meaning of washing. Be sure to change your scrubby with the equinoxes and solstices, and always buy one in a magical color: green for healing and prosperity, red for root chakra energy, blue for insight, violet for aspiration, and so on.

As you pour the shower gel on your scrubby, see it as magical gel. Know that you're working with magical liquid blessings. Start washing at your heart chakra, and move up and down your chakra column. You're scrubbing out misfortune, bad luck, pain, and disappointment. What are you scrubbing in? Good luck. Healing. Happiness. Prosperity. Success.

Rinse yourself in clean magical water that washes the bad things down the drain. As you dry yourself, focus on patting good things into your body and soul. You can even use magical bath powder.

Barbara Ardinger, Ph.D.

October 7

Monday

Color of the day: White
Incense of the day: Narcissus

Water Gazing

By candlelight, burn white sage around a moonstone and then around your body. Place the moonstone in a black ceramic bowl filled with water. Relax and gaze into the water as you call on the scorpion and the goddess of the moon. Inwardly, and directed toward the ether, ask the question *What visions hold clues that will be of value to my life path now?* Continue to gaze at the water. Let your gaze go out of focus and let your mind slip into an altered state. In the space between your physical eyesight and your inner knowing, see what you see. When you feel ready, open your eyes.

In the following weeks, whether you come to consciously understand your vision(s) or not, they will weave themselves into the fabric of your life, positively affecting your choices and life situation and leading you along the path of your dreamiest desires.

Tess Whitehurst

October 8

Tuesday

Color of the day: Red
Incense of the day: Geranium

Appalachian Bottle Tree Magic

Bottle trees are an old form of Appalachian folk magic that originated in Africa. Still used, they're found near houses to protect homes from evil spirits. Bottles of any color can be used, though blue is the favorite. The bottles are slipped onto bare tree branches, with the neck facing toward the trunk. At night, malevolent spirits are caught in the bottles and are believed to be destroyed in the sunlight the following day. According to folklore, on windy nights the spirits can be heard moaning in agony. Bottle trees are steeped in antiquity and are related to the occult belief of genies being trapped in bottles. Today an essence of bottle tree magic still survives in the form of the garden gazing ball.

Bottle trees are fun and easy to make. Just use your imagination. I've even seen them made using metal sculptures, and in this manner they resemble garden ornaments.

James Kambos

October 9

Wednesday

Color of the day: Brown
Incense of the day: Bay laurel

The Festival of Felicitas

On this day the ancient Romans celebrated Felicitas, goddess of good luck and joy. One of her sacred symbols was the cornucopia. You can use a cornucopia to add joy to your life.

If you have a cornucopia, place it in a prominent place in your home and fill it with fruit, gourds, and corn. If you don't have one, a basket will do. Next fill a bowl with nine pennies and set it next to the cornucopia. Pick up a penny and hold it in your hand, focusing on something that brings you joy. Visualize it completely until it brings a smile to your face. Drop it into the cornucopia. Repeat with the other coins, naming each one for a different joy in your life until they are all gone. You have just filled your cornucopia with nine joys!

Leave the cornucopia out as a decoration all autumn, refilling the fruit as you eat it, and watch your joys multiply.

Mickie Mueller

October 10

Thursday

Color of the day: Purple
Incense of the day: Nutmeg

Personal Pumpkins

Pumpkins are abundant now, from the roadside farm market to the big box supermarket. These squash come in so many shapes, sizes, and colors that the mind reels. Seasonal decorations lacking pumpkins are sad, indeed.

Be sure to include a few standard orange globes to welcome guests during this month of harvest. Leave some smaller pumpkins in an unobtrusive yet sunny spot for the winter. Allow rot to occur, right into the ground. In the spring be on the lookout for those telltale vines and golden-yellow flowers. With some assistance from nature, and bees, you will find your very own personal pumpkins growing in the yard. Say:

Color of the sun at noon,

Shape of the harvest moon.

Fair pumpkin, bless this home

Till summer again does come.

Emyme

October 11

Friday

Color of the day: Rose
Incense of the day: Alder

Service to Truth

We all know the story of George Washington and the cherry tree. After taking his hatchet to the garden and doing irreparable damage to the tree, the little boy confessed to his father, saying, "I cannot tell a lie."

Be inspired by this heroic deed today, making an effort to be of service to the conveyance of truth. First, however, a meditation on the nature of truth as it ties to your beliefs and values is a must. Spend a few moments too reflecting on what truth is in your personal cosmology. Then ask yourself, *What is it that nurtures truth?* Use a divination tool to deepen yourself into this question, perhaps allying with gods and goddesses who know this realm as you do so.

Take the wisdom you receive out into the world through word and deed. Journal on your experiences of this day before bedtime, and look for your dreams to carry messages of the boons of your work, helping to take what you have done into a more deeply embodied place.

Chandra Alexandre

October 12

Saturday

Color of the day: Black
Incense of the day: Sage

Navaratri Warrior Spell

Today is the second to last day of the nine-day Hindu festival of Navaratri. The festival celebrates the warrior goddess Durga, among other forms of the divine feminine in the Hindu tradition. Many devotees either ask for triumph of good over evil or express gratitude for a triumph they have experienced. Use today as a similar opportunity for yourself. You may wish to invoke Durga, and ask for her assistance in overcoming a difficulty you are experiencing or give thanks for something you have been able to rise above and overcome. Gather inspiration from her example as a divine warrior. Pause and recognize the warrior within yourself. A simple way to then show your gratitude and praise to Durga is to offer her incense and repetitive recitations of her mantra: *Om Dum Durgayei Namaha!*

Blake Octavian Blair

October 13

Sunday

Color of the day: Yellow
Incense of the day: Juniper

Cleansing Spell

Today is the Fontus Festival, the Roman celebration of the god of wells and springs. This day is highly beneficial for clearing and cleaning negative thoughts and emotions.

In the morning, fill a two-liter glass container with filtered water. Place a silk scarf over the bowl and set it in a window. Place both hands over the silk and repeat three times:

> With this water I cleanse my
> heart, my mind, my body, my
> soul. Every drop I drink dispels
> the darkness and restores
> health and happiness. I am
> clean and bright.

Move the bowl to the refrigerator and drink throughout the day, repeating the incantation over every glass. When you reach the bottom of the bowl, repeat the following three times:

> I am clean and bright, a shin-
> ing light. My heart is pure, my
> soul is right. My body's health
> is now restored. Thank you,
> water, for this and more.

Patti Larsen

October 14

Monday

Color of the day: Gray
Incense of the day: Hyssop

Columbus Day (observed)

Healing Invisible Wounds

Life is a pretty tough road sometimes, and it's not always pretty. We encounter things along the way that affect us deeply. Sometimes the hurt is so bad, we need help to get over it.

We should learn to ask for help when needed; we do ourselves more damage by not dealing with our injuries. You wouldn't dream of not going to the doctor when you have a broken leg, so why hesitate at the idea of seeking professional help to heal the wounds of your heart or mind?

If there is something weighing heavily on you that you can no longer deal with on your own, it's time to get professional care. Seek a trusted medical person to help you though this. And if you need to be sure this is the right thing to do, ask Hygeia, who is associated with mental as well as physical care.

Boudica

October 15

Tuesday

Color of the day: Black
Incense of the day: Basil

The Feast of Freya

Freya is a prominent Norse goddess famed for her beauty and grace and possessed of complex attributes. She is known as a fertility goddess but also represents power and wisdom. She governs the disir, land protection spirits said to be our ancient female ancestors.

October 14–15 is known as "Winter Nights" among those who observe Norse traditions: it marks the end of the harvest and the start of the winter season. To honor Freya's fertile gifts, pour a libation of milk, mead, or ale into the soil, to symbolize thanks for the harvest and ask for her protection. Sharing mead and speaking blessings aloud is a common ritual among modern Norse and Heathen practitioners, and such a rite would also be appropriate at this time.

Peg Aloi

October 16

Wednesday

Color of the day: White
Incense of the day: Lavender

Uniquely Me

It's said that we are ¼ genetic material, ¼ early life experiences, ¼ random luck and chance, and ¼ the result of choices we make and their results. We can't change our genes or early life experiences, but we can make choices that shape our experiences and actively influence luck in our lives. You wouldn't be who you are today without all you've lived through.

Take stock of the big experiences, learning, and relationships you've had. See how they've shaped you, making you unique. Give thanks. Chant joyously:

I am that I am, I am, I am, I am.

Now envision the future and see yourself engaged in happy, fulfilling, and meaningful activities. Know that where you're going is determined by where you've been and your present choices. Use the chant regularly to focus on manifesting your future vision:

I am that I am, I am, I am, I am.

Dallas Jennifer Cobb

October 17

Thursday

Color of the day: Crimson
Incense of the day: Mulberry

Stone Spell for Expansion

Today create a talisman for abundance and prosperity. Prosperity does not have to be financial—consider what you really want to expand in your life: knowledge, friendship, love, wisdom, spirituality, family, and so on. Select a stone that symbolizes the quality you wish to increase. Place the stone near a tree or potted plant, next to something that grows. Say:

> Like the plant that grows and thrives,
>
> With endurance it survives.
>
> Let my need be satisfied—
>
> Let abundance now arrive!

Ember Grant

October 18

Friday

Color of the day: Pink
Incense of the day: Rose

Full Moon/Lunar Eclipse in Aries

Lunar Eclipse

Eclipses only happen a couple times a year, and not everyone gets to see one each year due to weather, the time of the eclipse, and other factors. If you are fortunate enough to get to see the eclipse with your own eyes, take the opportunity to do some magick for other long-shot or rare opportunities. For example, if you're not currently in a good financial position but want a quick turnaround, try a spell for extra prosperity and use the energy of the eclipse to help bring it about.

Then do everything reasonable you can to make your desire come to pass. Keep it within perspective; don't sink all your money into a get-rich-quick scheme. However, if there's a job you want that you haven't applied for because you aren't quite qualified, give it a shot anyway. Use the eclipse energy to help turn things in your favor!

Lupa

October 19

Saturday

Color of the day: Brown
Incense of the day: Ivy

Returning to a Place You Love

I always carry a few energizing crystals with me when I travel. If I find a place that I want to visit again, I drop a crystal discreetly in the grass and say:

> Please call me back to this
> place.

If you are making a visit to a place where you want to live—and you're absolutely sure you want to live there—bury a crystal at the base of a mature tree and say:

> Bind me to this place.

Be sure to petition your deities for their help in your endeavor.

If you want to hold on to property that has been in your family for generations, take a strip from the oldest heirloom you own and tie it around a tree on the property. Petition your ancestors to help you keep the land.

Anne Johnson

October 20

Sunday

Color of the day: Orange
Incense of the day: Almond

Celebrating a Western Diwali

Diwali, the Indian Festival of Lights, is the beginning of the Hindu lunar calendar's new year. It covers four days, the last of which is auspicious for shopping, business, and starting new ventures.

Instead of stealing another culture's traditions, we can respectfully adapt Diwali. Begin by lighting at least four candles. With each one, be glad for new light in a month of growing darkness. Sit quietly before your candles and reflect on the joyful things that have occurred this year. See again the beautiful things you've seen this year. Yes, it's been a good year. Know that across the earth, people are lighting lamps and candles tonight to bring peace and harmony into the world.

In what endeavors do you still need to find success? Do some planning and decide what steps you can take to move this project forward. Know that with good work, you will succeed.

Barbara Ardinger, Ph.D.

October 21

Monday

Color of the day: Lavender
Incense of the day: Lily

Magical Autumn Decorations

Many of us enjoy decorating our homes with seasonal autumn decorations, but don't forget that many of the natural decorations we use also make powerful spell ingredients. Here are some spellcrafting ideas.

The bittersweet you may have hanging on your front door is good to add to love spells. Place a few of the dried berries in a love sachet along with crushed almonds and orange peel, then tie up in a piece of pink fabric. If you have any colored maple leaves on hand, place them on your altar during abundance or money-attracting spells. The Indian corn you probably have on display is considered to be among the most powerful of spell ingredients. Use it in fertility, abundance, or general good fortune spells. And don't forget chrysanthemums. Mums should be planted in the garden, in pots, or placed on your altar to repel evil.

James Kambos

October 22

Tuesday

Color of the day: White
Incense of the day: Bayberry

What's Gone Before

Today people in Kyoto, Japan, celebrate the Festival of the Ages, a grand parade that shows all of history, beginning with the twenty-first century. Take some time to reflect on where you came from.

On a big piece of paper, draw a timeline. Put yourself at one end, then mark points on the timeline that are important to you. These might be events in your life (relationships, achievements) or in the lives of your parents or family. But don't just stop with your family. Include the lives of favorite musicians or artists, when a hobby became popular, or dates important for your spiritual life and community or where you live.

Jenett Silver

October 23

Wednesday

Color of the day: Topaz
Incense of the day: Marjoram

Greeting the Sun

Today the sun moves into Scorpio, a water sign embodying mystery, curiosity, and intense focus. This charm from the *Carmina Gadelica* is an ancient Pagan prayer to the sun. The *Carmina Gadelica* is a group of folk rhymes, charms, and tales that reflect the lives of rural Scottish people in the late 1800s. Collected by folklorist Alexander Carmichael, the *Carmina Gadelica* provides a window into a past culture.

Face the rising sun—with head uncovered and palms facing up—as you repeat this charm:

> Hail to thee, thou sun of the seasons,
>
> As thou traversest the skies aloft;
>
> Thy steps are strong on the wing of the heavens,
>
> Thou art the glorious mother of the stars.

Susan Pesznecker

October 24

Thursday

Color of the day: Green
Incense of the day: Balsam

Mnemosyne: Mother of the Muses

Mnemosyne: a titan daughter of Gaia and Uranus, mother to the nine muses, and the goddess of memory. Though Mnemosyne is fully powerful in her own right, when she is called upon in conjunction with one of her daughters, great magick may be expected. Should you find yourself blocked creatively, adjust the following spell to suit your needs. Let the issue at hand dictate the candle color and food offering.

> Wondrous Mnemosyne,
>
> I call upon you and your daughter(s) (_____).
>
> I light this candle in your honor.
>
> I offer this gift to you as proof of my devotion.
>
> Allow my talents to break free from constraints.
>
> Allow your gifts to flow through me.
>
> I am but the conduit; I follow your lead,
>
> Blessed be.

Emyme

October 25

Friday

 Color of the day: Purple
Incense of the day: Vanilla

happy home Broom Spell

It's time to banish any bad vibes lingering around the house and raise the vibrations, bringing feelings of happiness and peace into your home. Start with a physically clean home. Decorate a cinnamon broom from a craft store with dried herbs such as yarrow, lavender, or rosemary; herbs for protection, cleansing, and love are all good choices. Wrap the broom handle with festive fall-colored ribbon and leaves, if you like, and dangle a few bells on the broom, since ringing bells release stagnant energy.

Now move from room to room, gently sweeping toward your back door. This is meant to be a spiritual cleaning, the physical cleaning having already been done. Sweep all negativity out your back door. Sprinkle your threshold with saltwater. Stomp your foot and say:

> Negativity, now you're out.
> You can't come back or hang
> about!

Hang the broom outside on your front door or prop it nearby.

Mickie Mueller

October 26

Saturday

Color of the day: Gray
Incense of the day: Sandalwood

Overcome Blockages

We all encounter blockages in some respect or another. We try to accomplish something and find halfway through the project that we have lost interest, can't figure some part of it out, or maybe become frustrated with it.

To regain your balance and find your spark of inspiration, I recommend a seven-day road-opener candle; the candle is there to remind you that you are seeking your center. When you see it sitting there burning, take a few minutes to rest and meditate. Allow your mind to clear of the everyday routine and find some quiet within. Many times we are just stressed out, and our imaginations shut down in favor of everyday needs. Allow your mind to roam. Clear away the cobwebs and invite the muses in to have their way.

Boudica

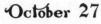

October 27

Sunday

 Color of the day: Amber
Incense of the day: Marigold

Sunlight Confidence Ritual

Go outside in the sunlight. Stand comfortably and take some deep breaths as you consciously tune in to the energy of the sun. Light three sticks of frankincense, one stick of patchouli or vetiver, and three sticks of cinnamon incense, and hold them together like a smudge stick. Safely smudge your body and aura as you say:

> I now release all fears, limiting
> beliefs, low self-esteem, and
> other seeming blocks to the
> perfect confidence that is mine
> by divine right. With fragrant
> smoke, and the light and bless-
> ings of the sun, I am cleansed.
> I shine, I radiate, I reign.

Now place the incense nearby (perhaps in the earth or a potted plant) and allow it to safely burn. Sit comfortably as you slowly drink a cup of cinnamon tea. Feel the sun completely removing and neutralizing all seeming blocks to confidence, and feel your true, brave, self-assured self emerge.

Tess Whitehurst

October 28

Monday

 Color of the day: White
Incense of the day: Neroli

Wishing on a Star

Rent or buy the 1940 Disney animated film *Pinocchio* and listen carefully as Jiminy Cricket sings "When You Wish Upon a Star." A star is a pentacle, one of our favorite Pagan symbols.

Buy a sheet of sky-blue poster board and cut out the biggest pentacle you can. Then go through all the mail-order catalogs you receive (and hopefully recycle) and cut out the illustrations of all the things you wish you had. Cut illustrations out of magazines or print pictures from online stores. Glue the pictures to your star. Add bright, glittery, significant stickers.

Now hang the star where you'll see it every day. This isn't just another "treasure map." Active wishing is not the same as wishful thinking. The purpose of your star is to focus your mind. Determine what you need, what you really want, and what can wait. Do both magical and mundane work to bring what you wish for into your life.

Barbara Ardinger, Ph.D.

October 29

Tuesday

 Color of the day: Scarlet
Incense of the day: Cinnamon

Banishing the Blahs

In the waning half of the year through the winter months, many of us experience a bit of seasonal affective disorder (SAD), to one degree or another. If you are having a particularly dreary day, here is a spell to help remind you that the light will return and to hopefully chase away some of the blahs.

Take a yellow candle and anoint it with an oil that has an uplifting effect on the mood, such as frankincense or lemongrass, and carve a sun symbol of your choice on its side. Light and visualize the glowing yellow light surrounding you while reciting:

> Candle of yellow, burning bright,
>
> Remind me of the sun's soon returning light.
>
> Assist me in chasing away this dreary plight.
>
> Help the mood of today become more light.

Allow the candle to burn itself out, or snuff and relight as necessary.

Blake Octavian Blair

October 30

Wednesday

 Color of the day: Yellow
Incense of the day: Honeysuckle

Mischief Night

The night before Hallowe'en is dedicated to the "trick" element of "trick or treat." Unfortunately this sometimes turns into some really destructive activities, like arson. Less damaging acts, like toilet-papering a house, are still disrespectful of the targets.

To counteract this harmful trend, spend some time today showing kindness toward others. Here are some ideas:

Get some friends together and plan to go out the next day, if possible, to volunteer to clean up messes left by the less scrupulous. Or do some general litter pickup and other helpful acts.

If you see someone committing vandalism, call the police. Give them as much information as you can—descriptions of perpetrators, license plates, and so on. The victims will appreciate the help.

If you have time and your neighborhood is safe enough, organize a family-friendly block party, to help with visibility and to get to know your neighbors.

Lupa

October 31

Thursday

Color of the day: Purple
Incense of the day: Apricot

halloween – Samhain

Samhain Cleansing Spell

Samhain is the time of the traditional harvest festival, a perfect time to release the old with the closing of the season. As you hover in limbo on Samhain between what was and what will be, take advantage of the sacred night to free yourself from burdens that no longer serve you.

Go outside into a garden or earthy space. Place four candles around you at the meridians: blue for north, green for east, brown for south, and red for west. Sit inside the circle of candles and light each with its own match. Make a small hole to cradle a bowl, and place the bowl inside. Pour a small amount of rubbing alcohol into the bowl, followed by a sprinkle of Epsom salts. Place the used and dead matches in the bowl.

Sit inside the circle with a pencil and a piece of paper, and write down all of the things you would like to let go of or have change. When complete, fold the paper six times. Light the alcohol saying:

> Spirits of the harvest, carry
> away the ashes of who I was
> and allow who I am to be.

Place the paper in the fire. Meditate in silence until the fire goes out, then scatter the ashes into the wind. Refill the hole.

Patti Larsen

Notes:

October Moon Table

Date	Sign	Element	Nature	Phase
1 Tue 2:52 pm	Virgo	Earth	Barren	4th
2 Wed	Virgo	Earth	Barren	4th
3 Thu 10:59 pm	Libra	Air	Semi-fruitful	4th
4 Fri	Libra	Air	Semi-fruitful	New 8:35 pm
5 Sat	Libra	Air	Semi-fruitful	1st
6 Sun 4:33 am	Scorpio	Water	Fruitful	1st
7 Mon	Scorpio	Water	Fruitful	1st
8 Tue 8:21 am	Sagittarius	Fire	Barren	1st
9 Wed	Sagittarius	Fire	Barren	1st
10 Thu 11:17 am	Capricorn	Earth	Semi-fruitful	1st
11 Fri	Capricorn	Earth	Semi-fruitful	2nd 7:02 pm
12 Sat 2:00 pm	Aquarius	Air	Barren	2nd
13 Sun	Aquarius	Air	Barren	2nd
14 Mon 5:06 pm	Pisces	Water	Fruitful	2nd
15 Tue	Pisces	Water	Fruitful	2nd
16 Wed 9:18 pm	Aries	Fire	Barren	2nd
17 Thu	Aries	Fire	Barren	2nd
18 Fri	Aries	Fire	Barren	Full 7:38 pm
19 Sat 3:27 am	Taurus	Earth	Semi-fruitful	3rd
20 Sun	Taurus	Earth	Semi-fruitful	3rd
21 Mon 12:14 pm	Gemini	Air	Barren	3rd
22 Tue	Gemini	Air	Barren	3rd
23 Wed 11:36 pm	Cancer	Water	Fruitful	3rd
24 Thu	Cancer	Water	Fruitful	3rd
25 Fri	Cancer	Water	Fruitful	3rd
26 Sat 12:12 pm	Leo	Fire	Barren	4th 7:40 pm
27 Sun	Leo	Fire	Barren	4th
28 Mon 11:45 pm	Virgo	Earth	Barren	4th
29 Tue	Virgo	Earth	Barren	4th
30 Wed	Virgo	Earth	Barren	4th
31 Thu 8:22 am	Libra	Air	Semi-fruitful	4th

Times are in Eastern Time.

November

November may appear to be a brown and dreary month, depending on one's particular climate, but it holds a quiet beauty. While in our mundane lives we're often preoccupied with planning for the upcoming winter holidays, this time of year, as fall begins to fully embrace winter, offers opportunities to observe wildlife, stargaze, and see aspects of nature that are sometimes overlooked. Observe the beauty of leafless trees; see their true form and shape. Look at fallen leaves, often etched with frost, and watch for trees bearing winter berries and cones. Walking through the woods in November can be eye-opening. Without the thick growth of underbrush, and biting insects, we can see a bareness of Earth seldom revealed. Work magic with the season's first snowfall, or save some snow for a future ritual. In addition, collect leaves, twigs, and nuts to make a wreath. Have a bonfire celebration; work fire-magic. Think of November as a special time of waiting, an interlude between the vibrant fall and the coming winter. This is a time of darkening days, but also a time for indoor work or, if weather permits, outdoor magic. Welcome the wonder of transition.

Ember Grant

November 1

Friday

Color of the day: White
Incense of the day: Orchid

All Saints' Day

So Much to Teach

Many cultures celebrate this day as a time to remember the honored elders and wise people in their communities—the people we want to become more like. Today create a simple altar to at least one person whose memory and wisdom you honor in your life. You might include photographs, drawings, letters, favorite items, or even favorite books or music. If you have the time and resources, favorite foods are especially good additions.

Spend a few minutes reflecting on what you've learned from this person. For most people, there's some good (the things we value and learned from them) and some bad (things we don't want to repeat). Take time to journal about your thoughts. You can leave the altar up as long as you feel it's useful to you, or incorporate the items into a larger altar for your beloved dead.

Jenett Silver

November 2

Saturday

Color of the day: Blue
Incense of the day: Ivy

Maneki Neko

You know those waving cat statues they often have near the entrances to Chinese restaurants? That cat's name is Maneki Neko, and she's a Japanese wealth-beckoning spirit. Although it seems like she's waving, she's actually beckoning: in many Asian countries the beckoning gesture requires one's palm to face out.

Placing a Maneki Neko statue near the entrance to your home or business—ideally so she's visible from outside (perhaps in a window near the door or pathway)—can help increase your affluence. When you place her, you can activate her magical potency by anointing her with a wealth-drawing oil, such as patchouli, jasmine, or cinnamon. Then chant an invocation, such as:

Maneki Neko, beautiful and
charming wealth-drawing cat,
I call on you and ask you to
dwell here in spirit. Thank you
for inviting and welcoming
blessings of abundance into my
home (or business) and life.

Tess Whitehurst

November 3

Sunday

Color of the day: Yellow
Incense of the day: Juniper

New Moon/Solar Eclipse in Scorpio
– Daylight Saving Time ends
at 2:00 a.m.

A Day of Change

Today the world will experience a rare event: a hybrid solar eclipse. This eclipse will begin and end as an "annular" eclipse. However, the path of totality will occur over the Atlantic, east of Florida, across Central Africa, and ending in Somalia.

You needn't live along the path of the eclipse to feel or work with its power. Eclipses are one of the few times when the masculine energy of the sun embraces the feminine force of the moon. The power of this eclipse is magnified since it occurs on the "Sun's Day," Sunday.

Since this eclipse falls in November, meditations dealing with banishment and ending bad habits/ relationships would be good. Most occultists refrain from major spellwork and decision making on the day of the eclipse, as well as three days prior and after. It's believed the earth remains in "the shadow" of the eclipse during this period.

To honor this eclipse, first light a white candle to represent the light before the eclipse. Then light a black candle to symbolize the total eclipse. Lastly light a second white candle to represent the returning light. Spend the day quietly thinking about the changes you wish to make in your life. Eclipses are all about change. Resume your spellwork in a few days.

James Kambos

NOTES:

November 4

Monday

Color of the day: Silver
Incense of the day: Clary sage

Money Drawing Spell

Place a coin in a glass jar and set a green votive candle on top of it. Sprinkle everything with dried basil. Visualize money coming to you. Light the candle and chant:

> Send me money, I'm in need!
>
> Bills and debts I must take heed.
>
> My request is not from greed,
>
> Of this bind I would be freed.
>
> Without harm I ask this deed.
>
> Let it manifest with speed.

Let the candle burn out.

Ember Grant

November 5

Tuesday

Color of the day: Black
Incense of the day: Ylang-ylang

Islamic New Year –
Election Day (general)

The Blessing Chant

> May the powers of The One,
>
> The source of all creation;
>
> All-pervasive, omnipotent, eternal;
>
> May the Goddess,
>
> The lady of the Moon;
>
> And the God,
>
> Horned hunter of the Sun;
>
> May the powers of the spirits of the stones,
>
> Rulers of the elemental realms;
>
> May the powers of the stars above and the earth below,
>
> Bless this place, and this time, and I who am with you.

From Scott Cunningham's "Wicca: A Guide for the Solitary Practitioner"

November 6
Wednesday

Color of the day: Brown
Incense of the day: Bay laurel

Spell of Mid–Autumn

This day marks the halfway point of autumn. As the days grow colder, shorter, and darker, it's important to take time to prepare for the coming winter. Most of us will spend less time outdoors, and may battle fatigue or occasional depression.

This spell will help you approach winter with enthusiasm and focus. Each day for the next week, light a candle at dusk. Look at the flame and say:

Give light and the darkness
will disappear.

Breathe slowly and let the candle's light fill you with warmth and hope. When winter's drab days threaten to overtake you, repeat the spell as often as needed.

Peg Aloi

November 7
Thursday

Color of the day: Green
Incense of the day: Carnation

Make the Money Stretch

There are hours of shopping on the horizon for all of us. Start protecting your financial assets by avoiding overspending pitfalls with this spell to help you make the most of the money you spend and hang on to as much of it as you can.

Get a bay leaf and a large bay-scented pillar candle. Turn the candle over and remove the sticker, then carve a pentagram on the bottom. Charge the candle and bay leaf with this charm:

Keep my wealth safe and sound,

Make the magic circle round.

With my bargain shopping
ways,

Money comes and money stays.

Burn the candle for one hour, then blow it out and put the bay leaf in your wallet. Before you go on shopping trips, burn the bay candle for at least fifteen minutes, then put it out. Focus on buying only what you need, and look for sales and bargains.

Mickie Mueller

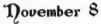

November 8

Friday

Color of the day: Coral
Incense of the day: Thyme

Winter Sanctuary

The summer sun has fled and night frosts have taken a toll. Leaves and acorns are falling, and it's time to put your little bit of earth to bed for the winter.

Before putting all the leaves and stalks on your compost heap, consider leaving some in the yard. They will be welcome shelter to our animal and faerie friends. Leaves afford warmth and protection to chipmunks and squirrels. Branches left to dry over winter make excellent kindling for next summer's fire pit. Withered annuals provide feed to rabbits. Announce your intentions so the wee folk will know they have a winter retreat. Bless the area, content in your love of mother earth.

Emyme

November 9

Saturday

Color of the day: Gray
Incense of the day: Pine

Finding Focus Spell

While indoors more at this time of year, spend some time envisioning the future you want to create. Get a large piece of paper, a pair of scissors, glue, and many old magazines. Close your eyes and breathe, welcoming your dreams and desires to arise. Envision your future. What do you love, want, need, desire, and fantasize about? Open your eyes and tear through the magazines, literally, pulling out pictures and words that "speak" to your deepest desires. Move quickly and instinctively; do not overthink. When you have a large pile, pull out the scissors and neatly trim picture edges and isolate meaningful words. Collage these on your paper, creating a vision board of the future you desire. Post it where you will see it often, so you can affirm your desires daily. With a vision of the future, now you can start to work on making these visions a reality.

Dallas Jennifer Cobb

November 10
Sunday

Color of the day: Gold
Incense of the day: Heliotrope

Reset Your Spirit

From our vantage point, as we move toward the farthest reach of winter's sway, the sun's warmth and light continue to ebb. And as we move toward the full moon, the moon's potency continues to grow.

Tonight honor the dance of both sun and moon and align with their power and grace by lighting your home exclusively with candle-light (and perhaps firelight) for at least one full hour. Electric heaters, if necessary, are fine, but leave off all electric lights, computers, televisions, and stereos and refresh your senses and spirit as you bathe in the sacred quiet. Once you've got your candles lit, say:

> As sun and moon dance
> through the sky,
>
> Exquisite balance ever nigh,
>
> As candle and flame shine
> gently bright,
>
> I awake my inner light.

Feel free to converse freely with loved ones, and allow the experience to be reminiscent of camping trips and the days of old.

Tess Whitehurst

November 11
Monday

Color of the day: White
Incense of the day: Narcissus

Veterans Day

Martinmas: A Day of Sharing

While on a journey, St. Martin is said to have given half his cloak to a beggar at the side of the road; that cloak is now a relic of the Church. The spiritual lesson today is not about charity, but about something we learned in kindergarten—the importance of sharing. We may not want to share or be comfortable sharing what we have, but we are reminded today of the sweet gifts that are ours when we give generously from our hearts.

Make a point today to share with others: your lunch, your time, your knowledge, your song. Whatever it is, do so with humility and without attachment. You will be blessed in return by the unexpected kindness of others.

Chandra Alexandre

November 12

Tuesday

 Color of the day: Red
Incense of the day: Geranium

Suffragette Goddess

On this day in 1815 first-wave feminist Elizabeth Cady Stanton was born. She was almost certainly not a Pagan, but if she were, her patron goddess might have been Artemis, who watches over women and supports their freedom and independence.

Artemis represents the concept that "female" does not have to equal "beholden to men." Her dalliances with both her female nymphs and the hunter Orion suggest bisexuality and a willingness to love where she will. Her role as protector of women in labor and childbirth acknowledges the danger inherent in the very act of bringing life into this world. And Artemis's influence may still be felt in the continuing work to liberate women around the world from everything from sexual harassment to assault to physical mutilation imposed by highly patriarchal cultures.

Therefore, today is a very good day to honor this goddess of women's rights in specific and social justice in general.

Lupa

November 13

Wednesday

Color of the day: Yellow
Incense of the day: Marjoram

Feast Spell

Today is Epulum Jovis, a Roman festival inviting the gods to a feast. Use this spell to bring balance and abundance into your life by offering sustenance to the gods in the form of the tarot.

On a black tablecloth place the Emperor card at the top, the Empress at the bottom, the Hierophant to the left, and the High Priestess to the right. In the center place the Hermit. Pour red wine into five small glasses and set on the right side of each card. Dip bread into olive oil and set to the right of each. Recite the following:

> Food and drink I offer you,
> Venture forth I ask, pray do,
> Take your fill of all you see,
> In its place leave wealth for me.
> Grateful am I for such wealth,
> I toast to you, your happiness
> and health.

Drink the wine and eat the bread, in that order, while sitting in gratitude.

Patti Larsen

November 14

Thursday

Color of the day: Purple
Incense of the day: Nutmeg

Money Spells

Here are some great little money spells:

Throw a silver coin in the water upriver from your house, so that money is always flowing in your direction.

Keep some silver coins in a cauldron on your altar, asking your deities to never allow you to be without enough cash to pay your bills.

Tossing a silver coin in a well on your property (if you have one) is supposed to always keep you from going broke.

Leave a silver coin at the grave of a wealthy person with a request that you attain wealth. Bury it in the dirt near the grave so no one else removes it.

Make a money pouch: use an old-fashioned change purse with a silver coin, a piece of citrine, a piece of malachite, some alfalfa, and some Come to Me Oil to keep the money always coming.

Boudica

November 15

Friday

Color of the day: Rose
Incense of the day: Cypress

Dispelling Possibly hostile Forces

Some people believe that hostile forces walk among us between Samhain and Yule. Ghosts and spirits may not always be friendly. Living people may not be friendly, either. Here's one way to protect yourself.

In your imagination, see yourself standing erect. Now see a golden ray coming out of your solar plexus. It looks like golden aluminum foil. Because in magic we can be inside and outside a vision at the same time, stretch the foil so it's as tall as you are. Stretch it another two feet. Now wind the golden foil around yourself three times, going sunwise. Seal it off. Use duct tape, if that makes you feel more secure. Don't forget to use twist ties to seal the golden foil above your head and below your feet. Let the foil become invisible so you can go about your daily life. Do this visualization at dawn for nine days.

Barbara Ardinger, Ph.D.

November 16
Saturday

Color of the day: Black
Incense of the day: Magnolia

hail to the hogboons!

My Eastern European grand-mother told me many tales of the hogboons, a variety of faery folk native to Scotland's Orkney Islands. The name may derive from the Old Norse *haug-bui* or *haug-buinn*, "mound-farmer" or "mound-dweller." The hogboons, also called hogboys, were mound-dwellers and much preferred the country to living in town. Unlike their trow (troll) kin, hogboons were appreciated for their relative benevolence. In exchange for a snug mound to live in on one's property, the hogboon would watch over the bounds and occasionally even worked, house-elf fashion, inside the home. My grandmother enticed her hogboons with dishes of butter and cream and swore they often lent a hand in her kitchen.

With the holiday season approaching, we could all use a house-hogboon! Create a small earthen mound in your yard, then set out a dish of butter and cream and invite the local hogboons to visit your kitchen.

Susan Pesznecker

November 17
Sunday

Color of the day: Amber
Incense of the day: Almond

Full Moon in Taurus

Tarot Journey for Insight

Today the moon is at its fullest, and it is a good time to gain illumination into areas and issues about which we are unsure, con-fused, or feel misguided.

The tarot is a wonderful tool for both meditation and guidance in uncertain situations. The Moon card from the major arcana is associated with visions and dealing with illusory perceptions. Pull the Moon card from one or several of your favorite tarot decks and lay them out on a reading cloth or your altar. Meditate by focus-ing on the tarot images and allowing them to serve as a catalyst to guide your journey for greater insight into those areas where you feel you are being mislead or need a clearer vision of the situation. If you feel you need further guidance into the situation represented for you by the Moon card, you may draw additional cards from the tarot deck, laying them down below the Moon. When you feel you've gathered enough informa-tion from your journey, you may wish to journal your experiences for further analysis in the future.

Blake Octavian Blair

November 18

Monday

Color of the day: Gray
Incense of the day: Rosemary

Power of the Pen

It can be hard to let go of what we think we should be doing in our lives, what we should be doing differently, what we should have achieved by now. Take a piece of paper and two pens, one black and one green (or brighter blue). With your black pen, freely write at least five things that frustrate you in your life right now. Include examples, but leave plenty of space around your writing (space between different words, lines, ideas). Next take your green (or blue) pen and look for ways to change your frustrations. Cross out words, draw arrows, add symbols or ideas, or list things you could do differently. When you're done, make note of anything you want to act on, and destroy the page (by tearing it into pieces or burning it safely) to release the new ideas.

Jenett Silver

November 19

Tuesday

Color of the day: Scarlet
Incense of the day: Cedar

I Am That

What is it you are willing to risk your neck for in this world? Where does courage need to come alive in order for your risk taking to be possible? Can you hold on to compassion in the face of failure on the road to success?

Let these questions percolate in your heart and mind; trust that they will help you connect to purpose and find support for your efforts to break new ground. Draw on the power of earth today as you solidify intentions to make change a reality. Remind yourself of your strength and determination by igniting charcoal in your cauldron and burning sage, dragon's blood, or pine. Visualize yourself already where you wish to be and affirm this by saying three times:

I am that.

Chandra Alexandre

November 20

Wednesday

 Color of the day: White
Incense of the day: Honeysuckle

A Self–Discovery Spell

A November night is a good time to perform a self-discovery spell to see if you're following the right path to achieve your goals. I've found that using only the major arcana portion of your tarot deck is a simple and effective way to do this.

Shuffle the major arcana cards, keeping them face down. Ask: *Am I following the right path to obtain my goals? Tell me what I should know.* Select one card at random and lay it face up. Look intently at this card. Really look closely at the details—observe the colors, the clothing, symbols, and so on. Remember, this is really your inner voice speaking to you. What advice has the card given you?

Put the cards away. During the rest of the evening don't try too hard to understand what the card has told you. Eventually messages will come to you.

James Kambos

November 21

Thursday

 Color of the day: Turquoise
Incense of the day: Myrrh

Jupiter and Expansion

Sagittarius is ruled by Jupiter, the planet of expansion and growth. Travel, education, family, community relations, and social networking are all ruled by this jovial god. One way to summarize Jupiter's influence is "more of the same." In other words, invoking Jupiter will not necessarily confer change, but may merely increase present conditions.

If your finances are struggling, use Jupiter to emphasize your other blessings: health or family. Focus on the positive aspects of your life. If you have properly sown your seeds, a fine crop will appear. You may use Jupiter for money spells during a waxing moon in an earth sign. Use something to represent abundance, such as a twenty dollar bill or silver coins, and place in a bowl or on a pentacle on your altar. Visualize them increasing and filling that space.

Peg Aloi

November 22

Friday

Color of the day: Pink
Incense of the day: Yarrow

harmony

Today work on building peace and harmony in any relationship you feel needs help. Or, if you don't have any relationship troubles (lucky you!), then focus on strengthening or enlivening a relationship. This does not mean only romantic relationships—we also have relationships with family, friends, neighbors, and colleagues that can benefit from a boost of harmony.

Find an object that represents the relationship, or simply write the person's name on a piece of paper. Light two pink candles, one on each side of the object. Visualize harmony and a feeling of calm unity between you. Say:

> Harmony between us,
>
> A bond that's strong and true—
>
> Together we are better,
>
> We see each other through.
>
> Harmony between us,
>
> To calm a stormy sea—
>
> Let nothing come between us,
>
> For good so shall it be.

Ember Grant

November 23

Saturday

Color of the day: Brown
Incense of the day: Sage

Fibonacci Day

Today, 11/23, honors Leonardo Fibonacci, who discovered the mathematical sequence 1, 1, 2, 3, 5, 8 ... to infinity. Each previous two numbers adds up to the next number. A Fibonacci poem consists of six lines. The syllables of each line correspond to the first six numbers in the sequence. As you go about your day, reflect on the wonder and magick of numbers. Be on the lookout for other sequences and seemingly random numerical oddities. Use the poem below or create your own Fibonacci poem for spellcasting today.

> Calm
>
> Still
>
> I rest
>
> Safely here
>
> The day complete now
>
> Lights out, thoughts recede, welcome sleep

Emyme

November 24

Sunday

Color of the day: Orange
Incense of the day: Eucalyptus

healing Altar

With the cold and flu season upon us, it's a great time to create a little nook, bookshelf, or table that you can use as a healing altar to send energy to loved ones feeling under the weather. Place representations of the elements, feathers, seashells, and so on. You can add a representation of a deity associated with healing, such as Quan Yin, Bridget, Asclepius, or whomever you connect to. Add herbs and stones associate with healing and keep candles nearby.

To bless and consecrate the area for healing, smudge the area with incense and hold your hands over the space, using this or a similar blessing:

> I hereby consecrate this healing altar. May it fill my loved ones and me with health, love, and blessings for the greater good and with harm to none. So mote it be.

Now you have everything handy to send quick healing energy anytime someone needs it.

Mickie Mueller

November 25

Monday

Color of the day: Lavender
Incense of the day: Hyssop

Elder Tree Spell

Today is the beginning of the Celtic tree month Ruis. Elder, known as the Goddess Tree, represents judgment and transformation, death and regeneration, and the crossing of thresholds. Tapping into the benefits of this tree helps in driving away malevolent spirits and refreshing health and happiness in the home.

Go to your front door and open it wide to the elements. Using a fine paintbrush of natural bristles, paint the lowest threshold with elderberry oil while saying:

> Evil spirits, creep you forth.

Now paint around the lock with the oil and say:

> Evil spirits, be banished and locked out.

Finish by painting a small pentagram above the door on the trim or wall and say:

> Evil spirits, you shall never pass.

Patti Larsen

November 26

Tuesday

Color of the day: White
Incense of the day: Ginger

Power over Bad Situations

When we need to be stronger than someone who is trying to control us, a little bit of Bend Over Oil goes a long way. It is also known as Command and Compel Oil, Be Gone Oil, and other such aptly named products.

Recipes vary, but I like something that smells wicked. I use John the Conqueror root (gives us strength over others who would mentally or physically try to suppress us) ground up into a little sambuca (sweet anise liquor that smells like licorice; used here as an expectorant to remove a person) and some frankincense oil (to give us control over our spiritual realm). Put a little of this strong, potent recipe on a poppet, and put it into the back of a freezer to remove the issue. Always be sure the mundane issues are taken care of before you start your magical work!

Boudica

November 27

Wednesday

Color of the day: Topaz
Incense of the day: Lilac

Watchdog Spell

Not everyone can have a real, live, flesh-and-fur dog, both as a companion and as an extra pair of eyes keeping watch at home. However, you can create a small substitute to help protect your home.

First either buy or make several small figurines of dogs. Get some red thread and an oil you associate with protection. Make a small collar out of the thread and tie around each of the dogs' necks, and anoint with the oil. Then walk around your home, showing the dogs every door and window. As you do, check the locks to be sure they work well, and anoint the sills and thresholds with the same oil.

Then place a dog by each door and window. For each, say:

*This window/door is now
your charge. Keep it safe and
guard it well, for this is your
home as well as mine.*

Lupa

November 28

Thursday

Color of the day: Crimson
Incense of the day: Clove

Thanksgiving Day –
hanukkah begins

The Thanksgiving Table as a Sacred Altar

Most of us call the hearth the center of a home, but the kitchen or dining room table may well be the family altar. As you prepare your table for the Thanksgiving feast, envision it as sacred altar space. Dress it with a freshly laundered tablecloth (your altar cloth). Set out silverware and carving tools (wands and athames), wine or water glasses (chalices), and candles (fire). Serving platters act as earthly panticles, ready to offer up your feast, while a centerpiece of fruits and flowers honors the seasonal cornucopia. Scented candles introduce incense-like aromas. Looking for a god/goddess representation? Use colored tapers, appropriate statuary, or, just for fun, a couple of Puritan salt and pepper shakers.

When the family sits down, pass a silver bowl of water and a towel for ceremonial hand washing. Offer a prayer or blessing, ring a bell to initiate sacred space, and enjoy an inspired feast!

Susan Pesznecker

November 29

Friday

Color of the day: Purple
Incense of the day: Violet

Black Friday Unwind

Today happens to be Black Friday. Many shoppers set foot in the world at early hours to fight crowds, prices, and time in order to start, or even perhaps finish, their holiday shopping.

If possible, stay home and use today as a day of sanctuary and respite before December's busy series of holiday events and gatherings. Instead of heading out into the retail-shopping rat race, engage your creative self in crafting a simple homemade gift for a loved one. Make yourself a calming cup of your favorite herbal tea or perhaps a rich cup of hot chocolate to enjoy during the process. Put your energy of love and well wishes for the loved one into the handcrafted gift. You can also use today to lovingly and innovatively wrap other gifts you already have. Make the day's focus a mini-retreat of sorts for nourishing your creative spirit.

Blake Octavian Blair

November 30

Saturday

Color of the day: Indigo
Incense of the day: Patchouli

Magical Water Cleanse

To cleanse your body after this month's excesses, and steady yourself for a healthy holiday season, perform this proactive holiday health and weight-loss ritual.

Begin with a warm bath in the morning, into which you have dissolved one cup of sea salt. Soak for at least forty minutes. Throughout the day (and during your bath), drink at least half your body weight in ounces of pure water, being sure to bless it and visualize white light in and around it before you drink. After dark, light a candle on your altar and diffuse essential oil of lemon. Hold a moonstone to your heart, close your eyes, and chant:

> As this moon doth now disperse,
> All excesses now reverse.

> As lunar glow wanes in the night,
> My weight and spirit now grow light.

For the next three days, keep the moonstone close and continue to drink water as recommended above.

Tess Whitehurst

November Moon Table

Date	Sign	Element	Nature	Phase
1 Fri	Libra	Air	Semi-fruitful	4th
2 Sat 1:35 pm	Scorpio	Water	Fruitful	4th
3 Sun	Scorpio	Water	Fruitful	New 7:50 am
4 Mon 3:14 pm	Sagittarius	Fire	Barren	1st
5 Tue	Sagittarius	Fire	Barren	1st
6 Wed 4:44 pm	Capricorn	Earth	Semi-fruitful	1st
7 Thu	Capricorn	Earth	Semi-fruitful	1st
8 Fri 6:30 pm	Aquarius	Air	Barren	1st
9 Sat	Aquarius	Air	Barren	1st
10 Sun 9:36 pm	Pisces	Water	Fruitful	2nd 12:57 am
11 Mon	Pisces	Water	Fruitful	2nd
12 Tue	Pisces	Water	Fruitful	2nd
13 Wed 2:39 am	Aries	Fire	Barren	2nd
14 Thu	Aries	Fire	Barren	2nd
15 Fri 9:49 am	Taurus	Earth	Semi-fruitful	2nd
16 Sat	Taurus	Earth	Semi-fruitful	2nd
17 Sun 7:07 pm	Gemini	Air	Barren	Full 10:16 am
18 Mon	Gemini	Air	Barren	3rd
19 Tue	Gemini	Air	Barren	3rd
20 Wed 6:23 am	Cancer	Water	Fruitful	3rd
21 Thu	Cancer	Water	Fruitful	3rd
22 Fri 6:56 pm	Leo	Fire	Barren	3rd
23 Sat	Leo	Fire	Barren	3rd
24 Sun	Leo	Fire	Barren	3rd
25 Mon 7:11 am	Virgo	Earth	Barren	4th 2:28 pm
26 Tue	Virgo	Earth	Barren	4th
27 Wed 5:00 pm	Libra	Air	Semi-fruitful	4th
28 Thu	Libra	Air	Semi-fruitful	4th
29 Fri 11:03 pm	Scorpio	Water	Fruitful	4th
30 Sat	Scorpio	Water	Fruitful	4th

Times are in Eastern Time.

December

December is a wonder FULL month! Bright sunlight on glistening snow that fills us with magical wonder can turn into a blizzard, or to slushy, slippery roads that make our hearts leap into our throats! Yet we embrace this month of extreme changes. The solstice will arrive, and we will renew the cycle of contemplation and new expectations. For many Pagans, this "winding down" of the old year encourages us to finish things we started and get our affairs in order. We look to the promise of the sun's returning, of days getting longer, and new possibilities hovering on the horizon. We celebrate this renewal by getting together with family and friends and sharing our optimism for the coming year. Sometimes the magic of December gets lost in a flurry of shopping, planning, and parties that have little to do with our religious beliefs, but we can't ignore the special feelings that pervade the spirit of the season during this magical month. It is the time of year that most strongly calls to us to remember our past and celebrate our future in tune with the cycles of nature. It can be harsh, but more often December nurtures our inner child to explore and embrace the hope and possibilities of life ahead of us.

Paniteowl

December 1

Sunday

Color of the day: Amber
Incense of the day: Hyacinth

New Beginnings Spell

The first of the month is a common day for moving. When leaving a home, discard your old broom, dustpan, mop, and pail. Don't take any old messes with you. Buy fresh equipment so your new home has a fresh start and a clean set of tools. Bless these tools before using. Charge them with the magical task of sweeping away old spiritual energy while cleaning up mundane messes. As you sweep the new space, repeat:

Sweep out the old, bad spirits gone,

Sweep in the new, good spirits welcome.

Gather all the dirt, put it in a bag, and tie tightly. Place it outside the main door. Say:

I release you, be it known,

That now I make this house my home.

Fill your bucket with warm water and four drops of lavender oil. While you mop, repeat:

Bless my home, day and night,

Keep it safe and sacred, always in the Goddess sight.

Dallas Jennifer Cobb

December 2

Monday

Color of the day: Ivory
Incense of the day: Clary sage

New Moon in Sagittarius

Releasing Anxiety

During this dark moon we move into the most stressful time of the year. Ahh, the holiday season. Take the energies of this new moon Monday to draw out anxiety and negative thoughts about the upcoming season, leaving you in a positive state of mind to deal with anything this month.

Print a calendar page for the month of December, then light a black candle and write down all your current obligations, shopping deadlines, and celebration dates. Using the juice of a lemon and a cotton swab, paint a large pentagram over the whole page, then sprinkle it with sea salt. Visualize anxiety from the dates being pulled into the lemon juice. Then say:

Lemon, absorb anxiety with your cleansing ways,

As I look forward to the coming holidays.

Salt clears stress, leaving only peace behind.

Any and all jangled nerves will unwind.

After the lemon juice is completely dry, shake off the salt. Hold the calendar page above the candle flame but not close enough to catch fire. As it warms, the pentagram appears in a calming shade of brown. As the lemon juice transforms, so does any stress that would have existed on your calendar, leaving only peace. Use the calendar page this month and stay ahead of your tasks, knowing that this will be the best December ever.

Mickie Mueller

NOTES:

December 3

Tuesday

Color of the day: Gray
Incense of the day: Basil

Understanding Scrooge

It's useful to learn, as Ebenezer Scrooge did, that spreading loving-kindness throughout the world is better than being mean and miserly. Early December is a good time to reread Dickens' *A Christmas Carol* and watch the three ghosts administering psychotherapy and tough love to old Scrooge. There's no way the book expresses Pagan ideas, but if we read closely we can see that its muscular Victorian Christianity foreshadows our Pagan belief in spiritual awakening. Scrooge gets a major attitude adjustment and turns into a good man who cares about the welfare of other people.

So … how did you come to your spiritual awakening? Did you have tough teachers like Scrooge's? Have you risen from misery and selfishness? How do you compare now with the good old man that is Scrooge at the end of the story? How can you become as kind and generous as he did?

Barbara Ardinger, Ph.D.

December 4

Wednesday

Color of the day: Yellow
Incense of the day: Lavender

Feast of Chango

Chango is the Afro-Caribbean god of fire, thunder, and lightning. Virile, passionate, and charismatic, Chango is the god who teaches us about our inner fire, our will and desire; he is a potent expression of the life force. His feast day falls in the middle days of Sagittarius, a potent fire sign. Chango is also a powerful warrior, and his weapons, the machete and sword, are said to allow him to create or destroy anything he chooses.

If you are not a Voodoo practitioner, you may still honor Chango on his feast day by drumming in your home—even better if you do so with a fire in your hearth or red candles. Chango enjoys offerings of alcoholic drinks (especially red wine), hot peppers or spicy food, tobacco (especially cigars), cornbread, or okra.

Peg Aloi

December 5

Thursday

Color of the day: Purple
Incense of the day: Jasmine

hanukkah ends

Earth Justice

Speak for Earth today as a member of Gaia's family. Bring mindfulness to your steps, your purchases, your intake of her resources and output into her embrace. Honor your part in the cycle of life in this way, and if you can, make a special effort to go on a hike, swim in the sea, climb a tree, or otherwise participate in nature. Ask yourself if you can reduce your carbon footprint in some small way, maybe by taking public transit, eating vegan or vegetarian more often, or turning off all the lights at sunset tonight. Find through your efforts one thing you can carry forward into your life every day, and dedicate this spiritual practice to Mother Earth on behalf of all beings.

Chandra Alexandre

December 6

Friday

Color of the day: Pink
Incense of the day: Mint

Generosity Spell

Today is St. Nicholas' Day, an old holiday honoring the kindly man who began the Santa Claus myth. He was known in his time for his giving of wealth to those who needed it. Time to tap into his energy. By giving, you open yourself to receive, often much more than you have granted others. The universe rewards such activity by making sure you are able to continue giving.

Lay out twelve red napkins on the table. Inside each, place a wrapped candy, a dollar, a toy trinket, and a hand-written note that reads: *Generosity feeds the spirit and opens the soul to abundance. Pass it on.*

Gather the four corners of each bundle and tie off with white string or yarn. Take them with you throughout your day and hand them out to those you feel would benefit, especially children. Feel the joy of the giving and the receiving.

Patti Larsen

December 7

Saturday

Color of the day: Blue
Incense of the day: Rue

The Break–Mirror Spell

Set a small round mirror on the floor. Stand over it, holding a large rock. Do not stand so that you can see your image in the mirror, but look at the mirror's face and visualize your enemy, bad habit, problem, or obstacle. Then drop the rock and watch the glass and your problem shatter into a million pieces.

Thus the spell is fixed.

From Scott Cunningham's
Book of Shadows

December 8

Sunday

Color of the day: Yellow
Incense of the day: Frankincense

Laughter Is Good Medicine

Need a quick mood boost? Laugh! Find something funny! Studies show that laughter increases chemicals in the brain and body that can help us feel better. Even if it won't fix all your problems, being in a better mood can help you function and troubleshoot things more effectively.

The Greek goddess Baubo is particularly adept at tough cases. She helped cheer up Demeter after Persephone had been kidnapped (though in a very ribald manner!). If you're feeling blue, say this little chant:

Baubo, Baubo, spinning 'round,

Help me create joyful sounds!

Help me laugh and feel such cheer.

There's a place for you; come join me here!

Then sit down and watch a funny movie, read a book of jokes or other humor, or even cruise the Internet for LOLcats and other lighthearted entertainment, and see if Baubo can't help you appreciate these more.

Lupa

December 9

Monday

Color of the day: Gray
Incense of the day: Hyssop

New Surroundings

This spell can be used for the home, office, or any place you feel needs to be cleansed. It's perfect for moving into a new space.

Make an infusion of rosemary and sage. After it cools, add a few drops of cedar or pine essential oil and a clear quartz point. Place the mixture in a clear container and set it beside a burning candle. Visualize the flame and heat charging the mixture with powerful energy to dispel negativity. After the candle burns out, spray the mist into any room that needs to be cleared of unwanted energy. You can also use it to anoint objects. Say:

Herbs and oil, fire and stone,

Cleanse this space, it is my own.

Dispel the past, and clear the way,

My presence here begins today.

Protect and guard all here within,

For good of all, let it begin.

Ember Grant

December 10

Tuesday

Color of the day: White
Incense of the day: Bayberry

Season of Lights

As we approach the depths of winter and the longest night of the year, the urge to kindle light is strong. Bringing lights into one's home at this time of year not only honors the season's festive nature but lifts the mood and creates a warm, inspiring atmosphere.

Hang strings of lights across the tops of doorways, around windows, and over bookshelves. Simple white lights provide light and a gentle glow, but you can also use specific colors for special effects: green for prosperity, blue for calm and healing, red for fiery energy, gold for the season's solar implications. You might also fill your home with candles of all shapes, sizes, and colors. Arrange candles on mirrors to magnify their effects through the illusion of reflection. Enjoy the luminous radiance and be filled with the light of wisdom, intuition, or other positive energies.

Susan Pesznecker

December 11

Wednesday

Color of the day: Brown
Incense of the day: Lilac

Odin's Day Travel Rune Spell

Wednesday's name stems from the Norse god Odin, also referred to as Wodin. Odin is said to be the inventor of the runic alphabet. Astrologically speaking, Wednesdays are energetically favorable for working travel spells. These two influences coinciding make for a wonderful opportunity to make a bind rune talisman for travel protection!

Gather an index card, markers, and some ribbon, or other art supplies you may wish to alternatively use in the construction. Pick two or three protective runes you are attracted to, and combine/connect them to form the bind rune. Raidho and Ehwaz are excellent choices. Remember to hold your intention of safe travel through the construction process.

Once you have your bind rune inscribed upon your card, make a hole in the top of the card and fashion a loop or ribbon through it. Hang in your car to promote safe travel. So mote it be!

Blake Octavian Blair

December 12

Thursday

Color of the day: Crimson
Incense of the day: Carnation

Abundance Check

The holidays are coming up, and if you need some extra cash for those holiday meals, Yule gifts, and Christmas surprises, then put an Abundance Check into play now for some extra spending cash.

Take a blank check, and on the date line place the absolutely last date you could receive the money by, say December 20. Where it says "Pay to the order of," write your name. On the $ line, do not specify an amount, but put $$$$.$$ to represent an amount. Where you write out the amount, just put the word *Cash*.

Sign the check with the words *Law of Abundance*. Put the event name on the memo line: *Holiday Fund*. Now fold the check and place it either under a statue of your favorite saint or goddess protector or in your cauldron of care, and leave it there. The Powers That Be will provide.

Boudica

December 13

Friday

Color of the day: Rose
Incense of the day: Thyme

Saint Lucy's Cats

We are fast approaching the time of year for Yule celebrations, and what is a celebration without sweets? Friday is for friendship and today is the Feast of Saint Lucy. Add pepparkakor (ginger cookies) and lussekatter (saffron rolls, or "Lucy cats") to your holiday baking. Dress your altar in white, and decorate it with stars of all sizes. Light silver and gold chime candles. Offer up your gratitude to Lucy, and ask her blessing on your work. Dress yourself in white (the better to hide the inevitably spilled flour). Gather your recipes, baking apparatus, and ingredients, and jump in. Be sure to bake any leftover dough or batter and place it in your winter garden for the wee folk. In the evening, while the candles burn down, relax with "cakes and ale"—a bite of the fruits of your labors and a glass of mulled wine.

Emyme

December 14

Saturday

Color of the day: Black
Incense of the day: Sandalwood

Don't Overspend Spell

This spell will prevent you from overspending during the holidays. You'll need one green and one brown candle, a money herb such as dill, a one dollar bill, and ribbon or twine. First light the candles while thinking of prosperity and balance. Then sprinkle the money-attracting herb of your choice on the dollar bill and roll it up. Grip it tightly and tie it with the ribbon. Hide the dollar bill inside your front door as you say this charm:

*Happy holidays and silver
bells, let me keep my money
until my pockets swell.*

*Let this be the place
where abundance dwells.*

If possible, don't spend any money for the next twenty-four hours. As you continue your holiday shopping, see yourself holding on to the dollar bill you used in this spell. You won't be tempted to overspend.

James Kambos

December 15

Sunday

Color of the day: Gold
Incense of the day: Juniper

Working Too hard

Today the Romans celebrated Consualia, in honor of Consus, a god of sowing and the stored harvest. During this day beasts of burden (horses, mules, and oxen) were given the day off. Like those animals, it's really easy for us to fall into habits of work. Where are you working too hard?

Take a deep breath and spend some time with your body. Listen to your feet, your ankles, your knees. To your thighs, hips, back, shoulders, neck, arms, hands, and face. Take a breath in each place, releasing tension and extra work. Do you clench your jaw, or use extra effort to sit a certain way? Find freedom in your movement. Throughout your day, check in with your body every hour or two, and release that tension. Find ways to go through your day with less effort, and give that energy to your other goals.

Jenett Silver

December 16

Monday

Color of the day: White
Incense of the day: Rosemary

Seeing More Clearly

Our winter sky is filled with bright stars. People have been gazing at them for millennia. We've always found inspiration in the stars. If it's not too cold tonight, go outside and look up. In Saint-Exupéry's novella *The Little Prince*, we learn that the stars sing. Can you hear them?

Buy a copy of Van Gogh's painting *Starry Night* and hang it where you'll see it every day. Study the swirling clouds, the luminous crescent moon and stars. How does the energy move you? Study the dark town. Who lives there? And the massive structure—is it a mountain? A tree? What does it signify to you? Why do we want to reach the stars?

Are you ready to climb up to the sky? Invoke your own bright stars:

> Blessed holy stars that sail
> above me—
>
> Enlighten my mind, my heart,
> my life.
>
> Show me what my path is,
>
> Lighten my way.
> > Barbara Ardinger, Ph.D.

December 17

Tuesday

Color of the day: Black
Incense of the day: Geranium

Full Moon in Gemini

Family Harmony Ritual

The full moon is a great time to perform rituals related to family harmony, and a Mars-ruled Tuesday is especially suited for dispersing discord and friction and opening the door to an even deeper level of peace. And what better time to perform such a magical working than during the holidays, when many of us reunite with our families (even if it's just in spirit)?

Gather one moonstone for each family member in question, including yourself. Wash the stones in saltwater and then run cold water around them for at least one minute. Fill a glass bowl with water. Hold the bowl in both hands and visualize very bright white light filling and surrounding it. Say:

> In this bowl dwell the cool
> waters of peace and harmony.

Place the bowl on your altar. Place the moonstones in the water. Carve the words *family harmony* into a floating candle. Float it on top of the bowl and light. Say:

> As this flame burns, all harsh
> energy is transmuted into peace.

Peace and harmony surround my family. Peace and harmony lend coolness and flow to our emotions. In my family, to the extent that it is in accordance with the free will and true wishes of every family member, peace and harmony prevail.

Allow the candle to continue to burn throughout the night.

Tess Whitehurst

NOTES:

December 18

Wednesday

Color of the day: Topaz
Incense of the day: Bay laurel

Wreath of Protection

Who says wreaths are only for Christmas? They can be made any time and used throughout the year. Save time and money by making your own. Get a coil of dried vine, found very inexpensively at dollar stores, and use it as the basis for a personalized wreath. Charge it with protection energy to oversee your home:

> *Sacred vines, coiled and curled, use your strength to protect our world.*

Make this plain wreath your own by adding color, texture, meaning, and magic to it. You can decorate for the season, adding small, meaningful bits to it each day so it's always changing. Invoke protection every time you add something new to the wreath:

> *Keep us safe each day that passes. I weave in strength with these grasses.*

Add ribbons, flowers, dangling balls, plastic fruit, or even some of your kids' action heroes. Magic comes in many forms. Make your wreath beautiful.

Dallas Jennifer Cobb

December 19

Thursday

 Color of the day: Green
Incense of the day: Clove

To Protect an Object

With the first and middle fingers, trace a pentagram over the object to be protected. Visualize electric-blue or purple flame streaming from your fingers to form the pentagram. Say this as you trace:

> With this pentagram I lay
>
> Protection here both night and day.
>
> And the one who should not touch,
>
> Let his fingers burn and twitch.
>
> I now invoke the law of three:
>
> This is my will,
>
> So mote it be!

From Scott Cunningham's "Wicca: A Guide for the Solitary Practitioner"

December 20

Friday

 Color of the day: Coral
Incense of the day: Orchid

Ahimsa above All

Typically we think of ahimsa, the principle of nonviolence, as a passive stance. However, there is nothing more active than a response to life that honors it fully. Ahimsa can be a philosophical position, an engagement in the world with care, a response to injustice, or all of these and more.

Consider today your approach to living a good life and the ways in which your choices impact others. To help you retain a powerful stance that encourages ahimsa from your core motivation to actual manifestation, do the following before you act. Find a white feather to represent connection to Soul. Holding the feather over white smoke, say:

> By this smoke be cleansed and strengthened that I may act in accord with the wisest of ways.

Lay the feather on your altar as a reminder of your commitment.

Chandra Alexandre

December 21

Saturday

 Color of the day: Brown
Incense of the day: Ivy

Yule – Winter Solstice

holiday Breather

This time of year, many of us are overwhelmed by all the activity and social obligations of the season. Introverts may be especially affected, though even extroverts may be feeling the pressure. Remember to take some time for self-care over the next few weeks. Here are some simple suggestions:

Make sure you get enough sleep and good-quality food, to the best of your ability.

Take a little extra time in your daily bath or shower. Visualize the stress—good and bad alike—oozing out of your pores and into the water, down the drain, and away.

If you can step away for just a few minutes—whether that's into an empty bedroom, outside, or even into the bathroom—give yourself a little alone time. Clear your mind, breathe deeply, and then head back in when you're ready.

Try to schedule a "downtime" day, or afternoon at the least, for a more extended break.

Lupa

December 22

Sunday

Color of the day: Orange
Incense of the day: Hyacinth

Charm for Balance

This is a good day to be mindful of keeping balance in your life. The holiday season is in full swing; it's easy to get caught up in the revelry, and before you know it, you've succumbed to excess spending, over-eating, or other bad habits.

Make this charm to keep your balance. Whatever need you have, focus on it. Select an item to remind you of your focus. This can be a piece of jewelry or a stone, or simply write your area of focus on a piece of paper. Hold your item and speak this chant four times:

Equal balance come what may,

Keep me on my path today.

Ember Grant

December 23

Monday

 Color of the day: Silver
Incense of the day: Lily

Spirit holiday Assistance Spell

Being in the midst of the winter holiday hustle and bustle of parties, dinners, and family gatherings can be stressful. Personality conflicts, differing religious beliefs, and even politics can add to the list of challenges. It might seem a taxing effort to maintain your inner calm; however, it is important to remember that assistance from the spirit world is available!

Today is a perfect day to pay homage to those spirits who enjoy lending a helping hand. This date is associated with the Roman goddess Larentia, guardian and mother figure of benefic and mirthful ghosts. Today set out simple offerings of food and drink for Larentia and her benefic spirits. Perhaps also light some incense and a candle, if you desire. Invoke Larentia and ask that she and her children of spirit bring their mirth and helpful energy when needed to your holiday schedule.

Blake Octavian Blair

December 24

Tuesday

 Color of the day: Red
Incense of the day: Cedar

Christmas Eve

Sadie, Goddess of Bargain Shoppers

Sadie, Sadie, bargain shopping lady, what treasures can you find for me?

Last-minute holiday shopping got you in a panic? Need the perfect gift, a special toy or just the right something for someone special?

Look for Sadie! She is that short, stout lady in the gray winter coat with a purple scarf carrying shopping bags filled to the top with treasures. Once you spot her, follow her through the store—she will stop at the priced-right bargain bins, closeout shelves, and treasure racks. You will find the perfect gift for that someone special for whom you forgot to shop or couldn't find the right gift. Don't worry; she will wait for you, leading you around the stores till your list is complete! Later at home make an offering of a glass of port or sherry and a foot bath for the goddess of discount shopping.

Boudica

December 25

Wednesday

Color of the day: White
Incense of the day: Honeysuckle

Christmas Day

In Defense of Santa Claus

Yes, Santa Claus (as we know him today) is a fairly recent development, culturally speaking. And yes, the Coca-Cola Company shaped his look. And yes, his image is often used to sell things. But rather than discrediting his existence and mythological importance, these things may be seen as proof of his aliveness, relevance, and magical potency.

Let's consider. Santa is derived from St. Nicholas, the saint associated with generosity. He's aligned with the energies of abundance, gratitude, and general jolliness. He works with the elves and has even been called an elf. He has a white beard, is near-omniscient, and stays far away for most of the year, so he fits the archetype of the wizard/hermit. And he grants wishes! You must admit that Santa is one magical fellow. To honor him today, consider placing a representation of him on your altar, making a Christmas wish, and donating even just a tiny bit to a charity of your choice.

Tess Whitehurst

December 26

Thursday

Color of the day: Purple
Incense of the day: Myrrh

Kwanzaa begins

Feast of Saturn/Saturnalia

Although this ancient Greek festival has largely been absorbed by Christmas, Saturnalia was once the best loved of the festivals of antiquity. Since Saturn rules structures and rules, Saturnalia became a time when the social order was relaxed and great freedom was permitted. Slaves were treated as equals, and drinking, dancing, games, and feasting took place every day for about a week in late December. Gifts were given, in particular wax candles.

As the holiday revelry surrounds you, think of the routines that guide you all year. Which of these rules and structures serve you well? Which ones need relaxing or discarding? Sometimes when we let loose, we learn just how strict we have been with ourselves or others. At this time, ask Saturn, the wise god of seeds and sowing, to bless the shape of your life, to help you reflect on where you're going, and to prompt you to change what needs changing.

Peg Aloi

December 27

Friday

Color of the day: Pink
Incense of the day: Rose

Quiet of the Year

One of the great pleasures of the deep winter for many people is the quiet and rest, especially before dawn. Today find a way to re-create that in your daily life. You might simply take a walk outside, if you're awake before dawn. But if not, create a little space of quiet. An eyemask and some headphones can create a wonderful meditation moment, even if your household is busy. Consider turning off the lights in your room a few minutes earlier, and resting in the dark, just listening.

Wherever you find your quiet in the dark, recite this chant to yourself:

Down in the darkness, I hear
a silence.

Down in that silence, I hear a
name.

Repeat the chant, letting the rhythm build in your mind to overflowing before it falls to silence. Listen in the dark to what was named, and what that name means to you.

Jenett Silver

December 28

Saturday

Color of the day: Gray
Incense of the day: Sage

Halcyon Days

On this final Saturday of 2013, we note the last of the halcyon days of winter. Said to begin every December fourteenth and lasting for two weeks, this time is believed to have been brought about by the alcyon, or kingfisher, bird, which nests on the ocean and requires calm seas to hatch its young.

The last two weeks in December have evolved into celebratory times in many belief systems; therefore halcyon days bode well for travel. Whether heading for home or out to visit loved ones, as you travel on this day offer up a spell of your own or use this simple chant:

Through air,

Over water,

On earth,

Toward home fires,

Spirits guide and shield me

To my destination gained.

Emyme

December 29

Sunday

Color of the day: Amber
Incense of the day: Juniper

Feast of Fools

Tired of the December holiday season? Ready for some loosely organized fun? It's time for the Feast of Fools. In times past, the uproarious events that seemed to pop up between the winter solstice and December's close were often called "Feasts of Fools." Scholars today agree that these were largely an attempt by Middle Ages people to escape the iron-fisted rule of the local church. The events—"misrules"— consisted of wild parties replete with food, drink, games, outlandish costumes, and music, always with an air of chaos.

Invite your friends and family to your own Feast of Fools. Play games, wear crazy outfits, enjoy good food and drink (or a meal served in reverse order), and elect and crown your own "Lord of Misrule." Imagine yourself in sync with your medieval brethren, raising a tankard to their memory. You'll emerge refreshed and ready to return to the "real" magickal world.

Susan Pesznecker

December 30

Monday

Color of the day: Ivory
Incense of the day: Neroli

The Chariot Spell

The Chariot card in the tarot is about moving onward and upward. Pulling it are four animals, representing the elements. Combining them guarantees victory.

Place four candles in a circle: blue for air, red for fire, green for water, and brown for earth. In the center, set a white candle for spirit. Beside the blue candle, place an empty glass. Next to red, a burnt match. For green, a glass of water. For brown, a saucer of dirt. And for white, a small wooden bowl. Light all five candles. Starting with air, breathe into the empty glass and dump the air into the center bowl. Then place the match (fire) in the bowl, followed by the glass of water (water) and the dirt (earth). Combine the ingredients in a slow clockwise stir as you say:

Elements and Spirit, light my way.
Bring me success from this day.

Send me every victory.
Elements and Spirit, hear my plea.

Blow out all the candles, whispering *thank you.*

Patti Larsen

December 31

Tuesday

Color of the day: Black
Incense of the day: Ginger

New Year's Eve

Snow Spell to Melt hard Feelings

No matter how hard you try to be nice, misunderstandings can end in hard feelings that you carry around. When this happens, take control of your feelings and take the high road. Try this spell to melt your anger, encouraging forgiveness in your own heart.

In a small bowl, gather snow, if it's available; if not, use crushed ice. Write what you're angry about on a slip of paper and put it underneath the snow in the bowl. Sprinkle a little sugar on top for sweetness. Place a floating candle on the top of the snow and light it. Say:

*As hard feelings melt I no
longer grieve.*

*Warm my heart this New
Year's Eve.*

As the snow melts, let go of your hard feelings toward the person. Holding on to anger will only end up hurting you in the end, so release it with love before the new year begins and move on.

Mickie Mueller

NOTES:

December Moon Table

Date	Sign	Element	Nature	Phase
1 Sun	Scorpio	Water	Fruitful	4th
2 Mon 1:31 am	Sagittarius	Fire	Barren	New 7:22 pm
3 Tue	Sagittarius	Fire	Barren	1st
4 Wed 1:49 am	Capricorn	Earth	Semi-fruitful	1st
5 Thu	Capricorn	Earth	Semi-fruitful	1st
6 Fri 1:53 am	Aquarius	Air	Barren	1st
7 Sat	Aquarius	Air	Barren	1st
8 Sun 3:34 am	Pisces	Water	Fruitful	1st
9 Mon	Pisces	Water	Fruitful	2nd 10:12 am
10 Tue 8:06 am	Aries	Fire	Barren	2nd
11 Wed	Aries	Fire	Barren	2nd
12 Thu 3:40 pm	Taurus	Earth	Semi-fruitful	2nd
13 Fri	Taurus	Earth	Semi-fruitful	2nd
14 Sat	Taurus	Earth	Semi-fruitful	2nd
15 Sun 1:40 am	Gemini	Air	Barren	2nd
16 Mon	Gemini	Air	Barren	2nd
17 Tue 1:17 pm	Cancer	Water	Fruitful	Full 4:28 am
18 Wed	Cancer	Water	Fruitful	3rd
19 Thu	Cancer	Water	Fruitful	3rd
20 Fri 1:48 am	Leo	Fire	Barren	3rd
21 Sat	Leo	Fire	Barren	3rd
22 Sun 2:19 pm	Virgo	Earth	Barren	3rd
23 Mon	Virgo	Earth	Barren	3rd
24 Tue	Virgo	Earth	Barren	3rd
25 Wed 1:17 am	Libra	Air	Semi-fruitful	4th 8:48 am
26 Thu	Libra	Air	Semi-fruitful	4th
27 Fri 8:58 am	Scorpio	Water	Fruitful	4th
28 Sat	Scorpio	Water	Fruitful	4th
29 Sun 12:37 pm	Sagittarius	Fire	Barren	4th
30 Mon	Sagittarius	Fire	Barren	4th
31 Tue 1:01 pm	Capricorn	Earth	Semi-fruitful	4th

Times are in Eastern Time.

Daily Magical Influences

Each day is ruled by a planet that possesses specific magical influences:

Monday (Moon): peace, healing, caring, psychic awareness, purification.

Tuesday (Mars): passion, sex, courage, aggression, protection.

Wednesday (Mercury): conscious mind, study, travel, divination, wisdom.

Thursday (Jupiter): expansion, money, prosperity, generosity.

Friday (Venus): love, friendship, reconciliation, beauty.

Saturday (Saturn): longevity, exorcism, endings, homes, houses.

Sunday (Sun): healing, spirituality, success, strength, protection.

Lunar Phases

The lunar phase is important in determining best times for magic.

The waxing moon (from the new moon to the full moon) is the ideal time for magic to draw things toward you.

The full moon is the time of greatest power.

The waning moon (from the full moon to the new moon) is a time for study, meditation, and little magical work (except magic designed to banish harmful energies).

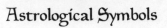

Astrological Symbols

The Sun	☉		Aries	♈
The Moon	☽		Taurus	♉
Mercury	☿		Gemini	♊
Venus	♀		Cancer	♋
Mars	♂		Leo	♌
Jupiter	♃		Virgo	♍
Saturn	♄		Libra	♎
Uranus	♅		Scorpio	♏
Neptune	♆		Sagittarius	♐
Pluto	♇		Capricorn	♑
			Aquarius	♒
			Pisces	♓

The Moon's Sign

The moon's sign is a traditional consideration for astrologers. The moon continuously moves through each sign in the zodiac, from Aries to Pisces. The moon influences the sign it inhabits, creating different energies that affect our daily lives.

Aries: Good for starting things but lacks staying power. Things occur rapidly but quickly pass. People tend to be argumentative and assertive.

Taurus: Things begun now do last, tend to increase in value, and become hard to alter. Brings out an appreciation for beauty and sensory experience.

Gemini: Things begun now are easily changed by outside influence. Time for shortcuts, communications, games, and fun.

Cancer: Stimulates emotional rapport between people. Pinpoints need, supports growth and nurturance. Tend to domestic concerns.

Leo: Draws emphasis to the self, to central ideas or institutions, away from connections with others and emotional needs. People tend to be melodramatic.

Virgo: Favors accomplishment of details and commands from higher up. Focus on health, hygiene, and daily schedules.

Libra: Favors cooperation, compromise, social activities, beautification of surroundings, balance, and partnership.

Scorpio: Increases awareness of psychic power. Favors activities requiring intensity and focus. People tend to brood and become secretive under this moon sign.

Sagittarius: Encourages flights of imagination and confidence. This moon sign is adventurous, philosophical, and athletic. Favors expansion and growth.

Capricorn: Develops strong structure. Focus on traditions, responsibilities, and obligations. A good time to set boundaries and rules.

Aquarius: Rebellious energy. Time to break habits and make abrupt change. Personal freedom and individuality are the focus.

Pisces: The focus is on dreaming, nostalgia, intuition, and psychic impressions. A good time for spiritual or philanthropic activities.

Glossary of Magical Terms

Altar: A low table that holds magical tools as a focus for spell workings.

Athame: A ritual knife used to direct personal power during workings or to symbolically draw diagrams in a spell. It is rarely, if ever, used for actual physical cutting.

Aura: An invisible energy field surrounding a person. The aura can change color depending on the state of the individual.

Balefire: A fire lit for magical purposes, usually outdoors.

Casting a circle: The process of drawing a circle around oneself to seal out unfriendly influences and raise magical power. It is the first step in a spell.

Censer: An incense burner. Traditionally a censer is a metal container, filled with incense, that is swung on the end of a chain.

Censing: The process of burning incense to spiritually cleanse an object.

Centering yourself: To prepare for a magical rite by calming and centering all of your personal energy.

Chakra: One of the seven centers of spiritual energy in the human body, according to the philosophy of yoga.

Charging: To infuse an object with magical power.

Circle of protection: A circle cast to protect oneself from unfriendly influences.

Crystals: Quartz or other stones that store cleansing or protective energies.

Deosil: Clockwise movement, symbolic of life and positive energies.

Deva: A divine being according to Hindu beliefs; a devil or evil spirit according to Zoroastrianism.

Direct/retrograde: Refers to the motion of a planet when seen from the earth. A planet is "direct" when it appears to be moving forward from the point of view of a person on the earth. It is "retrograde" when it appears to be moving backward.

Dowsing: To use a divining rod to search for a thing, usually water or minerals.

Dowsing pendulum: A long cord with a coin or gem at one end. The pattern of its swing is used to predict the future.

Dryad: A tree spirit or forest guardian.

Fey: An archaic term for a magical spirit or a fairylike being.

Gris-gris: A small bag containing charms, herbs, stones, and other items to draw energy, luck, love, or prosperity to the wearer.

Mantra: A sacred chant used in Hindu tradition to embody the divinity invoked; it is said to possess deep magical power.

Needfire: A ceremonial fire kindled at dawn on major Wiccan holidays. It was traditionally used to light all other household fires.

Pentagram: A symbolically protective five-pointed star with one point upward.

Power hand: The dominant hand; the hand used most often.

Scry: To predict the future by gazing at or into an object such as a crystal ball or pool of water.

Second sight: The psychic power or ability to foresee the future.

Sigil: A personal seal or symbol.

Smudge/smudge stick: To spiritually cleanse an object by waving smoke over and around it. A smudge stick is a bundle of several incense sticks.

Wand: A stick or rod used for casting circles and as a focus for magical power.

Widdershins: Counterclockwise movement, symbolic of negative magical purposes, sometimes used to disperse negative energies.

Moon Void-of-Course Tables

Last aspect		Moon enters new sign		JANUARY
3	7:15 am	3	Libra	8:11 pm
5	6:13 pm	6	Scorpio	1:09 am
7	6:31 am	8	Sagittarius	3:28 am
8	9:28 pm	10	Capricorn	3:54 am
11	2:44 pm	12	Aquarius	4:01 am
13	3:37 am	14	Pisces	5:49 am
16	4:32 am	16	Aries	11:07 am
18	7:40 pm	18	Taurus	8:36 pm
20	1:16 pm	21	Gemini	9:04 am
23	6:42 am	23	Cancer	10:00 pm
25	3:35 pm	26	Leo	9:20 am
28	11:59 am	28	Virgo	6:27 pm
30	8:59 pm	31	Libra	1:36 am

Last aspect		Moon enters new sign		FEBRUARY
1	8:03 pm	2	Scorpio	7:02 am
4	7:31 am	4	Sagittarius	10:45 am
5	3:42 pm	6	Capricorn	12:55 pm
7	7:44 am	8	Aquarius	2:16 pm
10	2:20 am	10	Pisces	4:20 pm
11	12:03 pm	12	Aries	8:51 pm
14	10:35 pm	15	Taurus	5:08 am
17	3:31 pm	17	Gemini	4:50 pm
19	1:48 pm	20	Cancer	5:45 am
21	9:08 pm	22	Leo	5:12 pm
24	11:50 pm	25	Virgo	1:52 am
26	1:13 pm	27	Libra	8:02 am
28	3:37 am	1	Scorpio	12:33 pm

Times are in Eastern Time.

Moon Void-of-Course Tables

Last aspect		Moon enters new sign		MARCH
3	4:19 am	3	Sagittarius	4:11 pm
5	10:28 am	5	Capricorn	7:14 pm
7	4:14 pm	7	Aquarius	10:01 pm
8	5:08 pm	10	Pisces	1:19 am
11	3:51 pm	12	Aries	7:17 am
13	4:02 am	14	Taurus	3:08 pm
16	7:11 pm	17	Gemini	2:09 am
19	1:27 pm	19	Cancer	2:55 pm
20	2:02 pm	22	Leo	2:50 am
22	11:28 pm	24	Virgo	11:49 am
25	8:46 am	26	Libra	5:32 pm
27	2:14 pm	28	Scorpio	8:53 pm
29	4:25 pm	30	Sagittarius	11:13 pm
Last aspect		**Moon enters new sign**		**APRIL**
1	1:00 am	2	Capricorn	1:35 am
3	6:35 am	4	Aquarius	4:41 am
5	1:22 pm	6	Pisces	9:00 am
8	12:10 am	8	Aries	3:02 pm
10	12:25 pm	10	Taurus	11:22 pm
13	8:30 am	13	Gemini	10:13 am
15	3:41 pm	15	Cancer	10:49 pm
18	8:31 am	18	Leo	11:13 am
19	5:06 pm	20	Virgo	9:08 pm
22	2:02 am	23	Libra	3:25 am
24	8:12 am	25	Scorpio	6:25 am
26	4:56 am	27	Sagittarius	7:32 am
29	12:37 am	29	Capricorn	8:21 am

Times are in Eastern Time.

Moon Void-of-Course Tables

Last aspect		Moon enters new sign		MAY
1	10:07 am	1	Aquarius	10:20 am
3	12:24 am	3	Pisces	2:25 pm
5	12:00 pm	5	Aries	9:03 pm
7	8:40 am	8	Taurus	6:09 am
9	8:28 pm	10	Gemini	5:21 pm
12	9:32 am	13	Cancer	5:57 am
15	8:14 am	15	Leo	6:38 pm
18	12:35 am	18	Virgo	5:33 am
20	12:48 pm	20	Libra	1:07 pm
22	3:35 am	22	Scorpio	4:55 pm
24	9:55 am	24	Sagittarius	5:49 pm
26	6:22 am	26	Capricorn	5:28 pm
28	2:40 pm	28	Aquarius	5:48 pm
30	7:57 pm	30	Pisces	8:30 pm

Last aspect		Moon enters new sign		JUNE
2	12:30 am	2	Aries	2:33 am
4	2:09 am	4	Taurus	11:53 am
5	9:25 am	6	Gemini	11:32 pm
9	4:29 am	9	Cancer	12:16 pm
10	5:15 pm	12	Leo	12:58 am
14	7:14 am	14	Virgo	12:26 pm
16	5:26 pm	16	Libra	9:19 pm
18	11:55 pm	19	Scorpio	2:38 am
20	3:16 pm	21	Sagittarius	4:31 am
23	3:08 am	23	Capricorn	4:08 am
24	10:24 pm	25	Aquarius	3:27 am
26	9:08 am	27	Pisces	4:32 am
28	8:16 pm	29	Aries	9:07 am

Times are in Eastern Time.

Moon Void-of-Course Tables

Last aspect		Moon enters new sign		JULY
1	2:48 am	1	Taurus	5:43 pm
3	11:51 am	4	Gemini	5:21 am
6	8:30 am	6	Cancer	6:14 pm
8	7:44 am	9	Leo	6:48 am
11	3:54 pm	11	Virgo	6:12 pm
13	11:26 am	14	Libra	3:41 am
15	11:18 pm	16	Scorpio	10:24 am
18	7:12 am	18	Sagittarius	1:54 pm
20	11:00 am	20	Capricorn	2:39 pm
21	11:53 am	22	Aquarius	2:07 pm
23	10:01 am	24	Pisces	2:22 pm
25	2:43 pm	26	Aries	5:29 pm
27	10:19 pm	29	Taurus	12:43 am
30	11:58 am	31	Gemini	11:42 am

Last aspect		Moon enters new sign		AUGUST
1	12:48 pm	3	Cancer	12:29 am
5	2:49 am	5	Leo	12:58 pm
6	5:51 pm	7	Virgo	11:57 pm
9	6:05 pm	10	Libra	9:08 am
11	9:29 pm	12	Scorpio	4:18 pm
14	5:30 pm	14	Sagittarius	9:04 pm
16	1:32 pm	16	Capricorn	11:25 pm
18	2:26 pm	19	Aquarius	12:07 am
20	9:45 pm	21	Pisces	12:43 am
22	9:38 pm	23	Aries	3:13 am
25	6:02 am	25	Taurus	9:13 am
27	6:58 pm	27	Gemini	7:08 pm
29	12:44 am	30	Cancer	7:33 am
31	8:06 pm	1	Leo	8:01 pm

Times are in Eastern Time.

Moon Void-of-Course Tables

Last aspect		Moon enters new sign		SEPTEMBER	
3	1:52 pm	4	Virgo	6:43 am
6	6:10 am	6	Libra	3:12 pm
8	4:46 pm	8	Scorpio	9:44 pm
10	5:21 am	11	Sagittarius	2:36 am
12	1:08 pm	13	Capricorn	5:56 am
14	7:17 pm	15	Aquarius	8:05 am
16	4:19 am	17	Pisces	9:58 am
19	7:13 am	19	Aries	12:58 pm
20	9:25 pm	21	Taurus	6:33 pm
23	3:13 am	24	Gemini	3:34 am
26	7:21 am	26	Cancer	3:24 pm
29	3:30 am	29	Leo	3:57 am

Last aspect		Moon enters new sign		OCTOBER	
1	12:48 am	1	Virgo	2:52 pm
3	2:57 pm	3	Libra	10:59 pm
5	6:28 pm	6	Scorpio	4:33 am
8	12:54 am	8	Sagittarius	8:21 am
10	6:10 am	10	Capricorn	11:17 am
11	8:04 pm	12	Aquarius	2:00 pm
14	4:28 pm	14	Pisces	5:06 pm
16	3:15 am	16	Aries	9:18 pm
18	7:38 pm	19	Taurus	3:27 am
20	5:02 pm	21	Gemini	12:14 pm
22	8:35 pm	23	Cancer	11:36 pm
25	4:31 pm	26	Leo	12:12 pm
28	8:26 am	28	Virgo	11:45 pm
30	10:48 pm	31	Libra	8:22 am

Times are in Eastern Time.

Moon Void-of-Course Tables

Last aspect		Moon enters new sign		NOVEMBER
2	8:47 am	2	Scorpio	1:35 pm
3	11:23 pm	4	Sagittarius	3:14 pm
5	11:48 am	6	Capricorn	4:44 pm
8	2:39 am	8	Aquarius	6:30 pm
10	12:57 am	10	Pisces	9:36 pm
12	9:34 am	13	Aries	2:39 am
14	3:57 pm	15	Taurus	9:49 am
17	10:16 am	17	Gemini	7:07 pm
19	10:59 am	20	Cancer	6:23 am
22	2:11 am	22	Leo	6:56 pm
24	3:59 am	25	Virgo	7:11 am
27	6:44 am	27	Libra	5:00 pm
29	6:13 am	29	Scorpio	11:03 pm

Last aspect		Moon enters new sign		DECEMBER
1	8:34 pm	2	Sagittarius	1:31 am
3	10:45 pm	4	Capricorn	1:49 am
6	12:31 am	6	Aquarius	1:53 am
7	7:11 am	8	Pisces	3:34 am
10	1:41 am	10	Aries	8:06 am
12	10:37 am	12	Taurus	3:40 pm
14	9:54 pm	15	Gemini	1:40 am
17	4:28 am	17	Cancer	1:17 pm
19	11:37 pm	20	Leo	1:48 am
22	8:25 am	22	Virgo	2:19 pm
24	10:55 pm	25	Libra	1:17 am
27	6:00 am	27	Scorpio	8:58 am
29	8:54 am	29	Sagittarius	12:37 pm
30	6:36 am	31	Capricorn	1:01 pm

Times are in Eastern Time.

Spell Notes: